Lodhi Road

The Puntland Assignment

By
Sanjay Kumar

Author's Note:

The name of India's foreign intelligence agency was chosen by the Cabinet Secretary, Dattatraya Shridhar Joshi, on 21 September 1968. Since its creation by bifurcation from the Intelligence Bureau, the Research & Analysis Wing has been responsible for gathering foreign intelligence, counterterrorism, counterproliferation, and advising the Prime Minister's Office on matters relating to national security and foreign policy. In the media the organisation is abbreviated to the R&AW or RAW. To maintain consistency, I have used the appellation, RAW, throughout the book.

Similarly, the RAW's ultra-secretive all-Tibetan covert paramilitary unit responsible for conducting clandestine operations which the government may not wish to be associated with, is given its formal name. Since its formation on 14 November 1962 by Nehru's spymaster, Bhola Nath Mullick, it has been known by many names including *Establishment 22* and the *Phantoms of Chittagong*. Again, to maintain consistency, I have used the formal name, the Special Frontier Force, or its abbreviation, the SFF.

Acknowledgements:

I would like to acknowledge the extraordinary debt I owe to those who shared their time and knowledge with me: the staff at the Vivekananda International Foundation in New Delhi; the South Asia Analysis Group in Chennai; the Indian High Commission in London; the Embassy of Israel in New Delhi; the British Embassy in Somalia; the Embassy of India in Djibouti; the Metropolitan Police Service in Westminster; and the Society of Jesus in Rome. I'm indebted to those associated with the China Study Group in New Delhi in helping me with this book.

I would not be able to get my work done without the continual support and vision of Elliot and Nathan at Wordsworth Writing House in copy-editing this book with enormous skill and precision and the team at Arlot Social for their infectious creativity and passion.

Finally, and most importantly, my parents. I am what I am because of you. And for that, I will always be grateful for the life I have.

Lodhi Road: The Puntland Assignment is a work of fiction. All incidents and dialogue, and all characters with the exception of some well-known historical figures, are products of the author's imagination and are not to be construed as real. Where real-life historical figures appear, the situations, incidents, and dialogues concerning those persons are entirely fictional and not intended to depict actual events or to change the entirely fictional nature of the work. In all other respects, any resemblance to persons living or dead is entirely coincidental.

First published in 2024 by Wordsworth Publishing House
Copyright ©Sanjay Kumar 2024
The right of Sanjay Kumar to be identified as the Author of this Work has been asserted by him in accordance with the Copyright, Designs and Patents Act 1988.
ISBN: 979-8-89397-149-1
www.sanjay-kumar.com

This book is sold subject to the condition that it shall not, by way of trade or otherwise, be lent, resold, hired out or otherwise circulated without the publisher's prior written consent in any form of binding or cover other than that in which it is published and without a similar condition including this condition being imposed on the subsequent purchaser.

Sanjay Kumar

This book is dedicated to the faceless heroes of the
Research & Analysis Wing of Lodhi Road who risk everything in the
service of Bharat.

Lodhi Road

Prologue

Bahawalpur Military Airbase, Pakistan 17th August 1988

The tall, stooped elegantly tailored Chinaman ducked through the door of the white and blue striped *Xian Y-7* passenger plane and momentarily blinded by the brilliant white sunlight, hesitated on the top step of the portable stairs. At over six feet, he was unusually tall for a Chinese man. His stoop, so it was rumoured around Islamabad, was from a childhood illness which kept him bedridden for months on end. During this time, his mother taught him the art of *shu*, the history and beautiful intricacies of Chinese calligraphy. His grandfather tutored him in the strategy game of *qi*. Before the boy reached the age of six, he had mastered the strokes, radicals, recensions, and phonetics of the Chinese written language. The disciple of learning, particularly the boy's mastery of the art of *qi*, was excellent training for his future career within the internal security apparatus of the Chinese Communist Party.

He had a busy schedule in Pakistan and was accompanied only by his aide cum-translator. The remaining passengers, world-class Russian, North Korean, and Iraqi scientists in various fields, including microbiology, virology, genetics, and bacteriology, will remain onboard to eat and rest.

In Beijing, it was understood by Politburo members that in all matters relating to state security, the enigmatic tall Chinaman was answerable only to The Eight Elders. Also referred to as The Eight Immortals, they were a group of elderly members of the Chinese Communist Party who made all Politburo policy decisions, usually from the home of Deng Xiaoping. Whenever the Eight Elders wanted a secret conveyed, they called for the Chinaman to act as their messenger; a task for which he was uniquely qualified.

The Elders had dispatched the Chinaman to the Islamic Republic of Pakistan to pass an urgent message to the army general in charge.

The thin metal dispatch case in his right hand was attached to the wrist by a discreet galvanised steel wire. Descending slowly down the stairs, he caught sight of the famous Pakistani army general lionised throughout the Muslim world. The Pakistani stepped forward and embraced the Chinaman awkwardly.

The Chinaman had been conducting business with Pakistan's army chiefs since the founding of the Islamic state. His late mentor, Kang Sheng, sent him on his first mission to Rawalpindi in May 1947 to create a working relationship with Pakistan's fledgling security apparatus, the Inter-Services Intelligence agency. The Chinaman had worked with the Australian-born founder of the ISI, Major-General Robert Cawthome to develop the Sino-Pakistani intelligence alliance. He knew all the generals. He had studied them all and written detailed psyche portraits on all: Ayub Khan, a vainglory army general who in 1958 assumed control of Pakistan in a coup d'état and lost the Indo-Pakistan War of 1965; the alcoholic Yahya Khan, who lost half of the country - East Pakistan - to India in 1971; and the psychotic General Tikka Khan, *The Butcher of Bengal*, the current president's predecessor.

The Chinaman had written detailed reports to Beijing, during his time at the Chinese consulate in Rawalpindi, of their peculiar peccadilloes. His analysis of their fear imagined and real; their ambitions and motivations; their vanity and grandiosity, all leading to military disasters ran to hundreds of pages. He had spent many a night discussing Pakistan and geopolitics in South Asia, especially the army generals while learning *qi* moves and watching his father play what he called *the surrounding game*.

"The key to controlling Pakistan is the careful orchestration of Rawalpindi's fear and paranoia of India being its existential threat. You must magnify the delusional fear of the retired generals living in Rawalpindi,' he murmured softly, making another adroit move on the board. "I read a report recently where the analyst concludes Pakistan is an army with a state, whereas India is a state with an army. Pakistanis enlist in the army in order to run the country, whereas the Indians enlist to defend the country. I agree with her."

As he walked, the Chinaman recalled the words of his mentor shortly before his passing. Mao's greatest spymaster, Kang Sheng, was in great pain with bladder cancer but insisted on seeing his protégé for the last time. "I congratulate you, Jiang, on your important work in Pakistan. I have read the detailed report you sent me and approve of your setting up of the organisation you call the Compact Accord" he wheezed, stopping for a moment to catch his breath. "I agree with you that Islam and democracy are incompatible. Always have been and always will be. I also authorised the budget you requested. The Compact you have created is a stroke of genius, I can now see this" he rasped, his breathing laboured.

Kang Sheng clasped his protégé's hand. "You please me, Jiang, with your service and devotion to duty to the Party. You please me greatly," said Kang Sheng gurgling from the back of his throat. "You were the hidden hand behind Pakistan's constitutional coup in 1953; it was you who initiated the 1958 military coup; and you helped our friend, Zia-ul Haq, execute Operation Fair Play, the coup which bought him to power in 1977," he recalled with obvious pride. "My dear Jiang, I have read carefully the blueprint you wrote and what you have created in the Compact is very sophisticated," Kang Sheng said with a thin papery smile. "I see the many hours spent teaching you *qi* moves have not been wasted. I can see you using the Compact members to execute what the Western media call our *"salami-slicing strategy"* in Pakistan. You make your dear father, Qiao Shi, immensely proud of you. Make our strategy a manifestation of the *weigi* game we played all these years. I shall miss our precious hours playing our beautiful surrounding game."

"Pakistan is a mere geographical expression; it's barely a state," said Kang Sheng emphatically. "It can only be governed by an oligarchy; the type of oligarchy with unique characteristics you have created in the Compact, fashioned out of Pakistan's military, bureaucracy, various leading clerics and their followers, and the powerful feudal families. You have succeeded in all this," nodded Kang Sheng with his eyes closed. "In creating the Compact, you have most definitely succeeded, my dear Jiang."

As one of the Politburo's senior members, Kang Sheng knew China's foreign debt-trap aid policy since 1949 was a deliberate one; a policy he was expected to execute worldwide. The Politburo was united in China's economic expansionism. "Pakistan is now ripe for plucking, like a fattened duck ready for the banquet table. We must have their resources, particularly in Balochistan. Go back to Islamabad and use the Compact to make Pakistan swallow all of China's economic plans we have for their country. Pakistan is nothing without China, make those army generals understand this simple fact of their lives. The Compact must be used to reinforce our message that India and only India is the existential threat to Pakistan and its people. This is the way we take Pakistani land and resources. The Islamic Republic of Pakistan must be totally dependent on the Communist Party of China within twenty years from now. Once Pakistan is made to become dependent on Beijing, and becomes our client state, we can begin the real task of surrounding the only thing in the way of China taking control in the region: India, the protector of the Dalai Lama."

"I understand, Master Sheng. Pakistan will be a well-trained, obedient attack dog owned by Beijing, and ready at our command to snap at Delhi's heels."

"You must take care, Jiang, that the balance of power is properly maintained between Rawalpindi and Islamabad; the prime minister of Pakistan must always be nothing more than the mayor of Islamabad. Real power in Pakistan must always reside with the retired generals in the Compact acting on orders from Beijing."

"We spoke of this during our *qi* games, remember? You must take control of the retired generals in Rawalpindi, or we will never be free from India's hold over China in the Malacca Strait. If this were to ever happen, then Delhi will forever have its hands around our neck. You must never allow this to happen. Never! You have always understood the greater game we are playing, Jiang. You know India can never be allowed to gain maritime superiority over China in the Malacca Strait. I know you will not fail me in our surrounding game; of all my students you are my most brilliant protege. You mastered the four arts of the Chinese scholar at such an early age, Jiang. I never told you, but I made sure every Politburo member knew this about you. All Eight Immortals know of this. You make me proud." Those were his last words to his protégé.

The Chinaman's beloved mentor Kang Sheng died peacefully the following morning, on 18th December 1975. It was the only time in his life he had shed a tear for another human.

Walking along the Bahawalpur runway, Mohammed Zia ul-Haq, the army chief who, in 1976, committed judicial murder by executing the democratically elected Zulfikar Ali Bhutto, taking control of the country, instructed the translator to tell his guest how honoured he was to welcome him back to Pakistan. The Chinaman caught sight of a group of elderly army veterans doing callisthenics and teaching cadets drill practice in a parade ground and nodded in approval. This was the Pakistan that Beijing wanted as its ideal client state in South Asia: an ideological state run by a rabid fundamentalist forever in search of a *jihad*. Turning back to Zia ul-Haq, the Chinaman focused his attention and offered the usual appropriate response: it went without saying that he was delighted to be in Pakistan and eager to meet the famous nuclear physicist, Abdul Qadeer Khan, at his Kahuta research facility. "I wish to shake the hand of the man responsible for creating the world's Muslim nuclear bomb. A great achievement indeed, General."

The two men made small talk, chatting – through the interpreter, a diffident young man, nodding at every word – about what they had been up to since their last meeting in Beijing two years ago.

They brought each other up to date on matters of common interest: with active assistance from the Indians, the Israeli Mossad was achieving considerable success infiltrating Pakistan's nuclear weapons facility at Kahuta. "It would appear, Mr President, the Israelis are helping their Indian friends plan a surprise air attack to destroy your Kahuta, in the same way the Israeli Air Force destroyed the Iraqi nuclear reactor in Baghdad during Operation Babylon." Walking slowly, the Chinaman also reported on the latest recruitment of two Pakistani air force officers in a false-flag operation by Indian intelligence officers: an alcoholic army captain working in Joint Intelligence North, the ISI bureau responsible for Jammu & Kashmir and the Northern Areas; and a colonel at the Directorate-General for Military Intelligence based in Rawalpindi; Beijing has concluded India is succeeding in lobbying for observer status at the Organisation of the Islamic Conference through an aggressive campaign of disinformation and propaganda aimed at undermining Pakistan's standing in the Muslim world; a former Pakistani ambassador to Saudi Arabia has been spotted twice in Rangoon in the company of a man the Chinaman believes to be an Indian agent operating in Burma; a member of Zia ul-Haq's cabinet, a former tank corps commander is having an affair with the wife of a member of Benazir Bhutto's party; if made public, this may harm Zia's ongoing Islamisation program for Pakistan.

Zia ul-Haq was keen to know about the Chinaman's views on the breaking up of the Soviet Union. Will Gorbachev lose all the Baltic States? Can the Chinaman shed light on press speculation about a possible coup to oust Gorbachev? Did the Russian reformer have any supporters left in the Politburo? What effect will the breakup of the Soviet Union have on India's military supplies? Will the KGB-RAW protocols remain in place after the dissolution? Will the Soviet Union honour the 1971 Indo-Soviet defence pact if Pakistan attacked India? Pressed, the Chinaman said he had no definite answer but offered his opinion: there will be no change in Moscow's pro-India tilt initiated by Leonid Brezhnev; India is a stick Russia uses to contain and control China's growth and prosperity. The Russians will continue to use the Indians as their useful idiots. "Moscow needs India's considerable influence in the Global South."

The Pakistani guided the Chinaman towards an American-manufactured C-10 Hercules transport plane standing on the runway of the secret military airbase. Stewards were busy boarding crates and trolleys of food, baskets of mangoes, and beverages onboard the plane decorated with the Presidential flag and insignia. Across the runway ground crew were fuelling a Cessna. The Cessna pilot will complete the final security check of the airbase and immediate areas before the security cordon around the Presidential plane can stand down. This was a routine precaution introduced by Army HQ ever since the unsuccessful missile attacks on Zia ul-Haq's plane in 1980.

On seeing the president's entourage approach, his batman snapped a salute and led the party inside. Sipping wine, bourbon, and orange juice in the front passenger seats were Herbert Wossam, a three-star general who led the American military aid mission to Pakistan. Sitting with him was Zia ul-Haq's intimate friend, Akhtar Abdur Rahman, the Chairman of the Joint Chiefs of Staff, one of the most powerful men in Pakistan.

Behind him sat seven top-ranking members of the Pakistani army and air force listening intently to an alcohol-flushed Arnold L. Raphel, the American ambassador. The ambassador was describing the goodwill of Arab nations he described for Pakistan on his recent Africa and Middle East tour. "Our brothers are with us in our jihad against the Communist infidels," the American diplomat reassured them, slurring his words slightly. His Muslim guests gave no indication of having noticed anything was amiss. The ambassador raised his glass, "Washington is also with you, never forget that gentlemen; Operation CYCLONE is the costliest covert action operation the CIA has ever funded. So far, we have paid nearly twenty-billion-dollars to uphold the Reagan Doctrine in Afghanistan. America pays you folks the big bucks because America knows that Pakistan, our most allied of allies, will bring home the bacon. All you boys need to know in Islamabad is that America will never break faith with those freedom fighters risking life and limb in Afghanistan to defy Soviet aggression. On that, you can count on me, gentleman."

The Chinaman's translator, eavesdropping intently in English, Urdu and Arabic gave no indication of understanding a word any of the non-Chinese passengers were speaking.

Behind the soldiers and diplomats sat Crown Prince Turcci of Saudi Arabia sipping sparkling apple juice and talking to Sheikh Khalid Omar, Zia ul Haq's *imam* and noted Islamic scholar. "We are matching the Americans dollar for dollar in Afghanistan," whispered the Saudi prince quietly as Zia ul Haq's entourage passed. "Yes, most of the funding is coming from oil exports but also our brothers and sisters in Qatar, Kuwait, and the United Arab Emirates have been particularly generous this year. Soon we shall be able to fund ninety per cent of the operating expenses of our jihad, *Inshallah!*"

Dressed in a brilliant white *thawb* and the traditional three-ringed black headdress, the presence of the crown prince in Pakistan was proof that the Kingdom of Saudi Arabia continues to provide a fertile recruiting ground for the jihadist groups and the unlimited petrodollar funds available to them. With the Saudi kingdom divided by power struggles between the ailing King Fahd and contenders for his throne, many of the royal family's six thousand princes lived in daily fear. "We all live in fear, my brothers, and sisters; all of us. We all fear the day when the dogs will topple the House of Saud, in much the same way Ayatollah Khomeini returned to Tehran to end the reign of the Shah of Iran", said the prince speaking with his mouth carefully covered. It was to prevent this nightmare scenario that many princes, like Turcci, provided jihadist groups with millions of petrodollars in the hope that when the Kingdom collapsed, they and their families would be spared in the violent insurrection which would engulf Saudi Arabia.

"Please tell the Governor of Riyadh Province and his brilliant young son, Crown Prince Mohammad bin Salman, we thank him for his most generous donations to our cause." Dressed in the garb of a Sunni cleric, Sheikh Khalid Omar was forty-three years old, a full-bearded and physically robust man. He lived and worked in a Deobandi madrassa on the outskirts of Islamabad and was by all accounts a devoted husband and loving father of nine children. Little was known about the cleric outside of Zia ul-Haq's inner circle. Hardly anyone knew, for example, that his madrassa was funded entirely by the Saudi prince and his family businesses. Cultured and soft-spoken, Omar was a little-known figure in the Islamic fundamentalist movement.

Walking slowly behind Zia ul-Haq, the Chinaman gave no indication of recognising either man. In fact, he knew Crown Prince Turcci and Sheikh Omar as ZHENNIAO and JIUFENG, respectively. The Chinaman and his son and heir, Kai Ling of Macau, followed Kang Sheng's tradition of using Chinese mythological birds as cryptonyms for his agents.

It was only when the veteran Chinese spymaster and his translator were alone in the sound-proof presidential quarters with Zia ul-Haq that they got down to the serious matters that necessitated the Chinaman's urgent visit to Pakistan. "I am here to address several issues which have arisen and have been brought to my attention," the Chinaman said without preamble.

Zia ul-Haq poured tea and watched in fascination as the Chinaman unbuttoned his jacket and produced a Cuban cigar. From another pocket, he brought out a British army Zippo lighter. Both his hand and a cigar between his lips trembled slightly as he bent his head to the flame. Although the act of lighting the cigar soothed his nerves, he was irritated the Pakistani had noticed his tremble. "I found this lighter on a Tommy during the Korean War," he said pocketing the lighter. "A boy from Wales who died defending Anglo-American imperialism; he was holding it in his left clenched fist if memory serves me correctly. He was crying for his mother as his innards spilled into the mud. He told me the lighter was given to him by his father."

"I have come to bring to your attention a critical danger to Your Excellency's presidency," he announced, speaking slowly and deliberately. He was always careful to address the former corps commander and army chief as "Mr President" or "Your Excellency" to maintain the façade he was chosen by the Pakistani people. Taking a small key offered by the translator, he unlocked the steel bracelet, opened the dispatch case, and extracted three red folders with security classifications marked on the cover in Chinese. He placed the folders on the table in front of him and sat with his hands resting on his knees, the same posture he always used when delivering grave news.

"The information we have gathered is too important, and too confidential, to risk transmission through our usual channels in Rawalpindi. We fear the Indians or Russians may be eavesdropping on our communications, or yours."

Sipping from a glass of mint tea, Zia ul-Haq sat across the Chinaman, a man he had known since 1969. He had changed not a bit since their first meeting at the Chinese Embassy in Aman, the capital city of the Hashemite Kingdom of Jordan, during the Black September insurgency of 1970. Tall and stooped with a lean haggard face, silver-haired, impeccably tailored with a blood-red handkerchief spilling from his breast pocket, he looked like someone in Lollywood would cast as a *goonda* boss. His age was impossible to guess. The secret slave camps in central China were filled with those who challenged him. Zia ul-Haq was, as usual, fascinated by the Chinaman's fingers. Long, skeletal, and beautifully manicured with fine tufts of white hair protruding from the joints below the knuckle and the large Siberian amethyst ring on the right pinkie, they drummed softly on his knees. They were the same fingers that, with a stroke of a pen, executed countless thousands of Tibetan and Uyghur dissidents, in the Xinjiang re-education camps. Zia ul-Haq had read General Rahman's reports over the years confirming the Chinaman was the chief architect of the cultural genocide in Tibet and Xinjiang.

"India is at this moment, as we are speaking, arming, and training a force of Balochi rebels to attack Chinese investments in the port city of Gwadar. These rebels include the original members of the Baloch Student Organisation, who travelled to India in 1972 for cash, arms, and training." He handed Zia ul-Haq one of the folders. "The operation was created in Lodhi Road by one of their best operatives, a maverick Hindu eunuch known as Golda. Her real name is Anita Kinnar. The details are in here."

Zia ul-Haq extracted some deciphered cables from a thick envelope and ran a forefinger along some lines of text. "So, India is using a Hindu eunuch spy runner to train those Balochis dogs, again? I am most happy to learn of this detail. I shall pass this information to my intelligence chief, General Hamid Gul, for immediate action. I will ask Akhtarji to take care of this for me personally."

Chairman of the Joint Chief of Staff Akhtar Abdur Rahman was the most powerful man in Pakistan after Zia ul-Haq. Rahman had headed the Inter-Services Intelligence, Pakistan's foreign intelligence service, for over ten years, until he handed over to Hamid Gul in 1987. Since 1979, Rahman had orchestrated America's proxy war – Operation CYCLONE - in Afghanistan against the Soviet Union. Towards the end of 1987, the American C.I.A. was paying over six-hundred-and-fifty million dollars a year to Akhtar Rahman to organise, train, and arm the mujahedeen guerrillas waging war against the Russians.

An acrid smirk made its way onto the Chinaman's lips. "Beijing instructs me to remind you of the importance of Gwadar in our win-win relationship, Your Excellency," he said staring directly at the Pakistani. The Chinaman paused to stub out the cigar. He glanced casually around the cabin. *He really is a true jihadist believer.* The austere quarter was decorated with icons and images of the holy places of Islam: ornate miniature paintings of the Kaaba and scenes from Mecca and Medina were decoratively arranged around a coffee table. Large photographs of the Prophets Mosque and Al-Aqsa Mosque in Jerusalem were also on display. The small bookcase contained an impressive collection of works on the philosophy of jihadism, including *The Neglected Obligation* by Muhammad Abd-al-Salam Faraj, the Islamist electrician who planned the murder of Anwar Sadat, the Egyptian president. The complete works of Sayyed Imam Al-Sharif were also included for Zia ul-Haq's pleasure, including *The Essential Guide for Preparation* and *The Compendium of the Pursuit of Divine Knowledge*.

"It is most important you understand why Gwadar is pivotal in our strategic relations, Mr President. I am authorised to tell you Beijing will not be able to proceed with our proposed investments in Pakistan's infrastructure, including our close and fruitful cooperation in nuclear weapons technology……"

"Please tell Beijing……."

The Chinaman cut in abruptly. "The only reason Pakistan is a nuclear weapons state is because China allowed you to have military-grade enriched uranium; we built your entire atomic weapons development program and infrastructure; Beijing allowed you to procure nuclear material via Chinese front companies in Sweden, Finland, Turkey, Japan, and Belgium; and I am allowing North Korea to supply your army with ballistic missile technology in exchange for the nuclear technology we gave you. When we land in Islamabad and I take leave of you, I shall be taken to see the great nuclear scientist, Dr Abdul Qadeer Khan, where I shall personally deliver special magnetics from our North Korean friends. All this cooperation will cease if Gwadar is not protected and Balochistan not secured. Beijing has instructed me to make this clear to you; I trust I have made our position clear to you, Your Excellency. "There will be no misunderstanding on this. Have I made myself clear on this?"

"Yes, you have," said Zia ul-Haq quietly. "Please tell me more about this planned attack by the Indians."

"All in good time, Mr President," snapped the Chinaman. "I remind you of the discussions we had during your 1986 visit to Beijing. We spoke about the importance of creating a seagoing highway for our goods and energy needs and we also discussed creating a land-based route from the ancient Silk Route. Do you remember this conversation, Mr President?"

"Yes, yes I remember of course," whispered Zia ul Haq meekly.

"Good, because the old Silk Route goes straight through Xinjiang travelling southwards until it connects to your Gwadar. Beijing will never tolerate threats to its economic development and the prosperity of the Chinese people. You promised me, Mr President, we can do business together."

"We can," squeaked Zia. His mouth had become uncomfortably dry. "We can do business. Please tell me about these Balochi rebels," he pleaded, feeling a sense of rising panic.

"The Balochi attack is scheduled for early in the month of May," said the Chinaman finally. "Current plans call for a freighter registered to a Yemeni shipping company in Bangladesh to ferry the rebels, to Gwadar port. The full details are in this second folder."

Listening intently to what his Chinese controller was saying, Zia ul-Haq reached out and pulled a sheaf of papers from the manilla folder. "We have a Bangladeshi agent among the stevedores loading the freighter, the *Red Dhow*, at its anchorage in Chittagong. We also have assets working at Al Mukalla port in Yemen. Their vessel is carrying large stores of Soviet-made arms supplied by the Indians, a sophisticated communications unit, and a quantity of gasoline."

"I can confirm the Indian agents are armed with guns and explosives of Russian and Czech origin. Half of the gasoline will be stored in tanks below deck, the rest will be divided into gallon drums tied to the deck's topside."

"Then these gasoline drums will be a perfect target for my Air Force pilots to use for target practice." Zia ul-Haq had always known the Chinaman had excellent sources of information in India and the USSR, but he had never realised just how excellent until recently. He was too professional a soldier to raise the subject, but it was clear to him that the Chinaman must be running an agent with access to the top four floors of Lodhi Road in New Delhi, the headquarters of India's foreign intelligence agency, the Research & Analysis Wing.

They discussed various details of the Indian operation that the Chinaman had knowledge of. He informed Zia of the arms and ammunitions that would be made available to the Balochi rebels inside the actual port complex, not the city; the communications channels that would be used from the port to the Indian boats out in the Arabian Sea; and the planned exfiltration of the rebels. "I leave it to your ISI people to fill in the missing pieces of the puzzle and extract the necessary information from the traitors."

Zia ul Haq said with a cold glint in his dark eye, "We most certainly shall."

Pakistan's president pointed with his chin towards the red folders. "There's the other folder you haven't opened yet," he said.

The Chinaman kept his eyes fixed on Zia ul-Haq. "We need to talk about our ongoing TUPAC operation, Your Excellency. I have made some changes to the original plan."

Zia ul-Haq's trimmed eyebrow furrowed. The black-dyed moustache twitched as the Chinese spymaster pulled a single sheet from the folder and began reading it aloud. Each phrase was carefully translated word by word into Zia ul-Haq's native Urdu. After he finished reading, he paused before handing the folder to Zia.

"You will carefully read the revised TUPAC II operation, Mr President. It is my masterplan for the destruction of our common adversary, India. The only other copy is in my private safe at Zhongnanhai. Thank you again for allowing me to join you onboard your plane, Mr President. I suggest we join your other guests. I look forward to hearing your thoughts on TUPAC II." The Chinaman stood up, followed immediately by the translator. The meeting was over.

As he walked behind General Zia ul-Haq he concluded the meeting had been satisfactory. The Chinaman took his seat and slowly fastened his seat belt as the plane began to move. What should he make of QUINGNIAO, the mythical Chinese bird which served as Zia ul-Haq's cryptonym?

Meanwhile, two middle-aged men sitting in the back of an APC Talha army personnel carrier approximately three miles from the Bahawalpur base watched as the Hercules lurched unsteadily in the sky. A third man, younger and wearing army fatigues and a maroon-coloured beret was standing outside but close to the personnel carrier. His sidearm was unholstered. The soldier was staring intently as the plane nosedived, burying itself in the desert after its fifth loop. The explosion was immediately followed by a huge ball of orange fire and thick black smoke. He glanced at his watch. It was 3.55 pm local time. After a flight lasting only six minutes, the Hercules had crashed killing all onboard, including the two Americans and the Saudi prince. He walked slowly back to the carrier.

Entering the vehicle, he took the driver's seat. "Golda has confirmed successful hit, Sir," Dressed in the regimental cap of the

Northern Light Infantry, the three-rank chevrons on the driver's uniform identified him as a *havildar*. "Zia is dead."

"Good cricket," said the older of the two men, a big-boned man sporting an immaculate Tagorean beard. He was dressed in the uniform of a colonel and carried with him documentation identifying him as Mehmet Assad Jurrani, an officer attached to the Joint Staff headquarters in Rawalpindi.

Although dressed in the garb of a Pakistani army officer, the man was neither Pakistani, a soldier, nor a Muslim. Inquisitive, acquisitive, manipulative, exploitative, and utterly ruthless, Acharya Bhairava was a veteran of India's clandestine foreign intelligence service. The former Hindu monk was recruited by Nehru's spymaster Bhola Nath Mullick in Benares in early 1969 and currently served as the hands-on deputy director of the Directorate General of Security. The DGS was the clandestine division based at Lodhi Road tasked with covert operations, tactical paramilitary operations, and covert political action.

"Zia was a true jihadist, a genuine believer. I am satisfied now he is dead; most satisfied indeed," murmured Acharya quietly. "I was surprised, though, when the MOSQUITO operation was approved by Ramji," said Acharya. "He always said targeted killing should exclude political figures like Zia. I know he will be relieved the deed is done. It's a better world with Zia gone."

The "Ramji" he was referring to was Rameshwar Nath Kao, the legendary founder-director of India's foreign intelligence service, the Research and Analysis Wing, popularly known in the media by its acronym, the RAW. Within the corridors of Lodhi Road, RAW headquarters since 1968, it was known by employees and insiders as The Wing.

"You are unusually quiet my friend, Robbieji. A penny for your thoughts, eh?" Common to men of his status, Acharya used the honorific suffix *ji* as a term of respect for his English friend.

"Apologies, my dear fellow," said the tall, languid Old Amplefordian. Impeccably dressed in a safari suit Robert Charles Gage took a long sip of Amrut single malt from an ancient, battered hip flask. "I feel I can finally breathe again, Acharyaji." He took another long gulp of malt from the hip flask. "I have not been able to breathe for the last ten years, not since the day Zia took away my boy Vivek," he said quietly. "I did this for him, you know. I'm not sure I care anymore if London finds out. I've had a good run in India, probably time to pack up my bags and bugger off back home. Besides, I don't have a reason to be in India anymore."

"Rubbish! India *is* your home," Acharya said emphatically. "Stop this self-pity, Robbie. Vivek would be disappointed to hear you say this. You are and always will be part of our Lodhi Road family. Vivek would have wanted you to be part of this mission," said Acharya softly to his close friend and colleague. "Stop this; stop it now!"

"Yes, you are right," said the British spymaster staring vacantly out of the window. He sighed. "Come along young Tariq, take us to base camp and the delightful Golda. I think we all deserve a decent meal to celebrate."

"Golda has already got Bilal started on cooking our supper", said Tariq smiling, "she said something about needing to feed her boys. It's her famous *panch thali tiffin*."

"In that case, you had better step on it, beta. Golda doesn't cook this meal every day. The last time I tasted it was after Operation Lal Dora in Mauritius," Acharya said smiling. Approved by Prime Minister Indira Gandhi in 1983, the mission called for the secret landing of Indian special forces taskforce to prevent an attempted coup from toppling the government of Anerood Jugnauth, the prime minister of Mauritius belonging to the local Hindu Ahir community.

"I can still smell, and taste Golda's five famous thali dishes she served up for us boys after the mission" said Acharya with his eyes closed. "*Qabuli pulao*; *chapli kebab*; *Lahori beef karahi* with tandoori naan; and *aloo mutter*. Ice-cold seasonal fruit *chaat* to cleanse the palate. Such a feast."

A lifelong foodie, Robert Gage nodded in approval. His summary of Acharya's deputy in a 1971 report to the SIS Station Chief read: "……. reporting directly to the deputy director of the Directorate General of Security Acharya Bhairava, Anita "Golda" Kinnar heads Research & Analysis Wings Special Services Bureau. A seasoned senior field officer, she currently holds the rank of Joint Secretary. She is a professional intelligence officer with a raffish charm, a lack of restraint, an ability to ridicule, to take imaginative leaps, to break the rules to work against a background of blending fact and fiction. Her operational cover for many years was the Press Trust of India. Anita Kinnar is a member of India's transgender *Hirja* community and a devotee of the Hindu goddess, Bahuchara Mata………"

Tariq Ahmad threw the carrier into gear and sped across the metalled tarmac and the fields beyond an airport gate guarded by a cordon of soldiers. Seeing the carrier approaching they hauled the gate open. A *naik* snapped off a smart salute as the vehicle whipped passed jounced up an embankment onto a wide access road and roared off in the direction of the Fareed Gate, a local monument in the city. Tariq's destination was the tree-lined *havelli* tucked away in a hidden lane which served as a long-time RAW safe house.

Speeding along a broad boulevard lined with cedar, Sgt Ahmad, who was a paratrooper in the Indian army, switched on the radio as the two spymasters chatted quietly in the back. To Tariq's delight the song *Julie Julie Johny Ka Dil Tumpe Aaya* from the 1987 Bollywood action film, *Jeete Hain Shaan Se*, soon filled the vehicle. It was the first film he saw with Sarita Khan. It took him seven pilsner beers to muster the courage to ask the formidable career-driven Intelligence Bureau officer out on a date.

As if reading his mind, he heard Robbie Gage say, "Never wait to tell someone you love them, Tariq my boy. It's the only thing that matters in the end. Who have I loved and who has loved me? It's the only question worth asking at the eleventh hour."

"I wonder how long it will be before dear Ramji summons us for the delicious ritual of squeezing the mango," murmured Acharya. "Squeezing the mango" was what Ramji euphemistically called the exhaustive debriefing of his bureau chiefs and agents at his club, McGregor's, on Safdarjung Road.

"God how I'm looking forward to a drink at McGregor's," said Robert Gage peering at Pakistani street life. "It's where I met Viv, you know. I think, my dear Tariq, you should invite the lovely Sarita Khan to McGregor's for a romantic dinner. Let me arrange it for you; as club steward, I am allowed certain privileges. I shall book the decadent Lakshmibai Room for you to entertain your love interest. It's where I took Viv for our first *biryani* dinner date. Unforgettable."

"From what I hear McGregor's is the place where many of us find our love interest. I think Robbie is correct on this issue. I also think you should ask her out on a *biryani* date," said Acharya with a twinkle in his eye.

"Thank you, Robbie, for helping us avenge our brother, Vivek's, murder."

The summons to meet Ramji at McGregor's came two days after the MOSQUITO taskforce was safely back in Lodhi Road.

1

Lewes Road, Brighton, England, 2024

It was a short walk to The Level from the Moulsecoomb estate where Jago lived. After another furious argument with his lover, Hari was grateful for the cold air; his migraine was beginning to throb less. *God, why does he look and sound so fine when he's angry? It drives me silly!* But on reflection, Hari acknowledged that watching the latest news bulletin of *StratNewsGlobal* immediately after making love wasn't perhaps the best of moves. "Dudes who go on YouTube immediately after a three-hour-fuck-session are selfish little cunts. That's you, Hari. Selfish and self-centred to the core. You lose all interest in me immediately after you shoot your load." Hari tried to explain that he couldn't possibly miss the episode because the brilliant Abhijt Iyer-Mitra was expertly explaining why Pakistan was a failing state and how that was a global problem. "He's one of the best geopolitical commentators in South Asia. Why don't you join me? You might learn something useful for once?" Jago's withering look told him that was also the wrong thing to say to his lover.

Until developers began turning it into a student ghetto, Lewes Road had been an unloved place, he thought, as he passed the old railway station. A muddle of buildings still lined the pavements. Crumbling Victorian terraces stood shoulder to shoulder with empty 1960s office blocks, which bled rust down the draining and facades. A few houses stood empty or gutted, their tiled roofs sagging, the red chimney pots leaning perilously. Pigeons flew in and out of broken windows. Walls served as urban canvases for local graffiti artists. In doorways, soggy food cartons lay among nests of rags and crushed cardboard boxes made by Brighton's homeless junkies. Jago often referred to the drug-infested Whitehawk estate, where he grew up, as the *Shitehawk* estate, so bad was the sanitation and drainage problems, causing weekly rat infestations. Jago's words, Hari discovered, were always perfectly delivered in any given situation.

Hari met Jago on a sunny summer day in Bevendean. Hari had just finished interviewing a Bangladeshi man at his home on Bodiam Avenue and was walking down the long meandering hill to wait for the bus to take him back into town. The interview was for background information on a murder in a flat in Sutton Hoo Street in Seaford, close to t*he Three Moon's of India* restaurant when he clocked a runner on Norwich Drive. The youth was jogging around the Bevendean estate, north-east of central Brighton. So captivated was he watching the graceful jogger with fine rangy features, Hari missed the number forty-eight bus. He shrugged, lit a pre-rolled marijuana joint, and waited outside a doctor's surgery for the next bus.

After a while, the jogger turned around, heading towards the bus stop. Hari cursed himself for not bringing his camera. He had a perfect view of the runner's tall, slim physique with long, slender limbs, his movements elegant and fluid. Hari adopted a pose, leaning against the bus stop, standing on one leg; his eyes fixed on the jogger with a soft gaze. He took a long slow drag, inhaling the sickly-sweet smoke narcotic deep down into his lungs for a few seconds before exhaling a huge plume of white smoke. The jogger slowed as he approached. He sniffed the air theatrically. "Ah, the aroma of Brighton, my favourite pong! Smells well nice. I need to rest for a bit; mind if I join you. I'm Jago. Jago J. Jarvis. Jay to my friends."

Tilting his head, Hari sized up Jago J. Jarvis walking towards him, absorbing every detail of him: his athletic rangy physique, and flawless carob-toned skin; the strong inverted triangular face; the long flat nose, with nostrils, flared slightly as he theatrically sniffed the air; and his large, liquid tiger eyes. Hari spent a few extra seconds absorbing the details of the elaborate tightly knotted pigtails hanging down the nape of his neck. "What's the J stand for?" asked Hari, admiring the laughter lines around the sides of his wide mouth, the repaired chipped front tooth, and the navigator glasses balanced stylishly on his head. Hari noted the details the details of the teenager's early attempts at shaving, the trendy brand-new trainers, and the *Nike* tracksuit bottoms.

"It doesn't stand for anything, to be honest. I only use it to impress the stylishly dressed, fit men with stunning green eyes I always seem to come across when jogging in Bevendean," he said with a smile that reached his eyes. "Not that I'm implying you're a stylishly dressed, sexy-ass, fit man!" Jago's eyes hadn't left Hari since he introduced himself. "My dad, my biological father that is," he explained eyeing the joint Hari held between his fingers, "was born in Santiago, Cape Verde and wrote it on the birth certificate because he figured it would make his son look important if he had a middle initial. Fuck man is you gonna pass that or not! Or are you waiting for me to beg you? Can't ya see I'm gasping for a toke? Tell me your name, yeah. I told you mine."

Hari began giggling, slightly stoned but feeling mainly intoxicated by Jago's theatricality, his farcical attempt at the Jamaican patois; his cocksureness, but his complete lack of vanity; his open, earnest face; the black-gold flecked tiger eyes and pigtails. But most of all, the infectious energy, which was then radiating out of him. "Hello, Jay from Bevendean; my name is, Hari K. Vandra from The Lanes, nice to meet you; really nice to meet you in fact," said Hari moving towards Jago, extending his right hand forward.

Jago took Hari's right hand in his, as per normal social etiquette, only held it for a tad longer than was the norm, his fingers stroking his wrist, paying particular attention to the area above his *median nerve*. "Did you, Hari, know that the human handshake is prehistoric; it was a gesture of peace to show the hands held no weapons." Jago's eyes never left Hari's and he refused to let go of the hand he was holding. "There look, I come to you unarmed, like the warriors of ancient times."

"I did not know that Jay, no, but thanks though," said Hari meeting Jago's gaze, enjoying the sensation of his fingertips on the inside of his wrist. "I live to learn and learn to live. I hope I always remain teachable."

"You're getting more and more interesting by the minute, Mr Vandra. I learned about the wrist thing from a film; cannot remember what tho' but of what I know, and love comes from the movies," Jago said smiling, but still refusing to relinquish Hari's wrist. "Hey Hari, what's the *K* stand for in *your* name?"

"The *K* in my name stands for Krsna. My father named me after the blue-skinned Hindu god of compassion, tenderness, and selfless love because he thought it would make his son virtuous, happy, joyous, and free. But to answer your earlier question; I probably shouldn't. Not to a fine specimen of male athleticism such as your good self, but do you fancy a drag of this, Jay? I like to share the good things in my life with friends."

"Blessed, yo! I'm tokin the sacred herb with a blue-skinned god, no less! Holy cow!" Jago exclaimed and as he reluctantly released Hari's hand from his, thus ending the marathon handshake, to take the joint passed, they're eyes locked, unwavering. Both stood their ground. Neither moved.

Hari recognised, immediately, the significance of the look Jago was giving him. He'd discovered at an early age he was able to communicate intuitively with other schoolboys using a special gaze, a sort of soft stare, which seemed unique to him at the time. Hari's parents had worked as international civil servants for the Commonwealth and the British Council, so Hari attended many embassy schools around the world, getting to know many different boys from many different cultures. During his teenage and adolescent years, he had spent days perfecting his ability to discern instantly from the returned glance, however fleeting, another boy's sexual nature. Jago's gaze was not only deliberately lingering, especially around Hari's face and eyes; it was also a visual probing; a search for recognition in Hari's face. "Thanks, and please call me, Jay," he said taking the joint, his eyes still not leaving Hari's face.

"So, Jay, what's your story? Are you a local, a genuine Brightonian?"

"Yep,' he said. 'Born in Brighton General, grew up in Whitehawk, and now living in Bevendean, over there," he said pointing in the general direction of a primary school. "I live with my mum; just the two of us."

"Bevendean looks like a nice place to live, to raise a family,' said Hari. 'I discovered the name Bevendean comes from "Beofa's valley", though I've forgotten who exactly Beofa was! I know this area is incredibly old; the manor of Bevendean – this all used to be farmland - is recorded in the *Doomsday Book* of 1086, would you believe."

"Is that the reason you're wandering around Bevendean looking fit with that leather satchel, you're a history buff?"

"I love history, always have, but no, it not that," said Hari, laughing at the lad's cocksureness. "I'm working; to interview a chap for an article I'm writing."

"It doesn't surprise me a bit you're a writer; you dress and talk like one. I don't hear guys talk about "chaps", not around 'ere anyways. So, what do you write about, Hari?"

"I've had a go at all types of journalism: news, mainly counter-culture issues; investigative crime reporting, usually gang-related issues, and drug markets; feature writing; reviews; and columns. Tried my hand at most things: personality profiles, living and historical; political: did one on Nigel Farage and another on Suella Braverman not so long ago; writing for women's magazines; but mostly I focus on crime reporting," he said, wondering, not for the first time, why he found it so hard to describe his work to strangers. "How do you spend your days, Jago?"

"Jay! it's Jay to my friends; especially those friends with green eyes like yours, never seen green eyes on a brown dude before. Quality! I insist you call me Jay! It's Jago to everyone else."

"Apologies, Jay!" he said, "names are everything. Christopher Hitchens was exactly like you; he became terribly upset when anyone called him Chris, instead of Christopher."

"Christopher Hitchens? Is he a friend of yours?"

"Well, not really, no; he was a writer and political polemicist who I've always admired." As Hari took the joint from Jago their fingers touched. "How does Jay spend his days? Pray, do tell."

"Not sure what a lot of that means but you sound really passionate about Christopher Hitchens and your work, Hari, which is a good thing; I need some passionate role models in my life. I'm not much of a reader I'm afraid, left school at fifteen because of undiagnosed dyslexia. How does Jay spend his days? Well, to make money I work as a day labourer on various building sites around the city. During my breaks I like to take photographs of the city from very high places. Some of the pictures are good, even if I do say so myself. My passion is trail biking across the Downs; I love it. Oh! I'm also in training for next year's regional slalom skateboarding races in London; any spare time is spent watching movies. I'm a film buff."

"That sounds nice……"

"Oh, I nearly forgot," he said quickly. "I'm an actor, actually; just applied to the Piers Farley School of Speech & Drama in fact, to join their foundation course in acting. They're in Lewes, you may have heard of the place; they're good on a whole different level. Waiting to hear back from them, in fact," he said his voice trailing off as he looked over Hari's shoulder. "I only mention the drama school because I didn't want you to think I was just a day labourer with no ambitions or prospects. I'd be pissed if you thought that about me. Your bus should be here any minute soon, Hari Vandra," he said. "Don't worry, it'll be here very soon to take you back to civilisation, and your home in the classy bit of Brighton."

"I think you'll make a great actor, Jay. Of that I have no doubt, *mon ami*. I'd love to come to see you perform........"

"Quality!" he exclaimed. "I was hoping you'd say that. Write down your digits, quickly before the fucking bus gets here," he said hurriedly as the number bus came slowly down Norwich Drive, stopping at the community post office. "I don't normally carry pen and paper when out jogging topless, so I'm hoping *Tintin* here is carrying a pencil and his trusty reporter's pad on him," he said pointing to Hari's satchel.

Hari took out his *Field Notes* notepad from his inner left jacket and jotted his home phone number. "I check the answering machine twice daily; just leave a message if I don't answer," he said pausing to look at Jago's eyes again, before writing down his pager number. "This is my mobile; you can get me on this at any time."

"That looks like an expensive pen," said Jago staring at the grey-coloured Montblanc, elegantly poised in Hari's right hand. "Hey, make sure you get mine; the number is......"

He wrote down Jago's number carefully, repeating it back to him twice. "It was a gift from my godfather, Robbie Gage when he last visited Brighton; he works at the British High Commission in New

Delhi." I can still remember him saying to me, "Now try not to lose the bloody thing, this time Hari! It's another Montblanc ballpoint pen to replace the one you lost in Bristol; this one's a *Writers Homage to Rudyard Kipling*, limited edition of course."

As the double-decker started to turn on the corner of Heath Hill Avenue, Hari turned back to see if Jago was still there. He was, standing very still, hands on hips, fading into the distance, but Hari could see he was still staring at the departing bus.

"You're a very beautiful young man; you also have a moxie, as we used to say," said an elderly woman sitting in the seat opposite, "and your friend, the one who couldn't stop looking at your face, is also beautiful; are you both alternatives?' she asked. 'Can I tell you something?" she asked taking in Hari's glossy jet-black hair, kept unfashionably long; his light-brown skin tone typical of north-east Indians; his strong, oval face, was framed by symmetrical cheeks; the almond-shaped eyes of glistening pools of green; thin, elevated arched eyebrows; an aquiline Roman nose with his slightly flared nostrils; the well-defined, laterally full cheeks; his lips, the lower lip slightly larger than the upper one; his firm jawline, and prominent, masculine chin; meant Hari Vandra was accustomed to turning heads.

"I have a funny feeling you're going to anyway," said Hari with a wry smile, as it dawned on him what she was alluding to with the word, "alternative."

"I love your eyes young man; I've never seen such beautiful green eyes as yours; they remind me of Ireland," said the woman. "I'm Gloria and I'm nearly ninety years old. I live on my own with three cats. I have seen many eyes on the faces of many men, but none as green as yours on a face so beautiful as yours."

"You're very kind, thank you for your compliments, Gloria; my name is Hari Vandra," he said, "green eyes are very rare; less than two per cent of the world's population has green, and I've yet to meet another green-eyed Indian."

"What colour are your beautiful friend's eyes," asked Gloria, "my eyesight is not as good as they were back in the 1930s,' she said with a sudden giggle. Is he also an alternative," she asked, "I'm assuming he is by the way he was holding your hand. He didn't want to let go of you."

"Well let me think," said Hari closing his eyes, remembering the natural contours of Jago's face. "Okay, the best way to describe Jay's eyes is large luminous liquid eyes, his irises flecked with specks of black and gold, rather the like tiger eyes; his rather girlishly long eyelashes definitely give a distinctly feline quality to him."

"It sounds as though he takes your breath away, the way you just described him to me," said Gloria looking at him. "I get that feeling when I'm on my allotment watching the peas grow, listening to larks, touching my plants and flowers. It's not how many breaths you take, but what takes your breath away; sounds like you're your friend back there took away your breath, Hari."

Later that day Hari was towelling off after a long, steaming shower when he heard the ringing of the landline phone. Normally he let the machine cut in, but something made him pick up the receiver. "Yo bro, Hari, sorry 'bout the late hour, but I was just thinking about you, so I called; you said I could call anytime, right?" Jago's voice sounded dreamy and playful. Soft reggae music played in the background. He could hear the familiar sound of Jago inhaling a drag of smoke, and then slowly exhale. After a very long pause, he asked, "Are you happy I called, Hari?"

"I'm incredibly happy you've called, Jay, you've been in my thoughts too; a lot actually" said Hari lying down on the bed. "The answer to your question is yes; yes, I do happen to know the Piers Farley School of Speech & Drama. I was invited to a fundraising event and ended up chatting with Piers Farley himself; we had an interesting chat on whether drama, as a category of narrative fiction, was intended to be more serious than comedic. Fascinating man, Mr Piers Farley! Surprised to discover how small he was, though!"

"Yeah, he's something alright. I've never seen him without a hat. Really gets into his passion. During my interview with him, he mentioned that the word *"thespian"* comes from the world's first actor, Thespis of Icaria. It was a good interview I thought," he said, the pride evident in his voice. "Piers asked me to perform a favourite scene from a favourite film, and I think he really liked my performance!"

"What did you perform?"

"I chose the part of Jules Winnfield played by my man Samuel L. Jackson in the film *Pulp Fiction*. The scene I chose was when Jackson blows away some scumbags uttering some seriously iconic words," said Jago, his voice like that of an excited little boy with a new toy. "You do know what I'm talking about don't you Hari? I only ask because you're quiet, real silent; not even making little sounds of silence, to show your listening, yo!" giggled Jago as he slowly got more stoned on his weed. "Hey Hari, in case you didn't know and you're quiet because you're too proud to admit you don't know something to someone younger; let me tell you: *Pulp Fiction* is, in Jay's most humble opinion, the best neo-noir black comedy crime film written by and directed by the genius that is, Mr Quentin Tarantino!"

Hari burst into fits of laughter. "Thank you, Barry Norman for that amazing critique of Mr Tarantino. And yes, yes, I do know about *Pulp Fiction*."

"Wish me luck with my application; don't rate my chances though."

"Really! Why on earth would you think that?" asked Hari.

"Well, that's a discussion for another time; like over a pint after a movie, for example. You down, yo?"

"You need to ask Piers Farley for some help with your Jamaican patois, Jay!" said Hari giggling like a schoolboy.

"I'm serious, man; I'm really interested in knowing more about what you know, Hari," Jago said, reverting to the dream-like voice he used earlier. "Nothing too deep, don't worry; well, not at the beginning anyway," he said, chuckling. "For example, I really want to know about the stuff you write for those women's magazines you mentioned. I want to know more about this story you're chasing, the reason you were in Bevendean today; the reason I met you. Also, I really think we should try to find out who this Beofa of Bevedean fella was; you mentioned he lived around 1086, right?" He started to giggle again. "Would you like to go and catch a movie with me this weekend, Hari?"

"You don't want to know much do you, Jay," Hari said, grinning broadly down the phone. "Yeah, I agree, I would love to watch a film with you, Jay. One condition: you allow me to take you out for a curry and Kingfisher beer where you can bombard me with all your questions. Hopefully, by the time we get to the desert, you can explain what makes *Pulp Fiction* a "neo-noir black comedy crime film." Hari's mobile emitted its distinct sound notifying him of a voice note. "Sorry Jay, some idiots just messaged me on my mobile…."

'Oh, that was me; I called both your numbers because I didn't want you to get the impression, I was in any way interested in kissing you or jumping your bones…."

A black refuse bag had been ripped open by seagulls and had spilt its contents across the pavement. Chicken bones, gnawed ribs, sweetcorn kernels, and yoghurt pots lay amidst a slick puddle of condensed Heinz mushroom room. The pavement had been fouled with dog shit, smudges and smears spread across the paving stones, causing pedestrians to skip around them like children playing hopscotch.

Hari realised he was at the end of Lewes Road. He reached the bottom of Elm Grove before taking a right towards the large parkland to his right.

The Level skatepark, surrounded by ancient elm trees, was a popular meeting place in Brighton for people walking their dogs or jogging. On the freshly cut lawn below, a fit-looking blond in his mid-twenties wearing a faded Sussex University sweatshirt played out the line that trailed off to a huge fluttering kite, which dipped and baulked and soared in the cold wind with gymnastic deftness. An elderly woman wearing a shocking, pink-coloured hat with feathers stood nearby with one hand on the back of a bench, trying to scrape dog poo off the sole of her orthopaedic shoes by shuffling her feet on the pavement.

Hari found the bench, sat down, and waited for his long-time confidential informant to arrive.

2

Gwadar Port City, Province of Balochistan, Pakistan

Chen Qiang sank into his seat and passed the time studying the Balochi people along the street. Despite the air-conditioning, he felt the stifling heat and extremely dry air. His armoured pickup truck was being chauffeured by one of the many uniformed militiamen poached from the Chinese Ministry of Internal Security to work in Pakistan, a dark man with little pig eyes and a peach-shaped face on the staff of his boss, Kai Ling of Macau.

After a while the truck turned onto a narrow one-lane road with a large sign at the edge reading in Urdu, Standard Chinese, and English, "China Pakistan Marine Shipping & Freight Forwarding Agency (Macau) – No Admittance." They drove for a few minutes through a small juniper forest. Through the trees, Qiang caught sight of a small, abandoned mosque, its door and window gaping open, its single onion-shaped dome in ruins. The truck swung into a driveway paved with fine white gravel and pulled up in front of a small brick outbuilding. A high electric fence topped with coils of razor wire stretched as far as his eye could see in both directions. A pack of black-tongued Shar Pei guard dogs prowled back and forth at the end of long chains tied to juniper trees. Qiang spied a Chinese border guard coming around to the rear window. A soldier with a QCW-05 bullpup submachine gun under his arm, its suppressor inserted, watched from behind a pile of sandbags. Qiang rolled the window down just enough to pass Kai Ling's card to the officer. The officer glanced at the card, then handed it back and waved the driver on. At the end of the gravel driveway loomed an early 19th-century British-era mansion. Around the side of the house a gaggle of little brown girls, barefoot and wearing short smock-like dresses were playing with dolls. Qiang tries to ignore the little girls knowing full well the fate that awaits them after his master, Kai Ling, grows bored of them and orders a new batch from Islamabad. A young man in a tight Mao suit, altered by the sentry guard at the gate, was waiting at the open door, his arms folded arrogantly across his chest, his shoulders hunched against the heat. "You are required to follow me," he said when Qiang came up the stairs. He preceded the visitor down a narrow hallway and up a curving flight of stairs covered with thick *Bokhara* and *Chobi* rugs, knocked three times on the door, threw it open and stepped back to let Qiang through.

Kai Ling, cooling himself in front of an air conditioner fixed in a window of the antechamber, was reading from a thin book. Kai Ling broke off reading when he caught sight of Lee Kung and strode across the room and clasped the hand of his young visitor in both of his. Behind Qiang, the door clicked closed.

"Do you have any idea where you are? What this place is?" Kai Ling asked softly as he gripped his protégé's elbow and steered him through a door into a large sitting room.

"I have no idea," Qiang admitted.

"This small estate was originally built by an English slave trader working for the imperialist East India Company who sold it to the Sultan of Oman. It was taken over by my father in the 1970s and has been used by us as a secret retreat ever since." He gestured with his head for Qiang to follow him as he made his way through a small archway and into a dining room with a large oval table set with fine porcelain and silver cutlery.

"The English imperialists certainly knew how to build their mansions," said Qiang looking around admiringly.

"The mansion is divided into three apartments – one is used by Pui Chui, who is head of our military intelligence operations in Pakistan. He comes to me from the International Liaison Department. The second is set aside for the Military Intelligence

Department officer responsible for liaising with the Pakistani Inter-Services Intelligence. He uses it as a hideaway when he wants to escape from the bedlam of Islamabad. There is also a small apartment for the Science and Technology Department who collect my signals intelligence." Kai Ling collected a rose-coloured bottle of sharbat and two glasses, each with a slice of lime in it, and continued to a spacious wood-panelled library filled with hundreds of ageing English-language volumes and several dozen portraits of long-dead colonial administrators. "I occupy the third apartment." On the single stretch of the wall not covered with bookcases hung a life-sized portrait of Jiang Qing, Chairman Mao's last wife and member of the Gang of Four. The painter's name, Tsu Pi, and the date 1939 were visible at the bottom right. Qing, wearing a rough peasant's shirt, had been posed sitting in a chair, an open book in her left hand. Qiang noticed that her fingernails, like Kai Ling's, were thick and long and squarely cut.

A large wooden table containing a neat pile of file folders stood in the centre of the room. Kai Ling set the bottle and glasses on the table and slipped into a seat. He motioned for Qiang to take the seat across from him. "Helu and his chief military strategist, Sun Tzu claimed that hot desert climates were an analgesic for his arthritis – more effective than any man-made remedies. Who can say he is not right?" Kai Ling lit one of his cheroots. "Would you like one? Our friend in Naypyidaw sends them to me from Myanmar."

Qiang shook his head.

A dour-looking, reed-thin man with a shaved head, wearing the uniform of the Baloch Regiment, appeared carrying a wooden tray. He set a plate of sweetmeats on the table, filled two chunky glasses with steaming milky *chai* from a thermos and set it down. "Talal is my housekeeper and cook. He brews the best *chai* in Balochistan," said the Chinese spymaster. When he had left, closing the door behind him, Kai Ling lifted his glass to his lips and began noisily drinking the *chai*. Qiang could see the Adam's apple, bobbing in sinewy neck. After a moment Kai Ling asked, "Tell me about Puntland." As usual, Kai Ling's words were a command couched as a gentle request.

"My meeting in Somalia was satisfactory. The Iranians, Al-Shabaab, and the Houthis are onboard. As are the Noth Koreans. I have transferred the funds according to your instructions. The Pakistani military trainers have already begun working with the new Houthi recruits in Puntland. Operation TUPAC II is on schedule," he said. Qiang had learned never to use long flowery words when reporting facts to his master. "Salim, the Somali pirate is working well in overseeing the monastery operations. The cargo is safe and ready for transportation. We have had no problems with the bioweapons. The recent toxicity reports from the scientists are most satisfactory." He handed a piece of paper to his mentor. "This is a list of the groups who will receive a share of the weapons. As you can see the lion's share will be given to the Maoist mercenaries operating in India's so-called Red Corridor. I will be leaving to meet the Maoist leader, Ganapathy, in two days. The rest of the weapons will be divided between the Kashmiri and Khalistan groups. I have allocated the extra amount to the al-Qaeda in the Indian Subcontinent, the AQIS, as you instructed."

Kai Ling nodded. He approved of Musharad's methods. "Seems the Compact is acting on the old Chinese proverb which advises: to rid yourself of barbarians, you must use barbarians. Kai Ling could hear the shrieks of his little girls as they played among the juniper trees. Deep in thought, he walked over to a cabinet and poured himself a glass of sharbat. What should he make of General Syed Musharad, he wondered. Kai Ling's gut instinct told him General Musharad was the right man to take over as head of the

Compact. But he could not shake off a feeling of uncertainty about the man. Did he have the nerve required for the many operations that made up TUPAC II: the long-term machinations to take the RAW over the edge, to destroy Lodhi Road from the inside?

He turned and smiled to his protégé. 'I think we chose the right man to manage the Compact for us. We will know if we have erred,'' Kai Ling said quietly. "Report back to me on your return from the Red Corridor, my dear Chen."

The door opened. "General Syed Musharad has arrived," announced Talal, the wraith-like Balochi manservant.

3

The Level Skatepark, Brighton

Somewhere close by the sensory garden someone was whistling in the dark. After a few more minutes a mixed-race man in his early twenties, of medium height and athletic build, dressed in smart urban streetwear and head covered with his trademark red bandana, smoking a marijuana joint, strolled around the pebbled path, passing the fountain, and settled onto the bench next to Hari Vandra.

"Nice night for it, mate," he said without looking in Hari's direction. "You looking for someone? Or something?" He passed the blunt to Hari. "I have this for you, also. Sorry about the blurry pictures; it was raining hard in Portsmouth, but the evidence is there. No doubt about it, Hari. Sir Ibrahim Ali and his Skinny Skoda Boys are deep in the drug trade. From what I can tell their speciality is crystal meth and fentanyl. Call me when you have looked the material."

"As a matter of fact, I am to answer your question," said Hari smiling with genuine pleasure. He placed the plastic envelope in his satchel, careful to ensure the straps were fastened. "It's a good night for it. It's so good to see you, Rhys. Looking in fine fettle, as usual. Thanks for your message. Give me a second to switch my voice recorder on; had some trouble with it last if you recall. Okay, I think I'm there. What do you have for me?" He took a long, slow drag of the heady, sweet-scented smoke and breathed it in deep. He listened intently.

Rhys Iyar was a long-time confidential source for Hari. A dedicated youth worker working for a local NGO, he helped organise a flourishing community mutual-aid society called *The Level Posse*.

Over time Hari discovered Rhys was self-educated, well-connected, and well-informed when it came to the subject of local gangs operating in Brighton's drug markets. He had a remarkable memory and excellent observation skills, which, when combined with his emotional intelligence made Rhys the perfect confidential source and informant. He also knew Rhys had served time in jail and was self-educated to a remarkably high level. Hari would always be grateful to Rhys because it was Rhys who provided much of the material, including photos, for the award-winning story which established Hari's reputation as a crime reporter specialising in British Asian gangs.

Three years ago, Rhys had contacted Hari through a mutual friend with information about a London-based Pakistani gang that had set up an elaborate immigration scam in Brighton. By the time Sussex police discovered that the English language school located in the affluent neighbourhood of Hove was nothing more than a front organisation, more than four hundred Saudi, Jordanian, Indian, Somali, Bangladeshi, Turkish, and Pakistani 'students' had been granted long-term visas and had already entered the country.

"A year later, forty-one of those bogus students had been charged with drug trafficking offences, eleven with firearm charges, one with rape and another with attempted murder. A further one-hundred-and-thirty were being detained on immigration offences while one-hundred-and-forty-nine remain on the run," wrote Hari in an article entitled, *"Immigration: Why Borders Matter?"* It was one of many articles Hari wrote and sold that year.

"Some of the Hove language school graduates still being sought here are known to have committed several terror-related crimes in the Middle East, Europe, and Pakistan. It is highly likely that some of these radicalised Muslims will target the United Kingdom at some point. I wonder how our government will deal with the threat of Middle East-style suicide bombers targeting innocent children at a pop concert or the happy revellers at a Gay Pride parade in Brighton? Will the Home Secretary put the security of all its citizens before social cohesion considerations?" he wrote in another feature-length article published in a national tabloid entitled, *"Jihadists-by-the-Sea given English lessons in Brightonstan."* The article was written before the Manchester Arena bombing in May 2017, when a terrorist suicide bomber detonated a bomb during an Ariana Grande pop concert. The jihadists killed twenty-two people and injured over a thousand.

Rhys Iyar was a child of the British care system. His mother, a Manchurian crack whore, worked the streets. "Mom was owned by a Nigerian pimp from the age of twelve onwards. He sold her to a saxophone-playing Jamaican from Montego Bay, a tall enforcer called "Big Sid" who got her into being a drug mule for the *Shower Posse* gang. The only thing Mom ever told me about my biological father is that they didn't call him Big Sid because he was seven feet tall," Rhys once told him in his usual matter-of-fact way. "Mom became one of Big Sid's best so-called body packers. I watched her, once, prepare herself for her smuggling trips by swallowing whole grapes dipped in honey." Rhys candidly explained that Big Sid paid his mother according to the number of pellets she swallowed. "Mom boasted to me she could swallow over a hundred cocaine-filled latex pellets. She told me how she used her other body cavities. She told me once as I was getting ready for school that Big Sid always lived up to his name and reputation and fucked her so thoroughly and professionally, she was able to hold over three-hundred pellets deep inside her anal canal. She was very free and frank about it all, the most open and honest woman I ever met; she never sugar-coated her life." Hari noticed Rhys's words were totally devoid of any resentment or self-pity. The thing he discerned most was a boy's love for his mother.

"In the end, it was the crack cocaine that got my Mom," said Rhys. "You see Hari when you mix crack and prostitution it becomes a crazy twenty-four-hour cycle, and Big Sid worked her hard. Mom went out every day and walked the streets long enough to get a rock, then she would find a place and use it, and then go out and do the same all over again. Mom said crack made her feel invincible," he said. "Eventually she would need some sleep, so she would come back to our little flat and take heroin to come down from the crack. Mom was always passed out when I came home from school. She would wake up as I was getting ready for bed. My Mom always made me a mug of Horlicks before she left for work; it was our little ritual," he said smiling at the memory of his mother. "Big Sid was no longer in the picture by this time. Crack had become Mom's new pimp and she worked harder than ever for it until the day I came home and found her dead on the sofa."

The sound of a couple laughing caused them to turn and look over towards the picante part of the park. They saw a couple embracing near a flowerbed.

"Those boys over there," said Rhys with an imperceptible nod of the head in the direction of a group of black and Asian youths sitting in a huddle in the middle of the concrete skatepark. Rhys had been observing them discreetly since he arrived. "A few of my boys got talking to them the other day. What they're telling me is not good news. They've been sent down from places like Southall, Crawley, Southampton, and Portsmouth. They're scouts, sent to tout new business opportunities in Brighton," explained Rhys, his eyes never leaving the youths. "As you know Hari, Southall is the centre of Britain's Sikh community where around ninety per cent of the locals are Indians, mostly from the Punjab. You also know there's a seriously dark side to Southall: it's the fast-growing centre of the heroin trade and the European headquarters of the Sikh drug lords. Brothers in Brixton I served time with tell me violence between the various communities has been exploding on and off for a few years and most are telling me it's only a matter of time before Southall implodes into full-scale urban warfare."

"Those scouts mean trouble, Hari. You mark my word, I've seen their type before; in prison," said Rhys. "Drug lords who can't compete in the big cities are moving out to new fields, small towns, and rural areas. Their usual trick is the same as those they use on their girls and baby mama's. Highly motivated young street dealers arrive in a town and quickly get together with local wets, and let's face it, Hari, Brighton has enough wets to go around. The dope peddler then enjoys a few weeks cuckooing with his new chick before getting down to the serious business of hustling drugs to the city addicts. They do this through extreme violence to break the girls in. That's how they've taken over the heroin and crystal meth street dealing in Brighton. You see the dealers working openly on London Road and St James Street every day, Hari. Everyday! Then the pushers begin giving away free crack with the smack until having created a whole new addict base, they rake in the profits by turning the addicts into prostitutes. Just like my daddy, Big Sid did to my Mom."

Working with Rhys, Hari had picked up a few words and expressions. For example, Rhys explained that *wets* were an acronym for a target, or 'bait', for cuckooing. It stood for White Estate Trash Slut. Rhys also explained the term cuckooing to Hari. "It's basically when a new drug dealer comes into town and takes over the home of a vulnerable person to use as a base of operation for county lines drug trafficking. It's becoming a serious problem in

Brighton, these pushers are targeting care-leavers in council accommodation, other youth workers are worried; very worried."

"Already we're hearing anecdotal evidence of out-of-town dealers baiting care-leavers, particularly those with learning difficulties and mental health issues, and quickly moving into their council homes. Other dealers arrive. The dealers control their victims by getting them addicted to drugs; ritualised violence; and extremely hard sex. It's not just about profit; it's also about power for these men."

"You gotta understand these gangs aren't hierarchical, Hari," said Rhys quietly, his alert eyes never wavering from the group of Asian boys near the skatepark. "It's more like a patchwork quilt. It's like a webwork of old relationships, hatreds, alliances, and blood relationships."

Hari nodded in agreement. He agreed with his informant's assessment of gang affiliations. "I read a Home Office report recently which said drugs are imported by several gangs operating in Britain. It said the Colombian cartels, which had diversified into poppy-growing and heroin due to a glut of cocaine on the American market, have been active in Britain, linking arms with the Jamaican Yardies and Posses, who dominate the UK drugs market."

"Exactly," said Rhys. "Yardies are mainly involved in pushing cannabis and crack cocaine. The hallmark of both Yardies and Posses is the proper use of weaponry to enforce territory and, most importantly, status. Respect is everything in gangland" Hari nodded in silent acquiescence. His local Special Branch source mentioned numerous times how Jamaican gangs base their respect for other gang members on the firepower of their weapons and the gang leader's willingness to resort to extreme violence. "For now, we don't need to worry about Jamaicans, they are largely restricted to the inner-city ghettos of London, Bristol, Manchester, Leicester, and

Birmingham. Also, they tend to rely on loose family-based links between Britain, the Caribbean and the eastern seaboard of the United States and Canada. The big problem for Brighton is the county lines drugs……….," murmured Hari. He noticed Rhys still scanning the Asian boys. "What's the matter, Rhys? Do you know who they are?"

"It's okay, it's nothing. I just thought I heard something in the bushes," quietly. Rhys shuffled a little closer towards Hari. "Blacks aren't the only groups active in the drugs market, not in Brighton anyway. I've noticed in the last few months a few Pakistani, Albanian, and Bangladeshi gangs specialising in the heroin and crystal meth scouting various parts of our city. I'm hearing that the gangs are seriously targeting the school kids, university students, and foreign language students. Brighton's lucrative market."

Hari nodded slowly as he digested the new information. "Pushing heroin makes perfect business sense. It's reasonably easy to import because of the close links between Britain and the Indian subcontinent, and the dealer's easy opportunities to launder money through cash businesses: taxi services, curryhouses, kebab shops and so on. Thanks for this, Rhys. You did well."

Hari was already thinking of the spinoff articles and features which could be generated by his *"Brighton's County Lines Narcotics Nightmare"* story. He had been working furiously on the piece about Brighton's seedy underbelly for the last seven months. It had all the right ingredients for a great story: the gruesome murder of a twenty-seven-year-old Pakistani waiter found dead in scenic Seaford after a cleaner saw blood seeping through the ceiling; two rival Asian business families engaged in turf war; the importing narcotics by a freight forwarding company in Southampton; Muslim grooming gangs and heroin dealers hiding in Portsmouth; the "county lines" supply and distribution of new, so-called "designer" drugs into

Brighton's clubs, targeting the commercial gay scene in particular; organised barebacking sex parties where affluent old men supply free drugs to teenage boys from the nearby sink estates in return for sexual favours; Brighton's student sex workers; and linked to that was the distribution, and sale of amateur pornography.

And it all led to one man: Sir Ibrahim Ali, a multimillionaire shipping mogul, a man who built a business empire having arrived in Britain a penniless refugee. A favourite of many business magazines, Sir Ibrahim was a tireless philanthropist, a good Muslim, known to remind believers that *zakat* is an important religious obligation of all Muslims, so they should give generously to charity; a trusted fundraiser for the Labour Party; an inspiring British Pakistani business leader who founded the PakUK Enterprise Fund, a specialist bespoke business coaching and mentoring service for British Asian youths from marginalised communities.

Hari on the other hand knew secrets about Sir Ibrahim. "He's my Napoleon of Crime," he would say to Jago on many occasions. "My Professor James Moriarty." With the help of Rhys and his other contacts, Hari was building a picture of Sir Ibrahim. The wealthy Pakistani ran his empire from his mansion in the Costa del Sol. His neighbour was none other than Monzer al-Kassar, the notorious Syrian arms dealer known as the Prince of Marbella. Hari was under no illusion that Sir Ibrahim Ali was the venomous spider in the middle of a complex web of narco-trafficking than ran from London to Lahore, from Paris to Peshawar. This would be his biggest story yet. Every editor will want to run it.

"Hey Hari, where the fuck are you, man," he heard Rhys say sharply, the voice cracking like a whip. "Wake the fuck up, bro!"

Embarrassed he had allowed his professionalism to slip, he quickly mumbled an apology. "Sorry Rhys, my bad. I've, um, got a lot on my mind about this story; I'll try not to let that happen again.

Promise." And he meant it. Rhys Iyar took an enormous risk every time he met Hari to pass on new information for his articles and feature pieces.

"No no, it's me who should be saying sorry to you Hari; shouldn't have snapped at you like that. I know how hard you've been working on this story," he said quietly, giving Hari a pat on the arm. "I just get edgy around those new pushers over there; they all carry knives you see," he said nodding towards the group of Asians. He frisked his jacket pocket took out a pre-rolled joint and lit up. "Hey, I want you to try this new hybrid strain, tell me what you think. It's very mellow."

According to Rhys, black and Asian scouts prowling around the Level were almost certainly members of one of the two gangs behind the Southall heroin trade. "They're known as the Khattis and the Banakis. The Khattis are controlled by members of a leading Pakistani business family with a lot of businesses, including a widely popular West London restaurant and most of the kebab shops in Portsmouth. The Banakis, also based in West London, have strong links with Yardies and Posses, who they hire as musclemen to carry out enforcement."

"Authorities learned of their activities in 1988 after the arrest of Khattis gang members, Ramidev and Brajindrah Aziz, known to the feds as the Skinny Skoda Boys after their physique and the boring cars they drove to avoid drawing attention to themselves."

"What were the brothers like?" Always a professional, Hari deliberately refrained from asking how his confidential informant came across this information.

"At the time of their arrest, they had become one of the most successful and ruthless drug syndicates in British history," said Rhys matter-of-factly. "While on the surface they deliberately adopted modest lifestyles, they were addicted to the good life. The brothers loved luxury. They always used to stay at the five-star Grand Hotel when in Brighton."

"Paid for, no doubt, by their Uncleji; our friend, Sir Ibrahim Ali."

"Exactly, Hari!' said Rhys. 'It's all in that package I gave you; I think you'll find it interesting, worth a read anyway. You were right; everything leads to Ibrahim Ali in Marbella. You'll find the answers on the Costa del Sol."

The sound of a couple laughing caused them to turn towards the picante part of the park. "Listen, Rhys, I think we're done for tonight. As usual, you've delivered some serious military-grade information. Come, walk with me for a while." They walked in companionable silence while Hari took his first few drags of the heady smoke. He could feel the familiar fuzziness around the eyes, followed by a deliciously warm floating sensation of total relation.

"You like the green? Looks like you do," Rhys said grinning widely.

"This is just the perfect end to the day. Thanks again for everything, Rhys. I'm not sure how I'll ever repay you for......"

"You don't need to thank me, Hari. I just need you to keep writing; to keep telling my Mom's story. She never had a voice while she was alive you see; the men in her life took away her voice. That's the reason Mom used crack you see; to stop the silent screams inside her head. I read that piece you wrote on Muslim grooming gangs in Portsmouth. That girl's story was just, God, it was awful to read, Hari. Those men kidnapping her in a taxi; injected those Pompey girls as young as nine with heroin; filming them being raped and sodomised above curry houses and kebab shops on the Albert Road; and then pimped out among their extended family all over Portsmouth and Southampton. Reading about the abuse was hard enough, but when I got to the bit where you describe the apathy of the police and council, that was when I got pissed off. How did we Brits become so scared of being branded racist than risk being wrong about children being exploited? I had to go for a long run along the seafront to calm down. When I read your words aloud, you know what I heard? I heard the echoes of my Mom's voice in my kitchen. Thank you for that, Hari. Oh here, I almost forgot," he said passing a cellophane bag. "Something for you and Jago. A small token of thanks from me for writing Mom's story. Now go home and chill."

4

Gwadar Port City, Province of Balochistan, Pakistan

"How exactly are we going to set India ablaze along the Red Corridor?" asked General Musharad in his heavily accented English. He was still relatively new in his position as Chairman of the Compact Accord, the most closely guarded concordat between the intelligence services of Pakistan and China.

"Operation TUPAC was an anti-India strategy developed by a team of analysts hand-picked by my late father, Jiang Chang Ling, from Bureau 05, the intelligence analysis division of the Ministry of State Security in Beijing. It was agreed that I would succeed him as the over-arching controlling officer of the TUPAC task force. We agreed the task force was to be manned and implemented by your Inter-Services Intelligence from their Islamabad headquarters. Please stop me, General *saab*, if you feel I have left something out."

"As you know, General, the main objective of the ongoing TUPAC operation is to use asymmetric warfare to exploit the exposed underbelly of our principal adversary: India," reminded the Kai Ling of Macau speaking very slowly, his dark almond eyes fixed on Musharad. "Specifically, General, we agreed on the K2 concept: a concept my father developed for Islamabad to use in helping your warriors wage *jihad* in Kashmir and the Khalistan movement in the Punjab. We agreed to establish sleeper calls and sabotage units within the local Muslim population in Kashmir and among the Sikh farming community in India's Punjab."

"Islamabad followed the letter of the agreement and quickly authorised Operation TUPAC to implement the first stage, as we agreed," Musharad said quickly. He wanted the Chinaman to know he was a reliable business partner and the incisive leader of the

Compact Accord. "Our asymmetrical warfare strategy in Kashmir you are already familiar with, but we have not been slacking on the Sikh issue either. The Compact is making good progress in creating our Khalistan movement overseas, particularly in Canada, America, and the United Kingdom. Our sleeper cells are doing excellent work in those countries."

General Musharad, always anxious to impress the Chinaman with the work of the Compact, slowly listed the actions taken by the ISI to date: funding the operating budget of the Khalistan National Council, a secessionist group founded by Jagjit Singh Chohan that wants to create a state for Sikhs out of both Pakistani and Indian Punjab; funding Khalistan separatist groups in the United Kingdom and Canada; creating militant and paramilitary outfits – Khalistan Zindabad Force, Khalistan Commando Force, Dashmesh Regiment, and the Khalistan Liberation Force - throughout Punjab; providing arms for militant Khalistani *kharku* groups, groups of Sikh youths on motorcycles armed with small arms, improvised bombs, and machetes; providing logistical support and bomb-making equipment for Khalistani militant attacks throughout the state of Punjab.

"That is all very well, General *saab*, but the fact remains……."

"That is not all," begged the Pakistani general. "Please, let me finish. My boys are doing fine work. The false-flag operations we have going within the Khalistan movement in Canada are producing excellent results. Pinning the death of that Nijjar fellow on Delhi was a stroke of genius. Even the Canadian prime minister is dancing to our tune. We are discrediting India on the world stage. Please, Master Ling, I know you are disappointed with our recent performance against India by losing the whole Siachen area, but I promise……"

"Please, General, calm yourself. I am not concerned about the Canadian prime minister's obsession with supporting Khalistan militant groups or that you have lost Siachen. Let us please remain on the TUPAC operation. Do not worry, you have my confidence still.' Kai Ling who in a previous life might have been a Buddhist monk permitted himself a thin smile, an expression so rare for him that it looked completely out of place. 'Yes, you and the members of the Compact have implemented the early stages of TUPAC adequately in Kashmir and Khalistan. The K2 concept is working well, as I knew it would. What I propose is we build on the success of K2, expand our original remit slightly and add two further elements into the TUPAC operation."

"This is all most sudden…."

"Here, let me explain; look at these maps," Kai Ling said passing a clear envelope of photographs and enlarged military maps. "These images are from our *Dongfanghong* satellite program; they were prepared specially by the director of the Xichang Space Center personally," said the Chinaman. He spread the enlarged photographs across the table.

"What I propose is we enlarge TUPAC to include this area here and that we also target this area here and here," said the Kai Ling pointing to a map highlighting the 1,652 miles of border between India and China. "This area marked in red – pointing to an area almost contiguous from the Indo-Nepalese border down the central and eastern states reaching to the top of Tamil Nadu in the south - is what I have selected as our revolutionary base area." My beloved father referred to it as the "Red Corridor. It is from here that we will wage an insurgency, a people's war, so fierce, the Indian army will be too distracted to notice the real danger facing them."

"Look at this magnified image here," he said passing the photograph across the table. "Notice that narrow area called the Siliguri Corridor. It is also known as Chicken's Neck. My revised plan for TUPAC calls for the construction of a highway here," – he pointed to the Doklam plateau in the Kingdom of Bhutan – "thereby controlling this tri-border area overlooking Indian military positions. As you can see this border is porous, easy to move men and arms across unnoticed by the Indian army patrols. It is rough terrain with heavy vegetation covering over seven hundred kilometres and touches four of India's Union States. Most importantly for Pakistan, it will allow your army to bring heavy armour closer to India, via the Chicken's Neck."

General Syed Musharad, who was educated at Shimla before attending Delhi University, knew the area well. At St Stephen's College, he consistently scored high in geography and natural history. He knew the area selected by the Chinese spymaster for inclusion in the TUPAC operation was almost eight per cent of India's landmass and encompassed eight of India's Union States. The region shared an international border with Tibet in the north, Myanmar in the east, Bangladesh in the southwest, Nepal in the west, and Bhutan in the northwest.

As Musharad read his eyes narrowed and he took a sharp intake of breath. He reread the passages again, noting sentences and phrases: "Working under Dr. Rihad Taha, the Iraqi microbiologist, Shireen Najarii will conduct research in the field of zoonosis…."; "With postgraduate qualifications from the University of East Anglia in Norwich in virology, parasitology, and bacteriology, Shireen Najarii, the daughter of one of Pakistan's ruling political families, completed her education at the London School of Hygiene & Tropical Medicine where as a senior researcher she had unrestricted access during the 1970's to research papers held at Britain's bioweapons research facility at Porton Down. From these papers, Dr. Najarii learned how to weaponize botulism, coronaviruses, anthrax, and other pathogens……."

Musharad continued reading: "asymmetrical warfare against India must include the use of biological warfare……."; "further research is needed into the mechanics of CaS9 and other kilodalton proteins….."; "…….the research conducted by Wouter Basson" from South Africa's *Project Coast* will provide the data required for the development of an India-specific so-called "ethnic bomb………"; "the effect will be to depopulate entire regions of the Indian subcontinent without damaging any of India's valuable infrastructure, resources and utilities……."

The Chinaman from Macau was sitting still; his eyes fixed, watching his host intensely. He knew the passage the Pakistani was reading. "Tell me, General *saab*, what you are thinking," he murmured. "The passage you are reading was written by a protégé of the brilliant nuclear physicist you affectionately call *Centrifuge Khan*. She is an unusual and brilliant research scientist, as you will discover very soon."

Musharad did not speak for an exceptionally long time. "What you propose is extremely high risk," he said finally. "I am worried about your plan to bring Dr Abdul Qadeer Khan's network onboard Operation TUPAC. I have certain reservations about his network. Since his death, his people have become unpredictable and reckless."

"That is what you said when I first mentioned my TUPAC plan to you when you took over the chairmanship of the Compact a year ago. Unpredictable is the exact word you used. I promised you the TUPAC operation would achieve results for Pakistan in Kashmir, the North-East of India, and the Khalistan movement. Do you not remember, General *saab*? The TUPAC operation is an ongoing strategy which requires nerves of steel if we are to succeed in our fight against our common enemy: India."

"Beijing will not tolerate Indian hegemony in the region. We made this clear to the Indians when Chairman Mao decided to teach Nehru a lesson by humiliating India in the Sino-Indian War of 1962. Have you forgotten your military history, General *saab*?"

General Musharad sat motionless.

"I remember my father telling me that it was an exciting year for a relatively young intelligence officer," said Kai Ling softly. "He remembered vividly the meeting called by Mao Zedong on the morning of the sixth of October with his senior military advisors. My father accompanied his mentor, Kang Sheng, to the meeting where Mao reminded them that China had crushed Chiang Kai-shek and his Nationalists, Imperial Japan, and the Americans and their allies in Korea, and now it was time to crush Nehru, who he called a whimpering Imperial British dog with a wagging Indian tail."

"We both agree, General, *your* need to humiliate India has arisen but Beijing is wondering if Pakistan is all rumble and no thunder. I think it is a fair point based on your army's performance in the Siachen Glacier in recent years, the Chinaman remarked dryly."

"Yes, I agree on the need to humiliate India after Pakistan lost Siachen," said Musharad quietly. "But what you are proposing is bioterrorism…. I am wondering if you have fully considered the total number of casualties from the outbreaks……I'm sorry, but I cannot risk retaliation from the Americans……."

For a few moments, apart from the ancient ceiling fans, there was silence in the room. Kai Ling leaned back in his seat smoking, his eyes never leaving General Musharad. In all his dealings with Musharad and his Compact predecessors, he remembered what his father always said to him during their *qi* games: "Everyone and anyone in Pakistan is your tool, my son. You will be able to lie to Pakistanis because truth is not part of your relationship with them.

All that matters is using them for the party's benefit. From the very start, my beloved son, you must learn this philosophy: Do what is right for your family, our mission and, always, for the party."

"During the 1981 USSR chess championship, my father successfully recruited the Russian scientists who once worked at *Laboratory 12* of the KGB's First Chief Directorate, the first poison laboratory of the Soviet secret police. These biologists were responsible for creating the Soviet bioweapons programs during the early years of the Cold War. Page six in the red folder gives you a brief history of *Laboratory 12* and how it was established in 1921 with Yagoda, the NKVD chief under Stalin taking over in 1926. I can tell you, General *saab*, that we have all the life science data I need to create biological and toxin weapons ready for deployment in asymmetrical warfare against our principal adversary: India. By 1939 the Russian biologists had successfully genetically modified and weaponised in their Moscow laboratories some of the world's deadliest viruses: smallpox, anthrax, Ebola, and baculavirus, among others."

"My father was responsible for expanding the good work carried out by Wouter Basson's *Project Coast* in South Africa working on genes responsible for specific sex, race, and other racial characteristics," he explained carefully. "Our bio-research labs are currently testing these genes on volunteers, mostly Tibetans and Uighurs, and the results are most promising. Turn to page eleven, please."

General Musharad obeyed the Chinaman's command immediately and began reading: ".......... the key to developing a successful India-specific ethnic bomb will lie in separating and isolating the minute but vital differences in the human genome. Although this difference is no more than 0.1% it accounts for over 4 million nucleic acid sequences, thus making ethnic comparisons relatively easy……."; "……this also makes comparisons possible among large and diverse ethnic groups such as those found in Northeast India……."; "…. the genetic differences between the various ethnic tribes of the Northeast make them exploitable as a weapon to be used throughout the Indian subcontinent…."

Kai Ling of Macau explained another weapon – an airborne toxin - was being developed at the Wuhan Institute of Virology & Microbiology which could be released into a crowd from a rucksack. "I can tell you we are interested in developing India-specific bioweapons created specifically to poison India's reservoirs and rural water wells; Beijing is now examining feasibility studies on how best to infect ordinary Indians by contaminating the food and drink and air conditioning systems of Indian Railways and Air India; we will target all public food distribution systems and granaries owned by the Food Corporation of India, and we will target all schools participating in the Indian government's famous school midday meal programme, and I do not need to tell you we will target all vaccine producing facilities", he explained carefully. "My people have compiled a comprehensive list of assets to target in India. Stop looking so worried, General *saab*. Think of this as a more muscular and sophisticated version of your disastrous 1965 *Operation Gibraltar* devised by your illustrious predecessor, Field Marshal Ayub Khan."

"I have the Russian and South African scientists working on this as we speak. Our India-specific weapons will become a reality, of this I give you my word, General *saab*. I shall have more scientific intelligence as more scientists leave the imploding and sick Russian Federation, South Africa, and Iraq for the greener and richer pastures of Wuhan in China. They will have access to excellent working conditions in our biolabs, and more money than they can ever hope to spend. We will put them to work in comfortable surroundings developing sophisticated miniature airborne delivery systems for things like botulinium and coronaviruses. These are the ethnic bombs your ISI scientists will use in the TUPAC II operation in Northeast India. Chairman Mao's protracted people's war in India continues, General *saab*."

"Where are these scientists exactly?" asked Musharad vacantly. He was slowly absorbing the full ramifications of what his Chinese overlord was saying. Indian Railways carried *billions* of passengers every year. He had read in the press recently that over a hundred million midday meals were served to school children of all faiths. How exactly will the Chinaman contaminate the stored wheat and rice held by the Food Corporation of India? He refocused his mind on what his visitor was saying.

"Some are spending time in North Korea working at Humbung University of Chemical Industry and the Songram-ri's Institute 398. They are well looked after in North Korea by my friend and colleague, Dr. Yi Yong Su, who runs the country's nuclear, biological, and chemical warfare programs for Kim Jong Un. The rest live and work at a special facility owned and run by my ministry located close to the Wuhan Institute of Virology where they have successfully created an India-specific ethnic bomb for the purposes of TUPAC."

After a long silence, General Musharad said quietly, "I do not think I signed up for this. I am sorry......"

"You clearly need reminding, my dear General, so let me do just that," snapped Kai Ling. "Pakistan continues to lose territory to India. In 1971 you lost half your country. In that year, India dismembered its nationhood and Indira Gandhi created Bangladesh out of East Pakistan. She then decided to take some more of Pakistan's land and authorised *Operation Meghdoot*. On the unlucky morning of April 13th of 1984, you, General, lost the Siachen Glacier, the Saltoro Ridge, and all the tributary glaciers as well. The man you sent to deal with the Indians, a mediocre brigadier-general, succeeded in giving India a total tactical strategic advantage of holding higher grounds. The result is you will never remove the Indians from Siachen."

"Yes, what you say is correct. The army failed in Siachen," said General Musharad miserably.

"Yes, it has. Pakistan is a professional and well-equipped army that has never managed to win any war with India. I wonder why that is?" asked Kai Ling rhetorically. "After you lost Siachen to the Indians, you came to me, General *saab*, after Benazir Bhutto suggested you should start wearing a *burqa* as you appear to have lost your manhood along with seventy kilometres of your land to India."

General Musharad furrowed his eyebrows again. "I'm sorry but I do not follow……."

"I took care of the problem for you, General," said the Chinaman. "I removed the source of your problem. I removed the person in New Delhi who authorised *Operation Meghdoot*." He kept his eyes fixed on the Pakistani general. 'I removed the Congress leader and prime minister Indira Gandhi by having her assassinated by her own Sikh bodyguards."

"What you tell me is new to me, I did not know this," said General Musharad.

"I did not inform you because you did not need to know. It was simple, really. I used the Khalistan movement to recruit the assassins of Nehru's daughter. So, you see General *saab*, TUPAC II does work. I made the Sikhs of India mutiny against their Hindu masters," he said.

"Now is the time for many more mutinies in India, General. This is the time to bleed India to death using a thousand cuts,' he murmured softly. 'It simply requires the necessary calculations and forward planning. The revised plan, to be known as TUPAC II, will work. I know it will work. With India busy fighting Pakistan's militants in the west, in Kashmir and the Sikhs in the Punjab, the RAW and their Intelligence Bureau will be too busy to notice what we are doing to them in the east; until it is too late for them to stop it."

"I am fully committed to TUPAC II, Sir!" barked General Syed Musharad almost coming to attention.

"Good. As I have already mentioned I have chosen my scientists from Abdul Quader Khan's research facility at Kahuta," said the Chinaman relocking the steel bracelet around his wrist. "She is something of a brilliant scientist, a British-educated Pakistani from a good Muslim family. Your good friend, *Centrifuge Khan*, introduced us during a visit to London. My father was responsible for supervising her scientific education."

"She is helping Pakistan's nuclear weapons program, no doubt," nodded General Musharad in approval. 'I receive regular reports from Dr Abdul Khan Institute on her work for the nation."

"Dr. Shireen Najarii is a biologist, not a physicist, General *saab*," explained the Chinaman. "She will join the team of microbiologists my father at the Institute of Virology in the city of Wuhan. It is a beautiful city which you must visit. I think you will find Shireen Najarii will do for Pakistan's bioweapons research program what Abdul Quadeer Khan had done for Pakistan's nuclear weapons program."

"Bioweapons research programme," mumbled General Musharad furrowing his eyebrows deeply. "I am sorry……I do not understand……"

"Forgive me, General *saab*, I am referring to matters before your time; let me explain," the Chinaman said. "Pakistan's army chiefs, including yourself, have long realised that your principal adversary, India, can never be defeated by conventional means. Never means never, General. I hope you have not forgotten the disastrous *Operation Gibraltar* which led to Pakistan's defeat in the 1965 war and India emerging as an Asian power."

"The 1965 war was the end for Ayub Khan. When I saw him for the final time, he was a broken man, very bitter. He finally agreed with me that the only way to bring the Hindus to their knees was through unconventional guerrilla warfare. What my late father called a protracted people's war in the heart of Hindu India."

"It was Ayub Khan who authorised Pakistan's bioweapons research?"

"Yes, General Ayub Khan, your predecessor, signed an agreement with me to engage Pakistan in bioweapons research for the defence of our nations. He signed the agreement after Pakistan's defeat in the 1965 war with India. An important part of our agreement was creating a pool of scientific manpower and resources to conduct bioweapons research at Wuhan. My father has created such a scientific pool for you," said the Chinaman.

"Thank you, Sir, for your careful explanation. Please reassure Beijing that all Chinese investments in Gwadar and elsewhere are safe under my watch," said General Musharad meekly. "You can trust me to execute TUPAC II, Sir."

"Read the revised TUPAC II operation carefully, General. My father wrote TUPAC II in his own hand. The only other copy is in my private safe at Zhongnanhai. Thank you for coming to see me at such short notice, General *saab*. I look forward to hearing from you after the Compact has voted on TUPAC II amendments." Kai Ling of Macau stood up.

The meeting was over.

5

The Lanes, Brighton

After leaving Rhys at the Old Steine Hari Vandra walked slowly up an ancient smuggler's alleyway so narrow that it was closed to non-residents and was longer in the *Brighton & Hove A-Z*; it was a cobbled cul-de-sac guarded at hits open end by two ancient bollards padlocked to the ground. A light rain which had started to fall minutes after leaving Rhys was getting a tad heavier. He began speed-walking home. Hari lived in a large, two-bedroomed flat in The Lanes, Brighton's popular quaint shopping district, above an antique shop specialising in military memorabilia. His parents had purchased the property in 1981 during the building of nearby Dukes Lane, a so-called 'reproduction street' constructed in 1979.

"It's a characterful former merchant seaman's house, prosperously plain, with a faint air of secrecy and exclusion about it, don't you think?" he asked during Jago's first visit. "Much of the window glass in this building looks original to me; warped, glinting and nearly opaque. Very Dickensian!".

By the time he reached his building, the drizzle had turned to a downpour. He hurried to the door located at the side of the building which gave access to the stairs to his flat. A small ornamental lamp glowed above it, and the rain dripped from the bare twigs of the climbing rose which surrounded the recessed porchway. He felt his heart lurch when he saw a figure huddled in the shadow on the ground, sheltering from the rain. Hari stared at the figure, trying to focus through the drizzle.

"Stax? Is that you? What the fuck are you doing in the rain? A hangover from your army days, I suppose."

"Shit Hari, I thought you weren't coming," he said in a tense voice, sniffing heavily. He stood tall and moved towards him. Stax was a colossal former army boxing champion, not only fantastically muscular but over six feet seven inches tall. He gripped his arms with his huge hands and pressed himself against Hari's body. The rain was starting to fall heavily on them.

"I didn't know you were coming here tonight. I thought we agreed you weren't to come here……," his voice tailing off. "You're soaking wet," said Hari in a practical tone. "You should have called or left a message to say you were coming." He freed himself from his grasp and fumbled for the door keys. "I think we both need a drink, Stax. Come on in and sort yourself out; you know where the bathroom is," he said, probably a bit too sharply.

As Hari wandered off to the open-plan living and dining area to look for a towel, Stax took his mud-cacked shoes off. He looked around the familiar surroundings. It was a narrow, dark hall, the stairs going up ahead to the right; an old-fashioned coat-and-stick stand filled with the collection of walking sticks gathered by Hari's father from all over the world; and the high, marble-topped table against the wall. On it was a salver with a letter stamped for the post addressed to Sir Ibrahim Ali of the *Fauji Shipping & Freight Forwarding Company of Southampton*. Above it hung an enormous ornate mirror in a gilt frame.

The rest of the panelled walls were covered with framed pictures, hung one on top of one another to the cornice, and going up the stairs too. There were watercolours of Indian birds, oils from the British Raj era, pencil drawings of Brighton Street scenes, and portraits, all mixed up. Stax was always drawn to the large painting of two, strong, muscular African warriors: Shaka, the leader of the Zulu Kingdom between 1816 to 1828, and his younger lover, Magaye. They are carrying an *ikiwa* each, the short stabbing spear with a long, broad, sword-like point invented by Shaka Zulu because he was dissatisfied with the traditional long-throwing *assegai*. In the background, young *udibi* apprentice warriors are shown in the 'bull horn' fighting formation made famous by Shaka, and the blue-robed figures in the background give the painting a sense of the vastness of the landscape. He remembered Hari telling him he purchased the painting with the proceeds of an article he had written on the African king's sexuality. It caused quite a stir at the time. As Stax ascended the stairs towards the bathroom, he noticed Hari had acquired two new pictures since he visited last: a framed poster of Quentin Tarantino's 1997 film, *Jackie Brown* hung opposite the bedroom. The other was a framed cover of *Tintin in the Congo*; the full-colour English version first published by Le Petite Vingtieme in 1946.

In the living room, Hari checked his answer machine: one message. "Hari, my boy," said the inimitably plummy, but noticeable drunk voice of his godfather, Robbie Charles Gage. "I can't stay on the line too long, my boy, just thought I'd stop by and say hello; been a while I know," There was a pause, followed by a static. "I'm coming back home; back to Old Blighty and dear Blayney. To be totally honest with you, Hari, India hasn't felt like home since I lost my boy, Vivek, to General Zia's bloodthirsty guttersnipes." A long burst of static was followed by, "So look out for my message; I'll call Padre at Blayney, of course, to make arrangements about my Q cottage; I left the storage details in the Zanzibar chest for you. Oh, one more thing, Hari *beta*, I've asked…." The machine cut out. Robbie always called him *beta* after a few drinks. He once explained that the English translation for *beta* was *son* and in Indian culture was an affectionate way an elder family member would refer to a younger member.

He then picked up the unopened mail he had tossed on the table that morning and began opening them: a membership renewal reminder from the think tank, *Civitas*; a phone bill; a letter from his solicitor Edward Carpenter & Co requesting Hari call "for an update of the ongoing investigation into the murder of your parents, Mr Ramsita Lal Vandra and Mrs Gopi Vandra, at Marlborough House, London on….."; his copy of the latest issue of *The Economist*; and a package containing a *"KatzEyez Kinetik."* Hari ordered the gadget a week ago after Jago sheepishly admitted he had "broken the kinetic rear light smashing it down Stanmer Park."

The arrival of the gadget was fortuitous; the gift might be a clever way to get back into Jago's good books. He walked over to the drinks cabinet and took out a frosted bottle from the fridge. He briefly admired the familiar smoked-glass bottle with its distinct blue label of birds in flight before pouring himself a generous measure of the *Grey Goose* vodka and a decent slug of *Mount Gay* rum for Stax.

The lounge was a modest-sized room; but it was crammed with books, most of them annotated with Hari's notes. "This place is a pyromaniacs wet dream and a dyslexics worst fucking nightmare!" Jago once exclaimed, skulking off to the kitchen after Hari told him off for smoking a joint in the living room. "No joints in here, Jay! Fire hazard! How many times do I have to fucking tell you! This is my workspace," he said in exasperation. "And stop slalom boarding in my hallway; I'm trying to fucking write for fuck sake, Jay!"

Hari's books were housed in an old, break-fronted bookcase with Gothic windows; a special bookcase housed his collection of signed copies from writers he has read and admired: Christopher Hitchens, Vikram Sampath, Salman Rushdie, Douglas Murray, J.K Rowling, Hanif Kureishi, Shahi Tharoor, Martin Amis; a large pile was sagging in the leather sling of the Butterfly chair in the bedroom; others were stacked on the three comfy armchairs, on shelves, on the Eames lounge chair and the Ottoman, and on tabletops. Well-thumbed books were stacked up like a Roman hypocaust, from the baseboard to the crown moulding touching the ceiling. Two entire shelves were taken up with first editions given to him by Robbie, when he finally sold his place in Brunswick Square. "Take whatever you want, Hari *beta*. I've spoken to Padre, and it's all arranged. I will move into Blayney Parke after my retirement from the Foreign Office," said Sir Robert loudly down the telephone line. "Sorry about all the background noise, Hari, but as you can hear Delhi is a very noisy place," he chuckled. "Padre has generously allocated Q cottage for me if I do my bit in the vegetable patch and pitch in with the beekeeping. He thinks the clean country air of Blayney Parke will do me the world of good after nearly three decades in Delhi. Anyway, I must dash Hari; I'm calling from my club, McGregor's, and I can see the pink gin being passed around. My love to you dear boy and all at Blayney. Not sure when I'll get to see you, Hari *beta*; problems in Lodhi Road, but I'll write to let you know…."

Sipping appreciatively, he remembered it was Robbie who introduced him to *Grey Goose* when he drove up to his university with a couple of bottles, a *Harrods* food hamper, and a huge tin of *Fortnum's* biscuits for Hari as a graduation present. "Well done for finishing journalism school, Hari. Finally finishing! I never thought I'd live to see this day," he said planting a wet kiss on his cheek.

"Here you go, Hari my boy, something decent for you to try with your handsome Garifuna fresher from Saint Vincent you've been mentioning an *awful* lot about in your postcards; a Garifuna from the island of Saint Vincent, if I recall correctly." In the background could be heard laughter and the clinking of glasses. "Do let me know if your Garifuna boy appreciates the Picardy wheat and calcium-rich water drawn from a natural limestone-lined spring water well located in the Cognac region," he said extravagantly, winking mischievously at his beloved godson. "Oh, it's vegan vodka apparently, tell him! The five-step distillation process renders the wheat gluten totally harmless."

Thank God for Robbie!

Stax was drying off after his shower. Naked on the floor, legs wide apart, one foot raised in front of him, he rubbed a towel between each toe and patted foot powder into the dry pink crevices. Hari approached him, drinks in hand, at an angle, noticing how his shapely buttocks spread on the ground, admiring the thick muscular band above his hips, and walking around him, glanced down at the prodigious, veiny bolt of his ruthlessly circumcised cock and balls resting on the floor. Stax looked up with his dark, bright eyes. "So, how's the story? Sir Ibrahim Ali is not exactly the easiest of men to investigate is he?"

"Mount Gay," Hari said, passing the tumbler to him. He remembered how struck he was that first night he spent with him by the contrast of his rocky, boxer's physique; the strange, crisp dryness of his short beard; and the beautiful, almost smothering softness of his black lips.

"Thanks, Hari," he said, glancing up again. He held the glass in the palm of his hand and swirled the dark spirit around the large bowl. "Sorry, about snapping at you earlier. Long day."

Hari rested a hand on the right side of his neck, whose shaft, thicker than his head, was buttressed by the hard-worked sloping shoulder muscles. Hari had never seen a single hair on the head; Stax religiously shaved his head daily and kept the beard on his broad, square face short and oiled. "You're looking noticeably bigger, soldier," he said, smiling at him teasingly. He was a notoriously difficult man to dress in civilian life and often went around Blayney Parke working with his torso draped in a torn old sweat-stained vest, a broad leather army belt unnecessarily supporting faded old jeans rubbed thin under his arse and inner thighs. "Certainly, bigger than when I first saw you in Blayney Parke…. what is now, coming up to five years now." The joint he had smoked with Rhys was making him distinctly horny.

He once showed Hari a picture of how he looked at fifteen – tall and uncertain, and indifferently built, Stax looks anxious, as if he's just winced. He was holding the hand of a grinning boy poking his tongue at the camera, aged around nine, standing beside him. Standing immediately behind Stax and towering over him was a tall, chunky, black man with a square face, bearing the faint scarification, a tradition practised in many parts of Africa. He had a distinctly military bearing; his hands were gripping Stax's bony shoulders. Standing next to the man, dwarfed by him was a timorous-looking blonde, white woman wearing a pretty, green dress and carrying a large red handbag.

"Sorry for surprising you like this, Hari," he said sipping his rum. "I had chores to do in town and needed to talk to you about something important; it couldn't wait. Grace dropped me off on the Old Steine and I came over. Bloody rain started, didn't it? I then realised Gizmo, who had hitched a ride with us, had my phone; I'd asked him to look at it for me while we were driving from the Parke into town, then forgot all about it!"

"I blame the boxing!" Hari said, squatting behind him. He wrapped his arms around Stax's neck and kissed his left earlobe. "You know my take on boxing and *dementia pugilistica*. We've had many bouts on this issue over the years, Stax. You helped me with those articles you sold to those extreme sports magazines, remember? You do remember those times with me, don't you? All those nights in your cosy flint cottage spent minutely dissecting your boxing prowess, and the finer points of your impressive musculature."

"So, how is the new story going? I know I'll get nothing from you, but I must ask," Stax asked his former lover getting up for a refill. He felt uncomfortable sometimes with Hari's overt flirtations. This was one such occasion. "Another?"

"This is one big fuck-off story, Stax. An eye-opening experience, a real fucking experience," exclaimed Hari, trying not to be too obvious in his admiration of the sheer physical strength of the former soldier. "It's clear that Sir Ibrahim is shipping huge amounts of narcotics, particularly crystal meth, and fentanyl into the country via Portsmouth and Southampton. Watching how the Skinny Skoda Boys operate has been an education that's for sure." He stopped talking suddenly feeling the sudden tiredness engulf him. "I'm glad you've cóme over, Stax, I've missed you." Hari walked up to him and tiptoed up to plant a hard, long kiss on his dark lips. "Stay with me tonight."

"Look, it's getting late Hari," he said reluctantly. "I should be getting back to the Parke; the others will be getting worried. I can just hear Padre now! If I can use your phone to call a taxi……."

Hari whispered quietly into his ear, "Stay," before wandering off in the direction of the bedroom. Stax remained in the bathroom, completely still. He knew Hari had rolled his usual bedtime joint because he could smell the sickly-sweet aroma of marijuana. After a few minutes, he walked into the bedroom and closed the door.

At around three Hari woke up needing a pee. After he was done, he stood next to the bed looking down at Stax asleep in the soft glow of the Jaspa floor lamp that fell across the blue pillows. His right arm was sticking out of the light duvet in a strange, ungainly manner as if he was shielding his face from an oncoming fist. Hari slid in beside Stax, rested his head on his broad chest and observed his strong face carefully. Closing his eyes, he inhaled deeply his natural male smell, the scent of the coal tar soap he used earlier, and minty mouthwash. As Hari reached up to switch off the Jaspa, he felt Stax roll towards him, his huge hands digging under him, as if wanting to lift him up and carry him away. Hari hugged him tightly, murmuring 'baby' several times. This caused Stax to tighten his grip more tightly, clinging to Hari as if in mortal danger. He murmured several times again before realising Stax had been asleep.

Despite the hard sex and his lover's athleticism and stamina in bed, sleep continued to evade Hari. Something was niggling him, but he lacked the clarity of thought to reason it out and was only half-conscious. It was only as he was nodding off that he realised what was bothering him. It was something Stax said earlier but Hari hadn't paid attention to it at the time.

Stax said he was in town because he wanted to talk to him about something important.

Hari was surprised to learn all three – Stax, Gizmo, and Grace – had left Blayney Parke to come to Brighton. That meant only Skeezy and Squeaky were left to manage the entire estate. This was highly unusual, and a breach of policy laid down by Stax shortly after he took over the management of Blayney Parke. The Five Aces, as they were known, were senior managers of the Parke estate, a spiritual retreat nestled deep in the rolling hills of the South Downs. For Stax to leave the Parke with Pinky and Gizmo must mean it had to be particularly important.

He turned to look at Stax sleeping soundly. Hari placed his hand on his chest, feeling it rise and fall, his breathing even. Lying next to Stax he suddenly had a moment of clarity.

Everyone I love in this world is connected in some way to Blayney Parke!

The four hundred-and-sixty-one acre estate contains a village with seventeen cottages, log cabins, a caravan site; an Ignatian spiritual retreat, built around the small Sacred Heart of Jesus church constructed after the suppression of the Jesuits in 1773; an orphanage, whose past residents include all the Five Aces; a ten-bed *Saint Juliana* AIDS hospice for Catholic priests; a business nursery providing logistical support to nearly fifty micro-enterprises operating on the site, including two award-winning micro-breweries supplying craft ales, the Edmund sloe gin, fruit flavoured liquors, and the signature Campion damson gin; a restaurant showcasing the best Sussex ingredients and the array of vegetables and fruits grown in the allotments and herbarium; Pizzey House, a women's refuge; the Hip Hop Garage Workshop; a farm shop selling its popular signature cheeses; a young person's residential drug and alcohol recovery house; a wildlife sanctuary; and an organic rare breed's pig farm. Blayney Parke was a hive of activity. For Hari, it was his real home.

Blayney Parke was run by the so-called *troika* comprising Reverend Father Ambrose Tyrell *a.k.a* Padre, a Jesuit priest, a committed liberation theologian, and former military chaplain to British special forces garrisoned at Stirling Lines; Sister Priya Ananda, a member of the Religious Sisters of Mercy and a medical doctor was a psychiatrist specialising in child sexual abuse accommodation syndrome; and Hari's godfather, Sir Robert "Robbie" Gage, a retired Foreign Office official and noted Indologist currently based in New Delhi.

Hari's move to Brighton coincided with Padre taking over the running of the Blayney Parke. In his typical Jesuitical manner, he quickly assembled a hand-picked team of men and women whose character, and abilities were known to him. Some he had known as children when they were residents at the Blayney Parke orphanage, COG House. Others, like Sister Ananda and Sir Robert, were friends and former colleagues from his army days.

Padre's team included Stax, a former Army Sergeant Major in the Royal Corp of Logistics, to take charge and manage the estate. Stax was short for Stacker, a colloquial term for members of the RLC. His baptismal name, which he never used, was Hamilton Duane Kingston. "Logistics trumps strategy! You of all people know this, Hamilton; therefore, I'm asking you to step up and develop a business plan for Blayney Parke. We must find a way to generate income in order to keep this place afloat. We must be self-supporting and never be dependent on Rome for the resources we need to do God's work at the Parke," Padre emphasised ceaselessly. A former member of the Adjutant General's Corps, Grace was inducted to manage Padre's busy office and to supervise the staff and residents on the estate. A former warrant officer (WO1) in the Royal Military Police, Grace was also responsible for all security matters. Padre bought in Gizmo, a former warrant officer (WO2) in the Royal Signals, to take charge of technology related matters. Finally, he appointed Skeezy, formerly a machinist sergeant-major in the Royal Engineers, and Squeaky, a former artificer sergeant-major in the Royal Electrical and Mechanical Engineers, to run the workshops vocational education. The Hip Hop Garage Workshop was their baby.

Stax opened his eyes to find Hari on his side looking at him. "You haven't slept have you," he said yawning. "I've known you long enough to know that means you've thinking about something all night?" He leaned towards Hari, cupped the back of his head, and kissed his lips for a long time. "I slept like a baby after what you made me do to you last night. I always do in this bed. We brought it the day after you moved in here, remember? I still laugh when I remember you telling the man you wanted a bed big enough to accommodate your five feet ten inches and my six feet and ten inches. It's all about feet and inches with us, you said to him. I was nearly pissing myself! Happy days! Good morning, Hari Vandra."

"Is everything okay at the Parke, Stax? Sorry I've been distant of late. I've meant to call Padre and the Aces, but I've just been so snowed under recently with the Portsmouth story," he said feeling first guilty then worried. "Is everything, okay? Last night you said you had something to tell me. What is it?"

Stax looked at Hari for a long moment then said, "I think we need breakfast. In the army we don't do anything before a solid breakfast."

6

Research & Analysis Wing headquarters, Lodhi Road, New Delhi

Secretary of the Research & Analysis Wing, Ajit Massey leaned forward and stared intently at the grainy black, green, and white image of a region in Somalia called Puntland. It was shot from the underbelly of a customised *DHC-7* four-engine turboprop. As part of a technical package from Israel, the plane was fitted with the Highly Integrated Surveillance and Reconnaissance System. Massey had recently ordered close monitoring of that country by the National Technical Research Organisation, India's premier technical intelligence agency known by its acronym NATRO. Following his recent appointment by the Cabinet Committee on Security as director of India's foreign intelligence agency Massey had inherited an ongoing agency operation code-named FLUENCY.

The ruling Bharatiya Janata Party had wanted the CCS to appoint someone from within the party hierarchy. However, the national security advisor to the prime minister, a former director of the Intelligence Bureau, had other ideas. The NSA called his former roommate from Agra University to take on the role of Secretary (Research) in the Union Cabinet Secretariat, as the director of Research & Analysis Wing is known. In return, Ajit Massey always had the ear and confidence of the NSA.

Since its creation by bifurcation in 1968, the RAW has held a controversial position within the union cabinet. The Secretary reports directly to India's prime minister and is not answerable to parliament. Massey had briefed the prime minister shortly after his appointment. He had been summoned to the Prime Minister's Office following an explosion close to where a local leader of the BJP was due to speak at a political rally. Massey had started to talk in very general terms about a task force which had been set up following the recent appointment in Pakistan of the new and relatively unknown chief to oversee an ultra-secretive concordat signed in 1957 between the intelligence services of Pakistan and China known as the Compact Accord. Had the previous Congress (I) government known about the Compact and had it authorised FLUENCY? The prime minister had wanted to know. Absolutely, Massey had replied in the affirmative; it wasn't the kind of operation RAW would undertake without prime ministerial approval, and certainly not on Massey's watch. He confirmed that director of the Intelligence Bureau, Bhola Nath Mullick had informed prime minister Nehru of the existence of the Compact Accord in October 1964. According to you Masseyji, this Compact pose a clear and present threat to national security, the prime minister had continued. According to your sources in Islamabad and Rawalpindi, the Compact has resurrected – your word, not mine - a plan to recruit, train and infiltrate thousands of jihadis and Afghan mercenaries into India-controlled Kashmir. You also write in your report that the Compact has a dangerously large cache of weapons stored somewhere in war-torn Somalia ready for distribution among Maoist insurgents operating in the Red Corridor. You state that biological weapons and dirty bombs will be infiltrated into India. Your memo speculates that al-Qaeda in the Indian Subcontinent may also be involved. In response, the RAW set up the FLUENCY task force designed to neutralise the threat posed by the Compact. You want to be careful Masseyji, the prime minister remarked, that we are fully armed with all the facts. Or else we run the risk of making too much noise at the United Nations and spilling so much blood in Puntland that everyone in the world will know India is behind this. The noise level, Massey had assured the prime minister, would have to be low enough to avoid pitfalls and high enough to send fear into the hearts of India's enemies. Is there a timetable? The prime minister had asked too casually. Two weeks said Massey.

"I see", murmured the prime minister. "It is early days for my government after the national elections. We must be cautious in a coalition; I'm sure you understand this Maseyji. National security is of the highest priority for the BJP," he mumbled to himself. "I will speak to my Cabinet colleagues on this matter." He scratched his chin. Anything else I need to be aware of? Massey had shaken his head. The prime minister shook his hand and his private secretary, who had entered through a side door, presented Massey with a volume of his recently published volume of Gujarati poetry. That was ten days ago.

The door opened and his long-time deputy, Shivananda Menon, entered without knocking. "Ready for the briefing?" His manner was diffident, the mellifluous voice more suited to a college lecture hall than dealing with Delhi's politicians and bureaucrats. The youngest son of a South Indian physicist from Tamil Nadu, his manners deepened the image of the quintessential Indian scholar. Although his hair was totally white Menon looked decades younger than his close to fifty-five years and there was a boyish quality about him. His every gesture while briefing his officers – the flicking away of hair from his forehead, the lengthy pauses between sentences, and the thoughtful stare – suggested a lifetime spent cloistered on a leafy university campus. Beautifully tailored clothes emphasised a figure-kept trip with regular yoga and a strictly controlled pescetarian diet.

In reality, Menon had been the intellectual guru behind many of the operations during the 1980s orchestrated by the RAW against India's enemies. His analytical skills had been accompanied by breath-taking nerves of steel, catching even the wariest in Beijing, Islamabad, and Washington with subtle and sly moves that quickly earned the respect of colleagues. Within the dry and featureless corridors of Lodhi Road, Menon was widely regarded as the epitome of the gentleman spy with the cunning of a Bengal fox. They walked in companionable silence for a while.

The fortress-like headquarters of the RAW is located close to Lodhi Gardens, the lush ninety-acre botanical park built in 1445 to surround the tomb of Mohammed Shah, the last ruler of India's Sayyid Dynasty. At the end of the corridor, Massey used his unrestricted electronic pass card to open the doors of the elevator which rose through the RAW's eleven floors.

Located between two Mughal mausoleums housing the tombs of Humayun and Safdarjung, the RAW headquarters was once described by an awed Israeli visitor as 'a bunker within a palace' with its own utilities – electricity, gas, water, sanitation – separate from the rest of the neighbourhood. The lower floors housed the communication centre which linked the RAW with other organisations in the intelligence community and with its field offices in South Asia and officers serving overseas; on the next floor came the offices of junior intelligence officers and analysts working on reports pouring in from nearly three-hundred embassies, High Commissions, trade missions, as covert stations and bases around the world. Upper floors were given over to senior analysts, planners, and operations personnel. The seventh floor was staffed by scholars, soldiers, and scientists engaged in the meticulous study of global trends in current affairs. The Secretary's office and conference room, and those of his senior aides, were on the top floor. The roof had a helipad and bristled with huge antennae. The area was secured and guarded by *4 Vikas* commandos from the Wing's own paramilitary unit garrisoned at Sarsawa Air Force Station.

The elevator stopped on the top floor and the two men entered a large conference room. Cool, spacious, and airy the floors were covered with Jaipur rugs. The only decoration in the wood-panelled office consisted of a large oil painting hanging on the far wall, an exquisite portrait of Rameswar Nath Kao, the founder-director of the Research & Analysis Wing. Painted by Kao's great friend and head of Vatican intelligence, the late Cardinal Luigi Poggi, and presented to Kao on his retirement in 1977.

Through the frosted glass door, Massey could see the FLUENCY task force members were already seated waiting for him. This wouldn't take very long. Massey had requested the meeting so he could tell them something. An armed security guard opened the door for him saluting smartly.

The FLUENCY task force sat under a large oil painting of a stern-looking Scotsman of the Victorian age. Known as the "father of Indian intelligence", Major-General Sir Charles McGregor was an explorer, geographer, and Quartermaster General of the British Indian Army. In 1885 he founded the Political & Military Intelligence Department of the British Army. This department, which was established to monitor Russian troop deployment in Afghanistan, was the precursor of all Indian intelligence agencies, including the RAW.

"Thank you for coming," said Massey. "I will be seeing the prime minister to update him on the operational status of FLUENCY. I feel that he should be made aware of just how much of a threat General Syed Musharad and the Compact is to our country. The prime minister needs to be told that Musharad's actions are tantamount to a declaration of war and that we need to take action immediately. Does anyone have any questions?"

The meeting had started.

7

Trafalgar Street, North Laines, Brighton

"I was standing right here when I took the photograph," said Hari, stopping outside a shop in Kensington Garden with an English Heritage blue plaque telling passing tourists the world's first Body Shop was opened by Anita Roddick in the shop on 27th March 1976.

"I remember the photo", said Stax, looking around the many boutique shops. "Went well with that piece you wrote, *"Greenwashing, Jon Entine, Pyramid Schemes & Frustrated Franchisees: The Body Shop Story"* He stopped to peer into the window front of Brighton's famous flea market, *Snoopers Paradise*.

"Where are we going? I'm starving; I need my porridge. Breakfast at Blayney Parke is served at eight."

"Stop moaning, you're in for a treat, Stax! I'm taking you to The Kitchen Café for breakfast. Neil cooks the best breakfast in town, and Sheila's sticky toffee pudding is to die for. Quick, find us a table before they're all taken," said Hari making his way to the counter to place their order. "And get me some chilled water from over here," he shouted over the noise of the bustle. The place was crawling with workmen tucking into plates of food and slurping tea from chipped mugs, ready for another day of hard labouring in the many construction sites nearby. A short, fit man in his mid-twenties with a craggy face, framed by a cropped ginger beard and wearing a reflector jacket emblazoned with the logo for, *"Crawley Scaffolding,"* finished telling a smutty joke to his four mates and then laughed at them so hard the entire table shook. "For God's sake, don't laugh at my anti-Tory jokes," he warned, wagging a finger at his mates. "Or Rishi will spank you and send you down for a ten stretch, just like the Birmingham Six!" Hari noticed the man had the bluest of eyes.

"That's better than a month living in one of those new high-rise flats we're building in this area," mimicked a man sitting opposite Blue Eyes, who had noticed Hari glancing in his direction. Blue Eyes took in Hari's dapper details: the pressed light-coloured chinos; a dark-blue River Island blazer over a striped Oxford shirt; and the casual loafers on his sockless feet. Smart casual, and fit-as-fuck thought Blue Eyes, with just a touch of class. "Fuck Rishi, mate! Fucker said the Tories will give millions for a regeneration scheme to improve inner cities. I bet Londoners get that dosh; we Brightonians won't see a fuckin farthing." Across the room, a bulky Sikh man wearing a blue turban with a plate piled high with thick-cut chips, fried eggs, and gammon in front of him, wiped his impressive beard with a napkin and sniggered in agreement. "Bravo! Well said, young man!" An electrician's toolbox was under his table. The Sikh's workingman's jacket was stitched with a cotton business logo, "Mandeep Electricals: Ditch The Cowboys And Call In The Indians."

"Wash out your filthy mouth, young man," said the short, energetic woman from behind the counter. "This is a family establishment not your local. Anymore gutter language and you can all fuck "orf"."

A roar of laughter reverberated in the small, tightly packed steamy cafe. "Nice one, Sheila! You sounded just like Maggie Thatcher after her elocution lessons; almost pitch-perfect, it was!" More laughter.

At a small table near the kitchen door, Stax lifted the mint leaf between his forefinger and thumb and dropped it on the red and white chequered tablecloth, angled his head back and, with his Adam's apple bobbing, drained off the chilled water in one swig. The tiles on the wall as well as most of the other fittings were original, or so it appeared to Stax. The walls were decorated with charming vintage Brighton art deco travel marketing posters published by the Brighton Tourist Authority after the Second World War. Wiping his lips with the back of his hand, he set the empty glass down next to a condiment tray holding bottles of ketchup, HP Sauce, sugar, salt and pepper pots, Tabasco, salt & pepper pots, and a nearly empty pot of Colman's English mustard. "I've ordered us Sheila's famous man-sized Full Monty, with double poached eggs; my favourite," he told his friend. "Hands down, this is my favourite greasy spoon. The meat here is locally sourced."

"Yes, I can see why you would want to eat here," Stax replied, watching a ginger blue-eyed, white dude with ginger hair try to make eye contact with Hari. "Listen, Hari, thanks for this......"

"Stop doing that, Stax!" snapped Hari. "Stop thanking me like that for fuck sakes; makes me uncomfortable, makes me feel as though we're strangers who have just met on the fucking pier......."

Stax fixed his eyes and, for a few moments, locked onto Hari's familiar face, drawn as always into those liquid eyes of his; a face he had studied, at one time in his life, as closely as he had studied the maps, acquisition reports, personnel files, and logistical plans of his former army days. He then poured mint-flavoured water into two glasses.

"There you go my lovely, double-fried eggs for you, as usual" said Sheila bringing a hot trolley to the table edge and laying two huge plates piled with Cumberland sausage, streaky back bacon, double-fried eggs, black pudding, baked beans, sauteed mushrooms, and grilled tomatoes on the table. "Oh, Hari love, we loved that review you wrote about us. Very clever the way you used *Breakfast at Tiffany's* and *Brighton Rock* to write about our little cafe. No wonder it got published in a national food magazine!" she said in an extremely loud whisper, making sure everyone in the café heard her.

Sheila was a bookwork, a passion she shared with Hari. The Kitchen Café served as the venue for the North Laines Book Club. "I can definitely see Graham Greene's evil Pinkie bringing poor Rose in here for our Tea for Two option: not sure about Truman Capote's Holly and Paul coming in here to be honest, though! Neil's ordered a picture frame so we can hang your article on the wall." Sheila quickly arranged the large rack of granary toast, butter and two big mugs of builder's tea around the centre of the table. We cannot wait for the frame to arrive; I want the article up on the wall so all my customers can see your "W*hy Pinkie Would Take Rose To Breakfast At The Kitchen Café*?"

"Tough one that, Sheila. Most of them lot cannot read," someone shouted followed by a roar of laughter.

"This place is really going down the chute; the quality of Sheila's punters is definitively diminishing. What do you say, Derek?

"I think our Hari should write more food marketing stuff for your greasy spoon, The Kitchen Café. What does everyone else think?"

Another roar erupted. "I agree! No one can fetishize food better than our Hari. I bet he's had something to those Cadbury's flake ads. Cor blimey, watching her take that flake in her mouth like that……"

"And two perfectly cooked healthy poached eggs for our Hari's handsome and healthy-looking friend. Hello love, I'm Sheila, nice to meet you, you've not been you in here; believe me I would have noticed," she said to Stax, looking at him closely with her sharp lively eyes. "You know, Hari love, your strong friend seems strangely familiar to me, somehow," she said placing a plate in front of Stax, still looking at his face. "It's funny you know, but when I saw you walk in behind Hari you looked like a bigger, well, much bigger version of one of my customers who is a regular here…."

"I'm glad you and Neil enjoyed the review, Sheila," said Hari quickly cutting across her. "I wanted to let you and Neil know that I've been commissioned to write a few more reviews of my favourite caff; it seems readers appreciate my style of food writing. I got a decent bottle of Rioja Reserva from my commissioning editor after finishing the piece I did for you. I'm putting the finishing touches on one I've just finished writing called," *"The Full Monty: How The Full English Breakfast Won."* It's all about your signature "Full Monty" I love so much.

"We cannot find Swarnjeet Agarwal; no one has seen her at Cog House for a week; she's missing from the Parke," said Stax after Sheila left taking the mustard pot with her. "We've searched all over the estate and turned up nothing. We think she's been taken. We think she's either in Rotherham, Derby, Portsmouth, or Southampton, in a sink estate somewhere."

On the other side of the room, Hari noticed Blue Eyes on his feet, ready for his shift. He lingered back, taking his time putting on his reflector jacket while his mates shuffled in a disordered line towards the exit door. Slowing as he passed, Blue Eyes made direct visual eye contact with Hari and smiled. "I think you'd better start from the beginning," said Hari returning Blue Eye's smile with one of his own.

"I will; just let me know when I have your undivided attention, Hari," he said stonily. "I did say that what I wanted to talk to you about was urgent."

"No Stax, you didn't actually. Last night you used the word *important*, not *urgent*. There's a difference. And, you have my attention; always have. You've had my attention since last night; there's never been a time when you haven't monopolised my attention, Stax," replied Hari with a smile that didn't quite reach his eyes. "Sorry, sorry, please tell me." He reached over and touched his forearm.

"You know Swarnjeet Agarwal's story, because you wrote her story in those articles you got published - *'Swarnjeet's Silent Screams in Southsea''* "How The Sikh Awareness Society Is Fighting Muslim Grooming Gangs" and "How Multiculturism Creates Muslim Grooming Gangs." he heard himself say, "They were some of the most powerful words you've written so, in my humble opinion. I know the other Aces thought so too."

"How's your food, boys?" asked Sheila. "Here's your mustard love, sorry about the wait, Angry Angie was getting a little stressed at the back; she's had problems with cystitis you see, caught it sitting on her daughter's filthy kitchen sink. Anyway, love, you know what it's like when we're just getting ready for our lunchtime rush, all regulars. They'll be famished those boys after using their blasting tools, hand tools, power tools, and air tools. Honest to God, I just don't know how those boys can spend all day handling those heavy, vibrating tools in their hands. Must make their bones jump around a bit."

"……erm, yes, yes we do Sheila; thank you for the mustard……"

"Sorry love, I've gotta rush, Neil needs me in the kitchen," she said hurrying off to the back.

They sat in silence until they had finished their eating, pushed away their clean plates and sipped their tea. "As you can tell Sheila loves what she does; that's why her customers love her back. Now, please tell me what's been happening at the Parke."

"As you already know, Swarnjeet had spent most of her young life in various foster homes in Leicester, Rotherham, then Portsmouth. She was targeted by a child grooming gang operating in Portsmouth, above an Indian restaurant on Albert Road. She was bought to Padre by members of the Portsmouth gurdwara who managed to rescue Swarnjeet from the grooming gang that had been pimping her in an attic above an Indian restaurant. She's been living with us at the Parke for the last eleven months and doing great. Or had been until a week ago."

"What makes you think she's been abducted? How do you know she's not run away?"

"I don't know for definite. Padre asked me to deal with this for him. So far, I've spoken to everyone involved in Swarnjeet's therapy and rehabilitation: Sister Ananda confirms she hasn't missed a single appointment; her recent drug test is negative for substances; and she is engaging with all therapeutic activities. Grace told me Swarnjeet recently joined the Brighton unit of the Sea Cadets and was making a lot of friends at the Sikh gurdwara in Hassocks."

"Do we know who might have taken her?" Hari had spent many hours interviewing Swanjeet

"Yes, I do", said Stax without any hesitation. "It was The Skinny Skoda Boys. I've spoken to Padre and the other Aces, and they all agree with me."

Sir Ibrahim Ali.

"What are you going to do, Stax?" Hari was feeling the guilt and shame of flirting with Blue Eyes when Stax had such serious news for him.

"The Aces will get back Swarnjeet and bring her back home, to the Parke. Where she belongs."

"How can I help?"

"I need information on two South Asian police officers working for the Hampshire Constabulary. One is Bangladeshi and the other is Pakistani. They're both affirmative action poster boys. Bent coppers on the take." He reached into his leather jacket and took out an envelope. "The details are in here. The envelope is for him."

"Him? Who are you referring to?"

"Look, Hari, one of our own has gone missing, a very vulnerable girl. This means the Aces pull out all the stops. You're one of us; you're an Ace. Please pass that to your Special Branch contact in Sussex police."

Hari bristled, stared at Stax with steely eyes, and said nothing for many moments. He sipped his tea.

"I'll go there now," said Hari suddenly, fumbling wildly for his wallet. "You're right Stax, let's get outta here. I need to see Charl..." erm, him... them, I mean. "Anyway, let me just get this." He hurried away towards the counter.

"Just let me get your bill, Hari love; give me a second," said Sheila. "Was everything okay? Did your friend enjoy his food?"

"Everything was beyond perfect, Sheila; as usual. Thank Neil and Angie for me, won't you?"

Did I just see Jago march down the hill? Didn't he say he was working on a site in Brighton Marina? What happens if he comes in here for a bite to eat and finds me with Stax? What will I say to him?

"Let's go in there," said Stax quickly walking towards a small, gated park tucked away in Pelham Square. "I need to sit for a few minutes to let that breakfast settle. That was a breakfast for champions; reminds me of the good stuff we got fed at Worthy Down Barracks back in the day," he reminisced, with a smile.

As they sat on the bench, Hari took out a pack of cigarettes and a lighter from his blazer pocket and lit up a Bensons & Hedges using his much-loved petrol lighter with the engraving of a spaniel holding a pheasant in its mouth.

"That stuff will kill you, Hari,"

"We're all dying, Stax; some of us quicker than others; it's the luck of the draw," he said, blowing smoke upwards, away from Stax.

He turned the lighter over in his right palm, caressing the cold grey gun mental and fine craftsmanship of the gift Jago brought him from nearby Snoopers Paradise after Hari sold his articles, "*How Old Blighty Became A Kingdom Of Addicts*," and "*How Tobacco Companies Use Subcultural Underground Marketing To Sell Tobacco Products To Gay Men*' to two different national publication on the same day.

"Hey, what happened back at the café?"

"What do you mean?" Hari said, admiring the neat, well-maintained gardens.

"You know what! Why did you break out in the café? It's not like you to lose your cool like that; I know you maintain course and direction in all areas of your life: self-contained, self-reliant, always self-controlled. So, what made you lose control in there, soldier?"

Hari sighed. He never could lie to Stax. "I didn't lose control, Stax, I very rarely do, as you just said. I got flustered because I was ashamed," said Hari, avoiding looking at Stax.

"Ashamed? About what? We were having a perfectly normal conversation over a great breakfast then you go all schizoid on me."

"I'm ashamed because I wasn't paying enough attention to you when you were telling me about what had happened to Swarnjeet Agarwal. I'm ashamed because instead of listening I was cruising that ginger chap, knowing very well that you would notice. I wanted to make you jealous. I was being childish. So, there you have it; I'm ashamed for feeling so infantile, still, around my feelings for you, and our unresolved business." He didn't mention the feelings of guilt at having cheated on Jago.

"We have no business left to resolve; everything is exactly as it should be. We've talked about this already."

"Look, I cannot sit here all day; I've got a story to write. I'm going to see if I can catch my source now to pass on your envelope," he said, patting his blazer front to check it was there. "I shouldn't be long, call me if there are any new developments on Swarnjeet," he said turning and heading for the gate.

The sound of a loud honk from a passing Vauxhall across the street made him turn towards the sound. Stax could see one of the street drinkers, the loudest of the group with a mane of filthy black hair, and a face as rough as a cat-scratched chair leg, standing on the pavement raising his can of larger to passing truck drivers and making incomprehensible toasts punctuated with the words "fuckers" and "you'se rotten cunts!" Next to him, a woman tramp sat on the kerb, picking at the flakes of dead skin hanging on the soles of her feet, occasionally laughing hysterically to herself.

After a while, he got up and walked over to the same phone box Hari had used earlier and placed a call to Blayney Parke.

"Any news on Swarjeet?" he asked Padre.

"Look, something's happened and I need you to get to Blayney Parke as soon as you can," said Padre, his voice unusually grave and solemn. "I can't go into details over the phone……"

"Padre, what's happened?"

"I'll tell you when I see you, Hamilton" the Jesuit said flatly. "Oh, and Hamilton, if you're with Hari please don't say anything to him. Just get to here quickly."

8

Brighton & Hove police station, John Street, Brighton

"According to my source, Charlie, we may have a problem with county-lines drug dealing in our bright and beautiful Brighton," said Hari looking around the cluttered broom cupboard which was the workspace of a special branch detective inspector. "I saw some black and Asian gang wannabees scouting the Level the other night. I suspect the crack and heroin is coming from the Sikhs in Southall Broadway and the Turks and Kurds in north London. My contact tells me the crystal meth is coming from Southampton. He also tells we will have a serious fentanyl problem soon."

"Sadly, this tallies nicely with the latest intel I've received from Scotland Yard," said Charles von Strett leaning back on his chair. Hari's long-time Scotland Yard contact hadn't changed at all since he met him five years ago, working on a story about the radical Muslim cleric, Sheikh Abu Hamza, who had preached in the Brighton mosques. They got to know each other over a drink after Hari sold *"Mad Muslim Preacher Worked As A Doorman At Brighton Strip Club,"* to a national tabloid newspaper. Originally from the West Midland, Charles von Strett was tall in stature with a long-headed, dolichocephalic skull; he kept his blonde hair short, often closely cropped; he had light skin and the palest of blues eyes. His face, with its high cheekbones, had a glow about it, with natural contours and highlights.

"As the price of cocaine continues to fall, so the use of crack and crystal meth is set to grow in Brighton, with all the usual consequences you write about. Apparently, it's becoming popular again with the Brighton middle classes and those wealthy enough in Hove to fund substantial drug habits without having to commit crime. It's a key finding in a report by our serious and organised crime unit that is being circulated around. I've put a copy in for you in my bag of goodies over there," he said pointing to a plastic Morrisons carrier bag on top of the filing cabinet. "I asked a colleague at Box 500 for help in getting the stuff you wanted on that Southampton shipping company and its owner, Sir Ibrahim Ali." Within the British intelligence community, Box 500 is a colloquial reference to MI5, after its official wartime designation, PO BOX 500.

Detective Inspector Charles von Strett made his mark as a Special Branch officer assigned to work in the St Paul's district of Bristol. "I arrived a week after local police had placed armed foot patrols on the streets to prevent a bloodbath between the city's homegrown drug gangs and the new influx of Yardie dealers who were fighting hard for control of the lucrative crack trade. If we're not careful we'll have the same chaos here in Brighton. Bad for the city, but good for you, Hari, because it will keep you in work."

"A bit ironic, considering crack was conceived and marketed at the working classes after the Columbian Cartels found they had lost the middle-class market," said Hari who had recently finished reading Guy Gugliotta's book, *Kings of Cocaine*, on the business models and operations of the Medellin Cartel and the role of Pablo Escobar within the organisation. The book was a Christmas present from Jago. "Anyway, I wanted you to know about these new county line dealers pushing crack and crystal meth because of Brighton's thriving sex industry. You know what I'm talking about, Charlie."

Charles nodded. "I've had colleagues here telling me teenage prostitutes are now offering sex for as little as a fiver to feed their crack habit. Underage hustlers on Saint James Street are offering passing men unprotected sex for ten pounds – the going price for a single rock in Brighton."

"I'm glad you came to me with this, Hari. Thank you. The last thing we want is Brighton turning into another Bristol. "I think I've already told you I found myself at the height of turf wars between the indigenous Bristol gangs," said Charles.

Hari laughed. "Weren't you the lucky one, Charles?"

"Not sure about being lucky. Not sure I want to repeat the experience either, to be honest," said Charles emphatically. "Definitely exciting though. During the nineties Bristol's drug trade was entirely in the hands of a ragtag gang called the Aggi Crew. I was part of the task force that caught them with more than two million pounds of crack cocaine."

"The vacuum left by the Aggi Crew was quickly filled by Yardies who not only picked up where the Aggi Crew left off but also brought new levels of violence and sophistication to the local drug scene. You're right Hari, we cannot have this in Brighton."

"It would be a nightmare if we allowed Brighton to become another St Paul's," said Charles. "I remember, instead of holding wraps of crack in their mouths, the street dealers operating from the Black & White Café placed drugs in old coke cans or milk cartons, which would then be left in the gutter or bins. After handing cash over, junkies would be directed to the nearest dustbin where they would frantically rummage around in the garbage and human waste until they found their wrap. We couldn't arrest gang members because they were carrying no drugs," Charles said regretfully. "Dealing in Bristol quickly reached epidemic proportions very quickly."

"The Black & White Café," whistled Hari, "fucking hell." He had read of the infamous café. Hidden behind deeply tinted windows, the café has a tiny mock-turtle counter with thick plated glass where you can buy traditional Jamaican food, like ackee, salt fish, curried goat, jerk chicken, and Swiss-style pork chops. "But no one went to buy food. Never."

"Exactly," said Charles. "Local junkies referred to the café as the hypermarket. I set up a network of low-level informants who told me about open dealing at a local pub and a curry house, but in terms of sales the Black & White Café was by far the most popular." The Special Branch officer was silent for a long while as he recalled scenes of countless armed robberies, stabbings, and shootings, and the many friends and colleagues injured or worse in the line of duty.

"Look, Hari, if what your informant is saying is true and there is some tie-up between Pakistani gangs and Yardies, then we have a shit storm heading for Brighton. There are always knock-on effects when two different gangs plan a joint enterprise," said Charles with urgency in his voice. "While the Jamaicans prefer firepower, the Asian boys prefer urban guerrilla tactics. In Bristol, we discovered Pakistani and Bangladeshi street pushers had started intimidating council utility workers and their families. We had countless incidents of maintenance workers, street sweepers and garbage collectors having guns held to their heads. The result was waste collection and road repairs stopped altogether because workers were too scared to turn up for work. The Pakistanis would then hide the cellophane-packed wraps of crack in between the pavement gaps as well as the dustbins."

"The dealers and pushers then turned their attention to workers attempting to install CCTV systems until they, also, gave up fearing for their lives and that of their families. An internal memo described Stapleton Road, another notorious shithole in Bristol, as the 'road of dread' with Pakistani pimps, Turkish dealers, teenage prostitutes, and street muggers operating with virtual impunity. Postal workers refused to deliver mail. I agreed with what the memo said, that the area had become a Third World cesspit."

Hari's mobile suddenly vibrated. "Shit sorry, Charlie, thought I had switched this bloody thing off," said Hari reading the message. "Can you excuse me for a minute, Charlie?"

He nodded absently and turned his head to face the whiteboard, staring intently at the spider-web diagram he had started soon after his arrival in Brighton. The intelligence gathered by Hari was a chilling fulfilment of a prophecy he made in an internal MI5 report he authored and was circulated in the Home Office in 1996. The Charles von Strett Report (as it came to be known) warned of a demographic time bomb of British Muslim and Sikh gangs who represent a clear and present danger to Britain's national security. The report shattered the long-held belief that Asian Muslims and Sikhs were the most law-abiding citizens living in thriving entrepreneurial communities in the country.

Charles had spent three months working on the report and the evidence was overwhelming: the significant increase in the number of Sikhs and Muslims in young offenders' institutions; the radicalisation of alienated youths by Saudi-trained imams preaching in Britain's mosques; small Asian businesses being used for money laundering purposes; and the lack of social integration. The report predicted that many of the groups that started out aiming to protect their community from racist attacks would soon evolve into full-blown criminal syndicates specialising in drug and sex trafficking. And so, they did.

Inspector Charles von Strett was considered a highflier, by both friend and foe. Born into a military family, Chares studied politics, philosophy and economics at Oxford followed by a year spent at Quantico, the FBI academy in Washington DC, before joining the Metropolitan Police national graduate scheme where he rose quickly through the ranks. Following the reorganisation of Operation Trident, set up to deal with gun crime, Charles was invited to join a multi-agency task force targeting home-grown criminal gangs operating within the British Asian community. "Someone in the Home Office had rummaged around in the cupboards and found the 1996 report I wrote while on sabbatical in Washington. The mandarins must have read the summary and key findings and decided I could be useful to the defence of the realm after all," he said to Hari over a drink one day.

"Listen, sorry Charlie, something has come up and I need to cut this short."

"No worries, Hari. I know the story always comes first for you. Always has always will. Let's stay in touch. Don't forget your bag of goodies," said Charlie, still absorbed by the whiteboard. "Oh, please put the Morrisons bag in your satchel please, Hari; there's a good chap. Neither of us would want our colleagues and peers to find you carrying confidential Scotland Yard reports; reports that I have printed off."

"Discretion must always be the better part of valour in our line of work, Charlie," said Hari carefully folding the carrier bag before placing it under the copy of *The Clash of Civilizations and the Remaking of World Order* written by one of Hari's political scientists, Samuel P. Huntington. "Let's do a long walk and pub lunch soon. And thanks again for looking into those two bent coppers in Portsmouth."

Inspector Charles von Strett had a twin sister who became a crack whore and in May 1988 overdosed in a council block in Handsworth in Birmingham at the age of 22. The flat belonged to her Turkish pimp. He had been studying the trafficking of crack cocaine into Britain ever since. A month after his sister's death, small traces of crack were found in a Liverpool squat. In September of that year, Scotland Yard raided and turned up the country's first crack factory in a south London flat on the Milton Court estate in Deptford.

"For those destined to get hooked on crack, like my twin sister Charlotte, the first ten-pound hit at first seems like a bargain but within minutes of the first puff, most users are begging for another hit," said Charles during one of the long walks he used to take with Hari shortly after he arrived in town having successfully taken down the Aggi Crew in Bristol. "Crack is truly diabolical because the high is so short-lived and sharp, junkies can smoke over three grands worth of crack and still come back for more. And if they cannot afford it, they'd quite happily beg, steal, or kill for it. For the dealers, it's an equally intensely pleasurable experience. An ounce of cocaine will produce around fifty decent snorting lines but some three-hundred-eighty rocks of crack. In other words, Hari, for the dealer, selling the cheaper product will on average quadruple their profit margin. It's important your readers understand this: it's all about profit."

"The speed at which crack spread in the UK surprised Scotland Yard," explained Charles who had been commissioned by the (then) assistant commissioner of the Specialist Crime Directorate to conduct a scoping study on the phenomena. "I understood all too well that it was pure economics. Crack dealers knew that pricing the new product was the key. In terms of global pricing at a hundred dollars a gram, cocaine was still having trouble in 1988 leaving its jet-set roots behind. At ten dollars a hit, crack wasn't just cheap, it was a miracle of modern marketing."

"What do you mean?" asked Hari staring out into the sea. They were walking along Telscombe Cliffs, near Peacehaven. Charles had agreed to provide background information on the pushers responsible for Charlotte's heroin addiction and overdose for Hari's feature-length article, *"The Future Is Black If The Sugar Is Brown."*

"It was innovative marketing which sold crack cocaine to the masses," said Charles warming to his subject. "We don't know who invented crack, but we know it was the Columbian cartels, led by the infamous Pablo Escobar, who pushed the drug into the ghettos. Crack was the perfect black ghetto drug, intense enough to pull the blacks out of the social deprivation they suffered."

"The effect of the drug alone was enough to guarantee its success." According to Scotland Yard, the instant euphoria a rock of crack produces lasts a few minutes at the most. But the high produced has no parallel. "Around seven per cent of cocaine users go on to develop an addiction, even then the process can take up to eighteen months. With crack, around eighty per cent go on to develop an addiction, usually within two weeks of their first pipe," he had explained to Hari on that day, standing on top of Telscombe Cliffs. "And now we have crystal meth and fentanyl coming in. cheaper and more potent than cocaine or crack."

An instructor once explained that drug markets are like the mythical, multi-headed, serpentine water monster: the Hydra. Designer drugs replace old drugs. Younger players replace old drug lords. New business models replace old drug cartels.

After many minutes of sitting still, staring up at the ceiling he got up to close his door. After sitting down, he reread the notepaper Hari gave him with the names, police number, and photographs of the two police officers. He opened a drawer, took out a well-thumbed *Filofax*, flicked through until he found what he was looking for and picked up the phone to dial a telephone number in London.

It began to ring.

It was windier when Hari exited the police station at Johns Street. "That interruption had better be for a good reason, Stax," Hari snapped, not bothering to hide his irritation. "I was working."

"Sorry, Hari, but somethings come up and I need you to get to Blayney Parke......"

"What's happened, Stax! You're not in the army anymore; you don't need my permission......"

"I'm sorry Hari I called you,' he said softly,' 'but I thought you'd want to know."

"Know what, Stax?"

"Robbie has had a heart attack; he's been admitted to a hospital in Delhi," he said. "I called you as soon as I got the news from Padre; he wants to see you at the Parke. He's waiting for you."

9

Secretary's Conference Room, Lodhi Road, New Delhi

Massey's regular budget meeting with section heads had been cancelled and an ad hoc council had been convened to discuss the FLUENCY operation before his meeting with the prime minister. Massey presided from the head of the large oval table. Present were those select few who were privy to the operation: Massey's deputy, Shivananda Menon; the head of the Directorate General of Security, Anita "Golda" Kinnar; and the section heads responsible for China, Pakistan, Africa, and the Middle East. The head of the Psychological Operations & Warfare Division was present. The national security advisor was represented by his deputy responsible for strategic and foreign affairs. A navy-blue folder embossed with the Lion Capital of Ashoka bulging with reports and photographs lay in front of each person. Next to each folder a full carafe of water topped with a glass was perched.

The joint secretary responsible for Pakistan, a thirty-year veteran, and a member of the Ismaili Muslim community, who had spent the week reviewing Massey's memorandum observed that, if initiated, TUPAC II would be akin to the bombing of Hiroshima and Nagasaki *and* the recent global COVID pandemic if bioweapons found itself in the Red Corridor. "The effect will be to annihilate entire civilian populations while leaving the valuable infrastructure intact. Musharad and the Compact must be insane."

"I would like to ask a question about the Somali angle?" said the hard-faced man, puffing away on his trademark long-stemmed pipe, sitting at the opposite end of the table.

"Please go ahead" said Massey to the formidable head of the China and Southeast Asia Division.

"Do we know the exact location of the weapons stored in Puntland?" he asked pleasantly. "According to some in my division you haven't made your case. I have read the report most thoroughly, Masseyji. Your memorandum seems to be strong in low and medium-grade intelligence, but weak in high-grade facts. My people feel we need to tread carefully with this Puntland plan," he continued in his usual measured tones. "Our relations with our QUAD partners can only survive this kind of risk if we're correct in our belief that there is in fact weapons in Puntland destined for the Red Corridor. This fact has yet to be established."

"No, we don't, not yet. We have no assets in Somalia because of the civil war. Locating that weapons depot is now a top priority for the Wing," Massey said carefully. He noted the concerned looks of his colleagues. "Problems arose when the Al-Qaeda-affiliated Somali group Al-Shabaab took control of Puntland and issued a *fatwa* that all foreigners are legitimate targets for execution," he explained. "In clan-based Somalia, strangers stand out." As a result, Massey had been unable to insert an infiltration agent into Puntland. "I'm waiting for a suitable infiltration point into the Al Shabaab stronghold."

The head of Psychological Operations & Warfare, a cool, aloof military psychiatrist by training and the in-house expert on disinformation who had more in common with the methodical intelligence gatherers than the Wing's covert paramilitary experts, leaned towards the cautious side. "Your report is intriguing," she told Massey in her usual calm manner, "but Prakash is correct – when you strip everything down to the bare essentials, all we are left with could easily be dismissed by the prime minister's office as a series of coincidences."

"And the prime ministers principal private secretary is not the biggest fan of the Wing," added the head of China & Southeast

Asia Divion. "He still holds Lodhi Road responsible for not preventing the Mumbai bomb blasts in 2008."

"For the Wing," argued Menon, the chief architect of the Puntland plan, "coincidences don't exist. And absolutely not when they relate to Islamabad and their paymasters in Beijing." In private Menon had always believed that the RAW had strong covert action capability, but it was weak when it came to analysis and assessment.

An elegant Gujarati, leaning back on his chair, his eyes half closed, allowed that Menon might be correct in his assumptions detailed in the report. The joint secretary responsible for Africa, the man responsible for maintaining the RAW stations in all African countries was a Brahmin from a family of scholars and intellectuals. He was an intimate of men in high places, from Cairo to Cape Town, who disliked anyone who rocked his boat. From his carefully groomed, sleek head down to his immaculate white cotton cuffs fastened with tastefully expensive silver links, he gave the appearance of a man devoted to the fine things in life. "Do we have any further information on the Pakistani mafia connection to these Somali pirates and the Compact," he asked, glancing down at the dossier, and reading from a note he'd jotted to himself. "Have we established what connects them together or are we still in the dark on this?" The FLUENCY task force had instructed the RAW station chief in Islamabad to place Haneef Hussani, a Pakistani national working for the Compact under full-service surveillance, meaning they wanted to know everything about the D-Company mafia point man. The station chief, an old RAW hand, got results quickly. It was quickly established that Haneef Hussani was paying a Somali soldier to store the weapons somewhere in Puntland.

"Yes, we have," said the head of the Directorate General of Security as she peered at her colleagues through her trademark ivory lorgnette. After the initial FLUENCY briefing, the DGS called to instruct her counterpart at the National Technical Research Organisation, India's secretive signal intelligence agency, to closely monitor all signal traffic in the Gulf of Aden region and the Red Sea. "NATRO intercepted a telephone conversation between Haneef Hussaini and a Somali pirate by the name of Salim. It was an interesting transcript; I'm still examining it all, including some very interesting cypher wireless traffic between Gwadar Port and Puntland," was all the DGS was prepared to say on the matter. Around the table, no one was prepared to question the indomitable Anita "Golda" Kinnar.

Menon positioned a forefinger along the side of his cheek. "When all the pieces lock into place," he said in his professorial manner, "we would be insane not to go to the prime minister with this. If we are wrong, then the fallout will be catastrophic. If the Compact is successful, it will make the three million deaths from COVID pale into insignificance. I remind you all again that we have the shadow of a bioweapons attack on India and the shadow is getting darker and larger. Am I the only one around this table to see this?"

"Do we know anything about this Somali pirate," asked the head of the Africa Division. "Salim, is it?"

Massey said, "The Somali is one of the pirate leaders, a member of a group calling themselves the Coast Guards of Puntland. We think this Salim fellow is ex-military, from Said Barre's regime. He likely served until 1985. Both Haneef Hussaini and Salim are fanatical members of Al Shabaab. Our analysts describe them as quartermasters, senior members of Al Shabaab. Hussani is responsible for transporting weapons for groups such as the Compact and Salim stores them somewhere in Puntland. This Salim is also responsible for overseeing the training of new recruits."

Menon added, "The training of the jihadists is outsourced to the Pakistanis. They are the same instructors who are busy teaching the Taliban how to use all the American weapons and equipment left behind after the fall of Kabul three years ago. The Americans fled leaving behind billions of dollars' worth of equipment." Everyone around the table recalled watching live footage of Taliban fighters in 2021 facing no resistance from the American and British-trained Afghan security forces.

"Just out of interest, why doesn't the Compact just store the weapons in Pakistan or Afghanistan like they used to? Why go to all the trouble of hiring a Somali middleman to store them in Somalia," asked the head of Africa.

"General Musharad cannot afford to take any chances," said Menon who was struggling to keep his annoyance at his colleagues from showing. He loathed the turf wars that permeated Lodhi Road. "The Compact won't allow it because the risks are too great for Islamabad, especially after the Americans discovered the Compact was harbouring Osama bin Laden in Abbottabad, within spitting distance from the Pakistan Military Academy. We now know the entire academy knew the ISI was hiding Osama bin Laden in that compound. Cadets were placing bets on how long it would take the National Security Agency to wake up in Fort Meade. The Compact knows what will happen if Washington ever discovers they are working hand-in-glove with Al Qaeda to smuggle bioweapons into India. Musharad will be crucified – literally," explained Massey. "He is unlikely to forget the fate of his predecessor who risked the wrath of Beijing. It's simply too risky to store weapons for Al Qaeda in Pakistan or Afghanistan, so the Compact outsources its warehouse requirements to Salim and the pirates to store it somewhere in Somalia, probably in Puntland somewhere. As we said, Salim is a senior quartermaster."

"This fellow, Salim, spoke English with what I took to be a Palestinian accent," the DGS offered after a long silence. "Which could mean he was brought up in the Middle East. There's a chance he might have worked in one of the Hezbollah or Hamas training camps in Beirut or Gaza. I will speak to my contact in Tel Aviv," Golda said.

"That's as good a place to start as any," Massey agreed, looking in the direction of Menon. "Now, let's get to the report about D-Company and its role in the Mumbai bombings?"

Adjusting her lorgnette and squinting through the lens, Golda, quick to clutch at any new nugget of information, demanded to know, "Which report are you referring to, Menonji?"

Menon said, "This came in late last night from the national security advisor. It was hand-delivered to me at McGregor's. Following the recent bombing involving BJP party workers the NSA asked for all files relating to the 1993 and 2008 Mumbai bombings to be sent to his office. He has concluded that D-Company, working hand-in-glove with Pakistani intelligence and the terror group Lashkar-e-Taiba, was ultimately responsible for all the bombings. The Cabinet Committee on Security concur with the NSA. I have read his report very carefully and I agree with him also."

The mood inside the room becomes subdued. Everyone was waiting for Massey to say something.

"The NSA wants two things from us. As well as putting together the FLUENCY taskforce to neutralise the threat of bioweapons being distributed throughout the Red Corridor by the Compact, we are also to neutralise D-Company using whatever active measures we deem necessary. The Prime Minister's Office is very clear on this," said Massey quietly.

Massey glanced at his watch. The meeting was well so far. Plenty of time before his meeting with the new prime minister.

"We still have to deal with the proverbial elephant in the room," said the head of the Africa Division. "Your report states that we have no assets in Somalia, and you have just confirmed this."

From the far end of the table, the head of the West Asia Division said, very quietly. "We do have an asset in Somalia actually. I recruited himself in Qatar and have been running him personally. He is quite brilliant. He's a photojournalist on the staff of Al Jazeera, and he's been delivering some interesting things."

The divisional heads around the table exchanged glances around the table. The head of the Africa Division leaned back further into his chair and eyed the man through a haze of pipe smoke. "I trust you're prepared to amplify and clarify that statement."

"You can trust me to do exactly that," he said and for the next forty minutes, he told them about his informer, Jabir Khanfari.

10

Chawri Bazar, Old Delhi

On a deserted dusty street running along one side of Old Delhi, a broad-shouldered middle-aged man known to the Compact only by his code name, QIPIAN, surveyed the neighbourhood through prism binoculars that could see in the dark. A former major in the Indian army his was a distinctly military bearing. Sitting motionlessly in the back seat of his car, he'd been surveying the area for over an hour. The courtyards and rooftops were filled with people. Some were lying in *charpoys*, snoozing away the last minutes of the working day before their evening meal. Others sat out on carpets beneath the shady trees enjoying the light breeze. QIPIAN was focused on the rooftops where the pigeon fanciers – the *kabooter baz* – gathered every evening. They stood on almost every terrace; hands extended into the air calling to their pigeons; *Aao! Aao! Aao!* Come! Come! Come! Above them, QIPIAN saw the sky was full of the soft rush of beating wings, clouds of birds dipping and diving in and out of the domes and minarets of Old Delhi.

As darkness settled, he spotted the dark Maruti Susuki with two men cruising the area. It vanished down a side street and emerged twenty minutes later from another direction. On its third pass around the area, the car eased to a stop near the entrance of a halal butcher, "Farooq & Sons." The headlights flickered out. For a long while the two men remained in the vehicle. Occasionally one of them would light a fresh cigarette from the glowing embers of the last one. Finally, the men emerged from the. One of the men tugged a large parcel from the floor of the car and entered the shop. The one chain-smoking cigarette turned his back on the shop and stood guard. His companion was in the shop for no longer than ten minutes. On their way back to the car, the two men stripped off the Congress Party poster pasted vertically across the side of the shop indicating that QIPIAN was ready to enter the butcher's shop and pinned a poster of the Communist Party India (Marxist) to indicate that the dead drop had been serviced. With a final glance around, they got back into their car and accelerating cautiously, drove off towards Turkman Gate.

QIPIAN waited another hour before making his move. He had been spying for the Chinese since May 1999 when he passed classified information about a Pakistani intrusion in the Kargil district of Jammu and Kashmir. Realising his seniority from the documents he provided, QIPIAN met his future handler in the Tengra district of Kolkata. Under the tutelage of Kai Ling of Macau, he quickly became a meticulous practitioner of tradecraft.

Back in 1999, when he had delivered his first cache of documents relating to what became the Kargil War, the motive was purely money. Many of his old army friends were earning a fortune working in the country's lucrative private arms industry. QIPIAN's government salary allowed him and his family to live comfortably, but he didn't see how he could possibly pay for the foreign education and marriages of his four daughters. Unless…. unless he came up with a scheme to supplement his income. The only scheme that seemed within the realm of possibility was peddling India's military secrets to the country's principal enemy, China. He followed his handler's advice to the letter to ensure he didn't fall into the hands of the Intelligence Bureau's formidable counterintelligence division. QIPIAN was careful not to attract attention. He drove the same Maruti family cars and vacationed in Kerala or at the same modest resorts in Goa. Curiously, it was only after he'd delivered the first few intel packages to the Chinaman that he understood the money wasn't the only reward he craved. He enjoyed beating the corrupt Indian system; he loathed the nepotism he saw all around him. His contempt for the Wing galvanised during the tenure of Ashok Chaturvedi. A hopeless alcoholic who ran Lodhi Road from 2007 to 2009, the Congress government refused to remove him from office despite clear evidence the poor man was not fit for purpose. The adrenaline rush flowed through him when he outsmarted the Intelligence Bureau that had been created in 1887 to prevent someone like him from doing what he was doing. His drab grey life, which was filled with boring routines, tedious paperwork and rigorous hierarchy, suddenly seemed a lot more glamourous.

QIPIAN could feel his heart beating faster as he let himself out of his car. He approached the halal shop and knocked five times. The door was opened by Farooq, the cutout working for Kai Ling. In silence, they walked up the stairs towards the rooftop where the birds were kept. Some were resting on the bamboo pigeon frames – horizontal slats of trellising raised on a pole – that Farooq's family had built.

QIPIAN was taken to the edge of the terrace, where his own pigeons were kept in a large coop. Farooq opened the wire mesh door and scattered some grain on the floor. Immediately the birds began to strut and flutter about, billing and cooing loudly with pleasure. Farooq pointed out the different varieties in his collection. "These are the *Shiraji*," he said pointing to three birds with red-dish wings and blackened breasts. "They are the fighter pigeons. Those are very good: they have won many fights. And you see these?" Farooq was pointing at some large blue-grey pigeons. "These were delivered recently. They are the *Kabuli Kabooter*. They are the strongest pigeons in Asia. They are not very fast, but they can fly very high and for up to eight hours – sometimes more. This is the one you will be needing tonight, the red one over there. This is the *Lal Khal*; it is the fastest of all *kabouter*."

With a swift movement, he picked up one of the *Lal Khal* and stroked its head. Then turning it over, he pointed to the metal bracelets fixed to its ankle. "Look!" he said. "I have made a false *ghungroos* anklet to insert the radio-frequency identity chip. The anklet is weather-proof. You will have nothing to worry about. *Lal Khal* will carry the chip to its destination in no time."

"You have something for me?" He carefully inserted the RFID chip into the *ghungroos* anklet.

"Yes," said Farooq. "They left a bag under that bench over there along with Lal Khal."

Walking soundlessly on his rubber soles, QIPIAN squatted next to the bench and worked an old leather bag from under the bench. He could make out the wads of bills and used two and five hundred banknotes bound together with rubber bands, through the paper. This Chinese handler will have left him $5,000 in total, compensation for the intelligence he'd passed the month before that included the latest developments in the QUAD and India-USA military relations. The internal workings of the BJP government. The payload included the identification of three Chinese diplomats serving in Tokyo who were spying for Naicho, the Japanese foreign intelligence agency. QIPIAN also included the latest intelligence on the secretive FLUENCY operation. Kai Ling had made his interest in FLUENCY very clear.

Back in the car, he jammed the leather bag under the dashboard behind the dashboard and started the engine. Threading his way carefully through the maze of ancient streets in the direction of home he allowed himself a smile. The double game he was playing had become the only game worth playing.

11

Raisina Hill, South Block, Government Secretariat, New Delhi

The normally empty space on the plain below Raisina Hill, a huge broad avenue which sweeps up from the east, was swarming with "family members" of various Hindu nationalist groups. The parent of the family is the Rashtriya Swayamsevak Sangh the Organisation of National Volunteers – which has between eight and fifteen million members, depending on whom you ask in New Delhi. Even the lower number would make the RSS the second-largest political movement in the world, after the Chinese Communist Party. One of its many offspring is the Hindu nationalist Bharatiya Janata Party which had been in power since May 2014. Since January 2024 the BJP led the National Democratic Alliance, a coalition of centre-right and neoconservative Indian parties.

A swarm of Rashtriya Swayamsevak Sangh (RSS) volunteers, each wielding an iron-tipped bamboo stick known as a *lathi*, blocked the path of the visitors as they walked along the corridor leading into the Prime Minister's Office (PMO). They were dressed in the standard kit of the RSS volunteer: a plain white shirt, khaki shorts held up by a sturdy black belt, yellow socks, and black shoes. Most were wearing the trademark RSS black cap, an inversion of the traditional white Congress cap made famous by Jawaharlal Nehru.

"Would you gentlemen kindly identify yourselves," said the head volunteer.

Massey, limping because of an attack of arthritis, seemed insulted. "I'm the Secretary of the Research & Analysis Wing," he said stiffly. "You will find me on that list under Secretary (Research). We have an appointment with the national security advisor."

"Kindly produce your security clearance card please," the unsmiling volunteer insisted.

Massey and Shivananda Menon both produced their biometric ID cards from their wallets. The volunteer studied each photograph and then looked up to compare it to the face in front of him. At the end of the corridor, a young aide holding a clipboard checked off their names and led them through to the Prime Minister's Office, a vast suite of thirty ornate Raj-era rooms overlooking the grandeur of Rashtrapati Bhavan. Passing the majestic Travancore Room, Massey caught a glimpse of a group of elderly volunteers giving the unmistakably fascistic RSS salute: standing to attention and moving the right arm across the chest with the palm of the hand facing down. Up ahead he could see India's first bachelor prime minister talking to his bald-headed, *dhoti*-clad principal private secretary, his closest political colleague. Known as The Skull due to his cadaverous features, the PPS was arguably the second most powerful man in Delhi after the prime minister. The two men had known each other since they were children. The national security advisor was nearby, talking to a journalist.

Menon, trailing behind Massey, murmured, "I hear our prime minister has big plans for the intelligence community. I bet you the first words out of his mouth have to do with the Sukma-Bijapur attack by the Naxalites."

"It's a good bet," said Massey. "It's a very good bet."

The septuagenarian prime minister, dressed in *dhoti* and an immaculate white shirt and looking relaxed rose from the wicker chair to greet Massey. "Congratulations on your appointment as director of the RAW, Secretary Massey. I take it you saw the article in the papers," he said, clearly annoyed. He pulled a copy off a stack of newspapers on a low table. "Front page, no less. Also, the social media." *"Suicide bombers target BJP minister in Sukma-Bijapur."* Jai

Ram, Masseyji. What is happening to our country? What is happening to Bharat? "What is our intelligence community doing?" he shook hands with the RAW men. "Menonji, good to see you again. I remember you briefed me in Gujarat back in 2014." The prime minister was known for his phenomenal memory skills. As the prime minister waved the RAW officers to seats his national security advisor wandered over from the adjourning conference room and took the last of the chairs. The prime minister settled back into the wicker rocker. "Why don't you begin Masseyji"

"Prime minister," Massey said, opening the briefing, "you asked me to update you on the details of Operation FLUENCY that your predecessor authorised. The late Vajpay……."

"Forgive me, Secretary Massey, my understanding is that Lodhi Road was authorised to draw up plans for a possible operation, as opposed to actually authorising any such operation," commented the Skull in his distinctive rasping, metallic voice.

Massey cleared his throat, "I was under the impression that was what I said, Sir."

The Skull, rocking gently in his chair, murmured softly, "Clarity is everything, Mr Secretary. I simply wanted to make sure we are talking about the same thing, Masseyji." He nodded for Maasy to continue with the briefing.

Massey, flustered, looked at the notes he had jotted on the back of an envelope. "There is no room for doubt prime minister; the group known to us as the Compact is stockpiling huge quantities of Chinese manufactured weapons somewhere in Somalia. We know that the new Chairman of the Compact, General Syed Musharad, is working with the Pakistani mafia, D-Company, to distribute these weapons to Maoist groups throughout the Red Corridor. One of those groups is the same rebel group that attacked your party workers and their security convoy in Sukma-Bijapur earlier this week. Our sources inform us that the Compact is being directed from Beijing. We suspect the Pakistani's controlling officer at the Ministry of State Security is a professional intelligence officer by the name of Kai Ling of Macau. His father, Jiang, was onboard the sabotaged plane of the late Zia ul-Haq. These plans are expected to become operational in less than three months. The Pakistanis even have a name for the infiltration. It's codenamed Operation TUPAC II. We know the Pakistanis are hiding huge stockpiles of weapons in Somalia — in Puntland ready for TUPAC II. And if all this isn't reason enough to go after him, the RAW has gathered extensive intelligence proving that General Musharad has stockpiled bioweapons as well as conventional weapons for distribution. This is a clear violation of the Biological Weapons Convention of 1975. Working hand in glove with the Chinese, General Musharad's ultimate aim is to destroy Bharat from within."

The Skull rearranged the folds of his white, silk *dhoti*. "No one doubts that the Pakistanis are troublesome fellows, Secretary Massey. We've known this since the 1946 Indian provincial elections," he said. "Question is: What is the Bharatiya Janata Party' — the veteran bureaucrat managed to linger over the words *Bharatiya Janata Party* — "going to decide to do about it?"

Massey said, 'The anti-Compact operation, codenamed FLUENCY, is directed by my deputy, Shivananda Menon. I will ask him to explain."

Menon, in his element began speaking without notes, his toe drumming impatiently on the floor, and began walking the group through what he called "the Puntland plan." "We are thinking along the lines of putting up to fifty men in Puntland, where we believe the weapons stockpiled for TUPAC II are hidden in an abandoned Coptic monastery. The men will be carefully selected by the Armed Forces Special Operations Division in Bengaluru. The AFSOD has shortlisted the Special Frontier Force with MARCOS playing a supporting role. The dawn landing will be preceded by a series of air strikes launched from one of the frigates we already have patrolling in the Gulf of Aden and in the Red Sea. Our navy is currently taking part in the NATO anti-piracy initiative, Operation Prosperity Guardian. The operation is a multinational military operation formed in December last year in response to Houthi-led attacks on shipping vessels in the Red Sea."

The Skull mocked. "You failed to find the weapons in Bombay in 1993, you failed Mumbai in 2008, and you failed to find the weapons in Sukma-Bijapur a few days ago, your success rate at locating weapons hidden by terrorists is not particularly good, is it Mr Menon?"

Shivananda Menon wasn't accustomed to being interrupted. He turned toward the civil servant and asked coldly, "Did you say something, Sir?"

The Prime Minister said quickly, "Please go on, Menonji."

Menon kept his gaze on the bureaucrat for a few seconds more and then turned back to the prime minister. "As you are surely aware, Prime Minister, there is no functioning government in Somalia; the place is run by clan-based gangs and various al-Qaeda affiliated Islamic terrorist groups, notably the Al Shabaab. We don't expect the Somalis, even with tactical air support from the Pakistanis, to defeat our Special Forces unit. But we do expect a fight and for that, we will be prepared."

The prime minister resumed his rhythmic rocking. The two intelligence officers exchanged looks; it was hard to judge how the briefing was going. From beyond the beautifully manicured lawns came the sound of elderly men singing *"Vande Mataram"* – Hail Motherland – the Hindu nationalist anthem. "Beautiful music for the soul," said the prime minister with a deep sigh. The Skull nodded in agreement.

"Naturally, we don't expect an answer until you've had an opportunity to mull FLUENCY over," Massey said, glancing discreetly in the direction of the national security advisor. The NSA was, as usual, inscrutable.

The prime minister kept the rocker in motion. He nodded to himself. He looked up at his private secretary, who raised his eyebrow. "Too much sound and too many men," the prime minister finally said.

Massey leaned forward. "How is that prime minister?"

"I have been at the heart of politics since The Emergency imposed on our country by Indira Gandhi and her son in 1975, so I am fully aware that the smaller the political risk to South Block, the greater the military risk to our fighting men and women," the prime minister said. "We learned that painful lesson in 1962 in the war with China, no? We need to find the correct balance between the two. Your Puntland plan is too spectacular and far too loud. It is like a Holi celebration with brilliant fireworks, no? The entire operation sounds too much like the Battle of Mogadishu," he said referring to the two-day battle, part of Operation Gothic Serpent, between the United States Marine Corps and Somali militia fighters loyal to Mohamed Farrah Aidid. "I would like you to reduce the noise level. Work with our navy on this. I would feel more comfortable if this business were a quiet landing on a remote beach, preferably at night. By dawn, I want all our Special Forces boys out of sight over the horizon and heading back home. That way we can plausibly deny any Indian involvement – a group of Somali pirates kidnapped some Indian fishermen on a beach, one of our patrolling warships heard a cry for help and gave chase and opened fire, that sort of thing."

"We have just held the elections, Secretary Massey. The prime minister does not want images of body bags during primetime television," the Skull rasped, glaring at the two intelligence officers.

"Prime minister, if I may……."

"See to it, Secretary Massey," the prime minister said with finality in his voice. "That is all for now."

The Skull shook his head. "What are you people doing about those criminals – this Chinese fellow living in Macau, is it - responsible for supplying all these weapons and biological agents? He ought to be assassinated before this operation or it will fail. The same goes for those Muslim terrorists in D-Company. Why are they still walking free in Mumbai?"

An embarrassed silence fell over the group. Menon opened his mouth to say something, but Massey touched his arm and he shut it. The NSA stared at the huge portrait of Sardar Patel hanging on the wall immediately behind the Skull. The prime minister told his friend, very gently. "I don't think that is the kind of thing I want to get involved in right now. We have to prepare for the India-EU Summit in Italy, my visit to Saudi Arabia, and then the QUAD Summit in Tokyo."

The civil servant immediately got the message. "Yes of course prime minister. I withdraw the question."

Moving the meeting forward, the prime minister fired questions about the nuts and bolts of FLUENCY. Menon provided answers. Yes, our long-time source in Islamabad confirms all weapons destined for the Red Corridor were definitely stored somewhere in Puntland; it was a matter of time before the RAW located the exact position. All weapons were supplied by a Chinese national called Kai Ling of Macau, a former military intelligence officer who acquired a notorious reputation in Tibet and Nepal for his anti-India activities. Absolutely, the RAW will execute the mission without assistance from Indian jets flying from aircraft carriers. No question about it, morale was high at the Chakrata barracks and combat proficiency among the Special Frontier Force was excellent. Yes, it was true that the RAW had yet to locate the exact place where the weapons were stored but as already explained it was simply a matter of time.

As the briefing dragged on, the Skull looked at his watch and reminded the prime minister that, in ten minutes, he would be talking on the telephone with Israel's Benjamin Netanyahu about the ongoing war with Hamas in Gaza and Indian assistance to Tel Aviv. The prime minister thanked the RAW men for coming down and asked Massey to walk with him along the corridor. "My cabinet colleagues and my national security advisor are all urging me to go ahead with this," he told Massey, who limped along beside him. "My coalition partners are onboard, but I want you to remember two things. Under no circumstances will I authorise overt Indian military intervention. Everything my government is trying to do in India: our economic initiatives with the free trade agreements the finance minister is currently negotiating, our relations with our QUAD partners, our friendship with Saudi Arabi and the United Arab Emirates, and our soft diplomacy in Africa, will be negatively affected if we are seen to be militarily aggressive. The BJP is quietly assertive, never overtly aggressive. Please remember this, Masseyji. The FLUENCY operation has to sink or swim on its own. Also, I reserve the right to cancel the operation right up to the last moment if I decide the risks are unacceptable. Do I have your word on this, Masseyji?"

Behind them, the Skull walked with Menon. He knew Menon was being groomed to step into Massey's shoes as Secretary when the spymaster retired, which made Menon a man of influence in Delhi. The prime minister will need the RAW's support in the

National Security Council Secretariat for the wholesale changes he intends to make to the country's intelligence community. He definitely did not want to get on the wrong foot with Menon. The man had a formidable reputation. At the same time, he wanted to ensure that Menon, like everyone else, understood that he was the second most powerful man in Delhi.

"I thought your briefing was very effective," he told Menon. "I like the Research & Analysis Wing - I was saying to the prime minister earlier if you need to know something fast Lodhi Road is the place to call. Our IAS officers take four days to answer a question with a simple yes or no," he said.

Through a partly open door, the prime minister could be seen talking animatedly on a telephone while the *Sarsangchalak*, the supreme leader of the RSS, stood by, his arms folded across his chest, listening intently to the conversation. "Let's be clear about one thing," the prime minister's enforcer went on. "The War on Terror is my number one priority. Tackling these Muslim pigs who bombed our beloved Mumbai in 1993 and 2008 and those dirty rats that murdered our BJP party workers in Sukma-Bijapur is at the top of our agenda. Everything else plays second fiddle. No time, no money, no effort, no manpower is to be spared. We want you to destroy D-Company for bombing Mumbai. Destroy them all, every one of those dogs." The bureaucrat stopped and grabbed Menon's arm, gripping it tight. "What happened in Mumbai must never be allowed to happen again. Do whatever it takes." His eyes narrowed; his voice becoming softer, more precise. "We're in a hurry, too. We must start the government by sending a clear message to the Indian masses that we are tough on terrorists and will hunt them down wherever they are." He looked hard at Menon. "Frankly, I'm a little concerned that the RAW may not cut the mustard – as our British friends would say – and lose its nerve."

Menon, let a faint smile work its way onto his lips. The prime minister's consigliere had rubbed him the wrong way. "I never lose my nerve," he muttered. "But I'm worried you and your South Block bureaucrats might."

Looking directly at him, he said, "Find the exact location of those weapons and finalise the Puntland plan, and I will make sure the prime minister authorises FLUENCY. We must work together Menonji. For India. For Bharat."

In the armoured Maurati car on the way back to Lodhi Road, Massey sat lost in thought. He hated this part of Delhi. There was something eerie, authoritarian, and inhuman about the whole area. A bit like Nuremberg. Its silent emptiness always reminded him of the famous *bon mot* uttered by the former French Prime Minister, Georges Clemenceau, visiting India in the 1920s: that the great buildings of Imperial Delhi would make magnificent ruins. The Viceregal palace was not, as Mahatma Gandhi would recommend on the eve of Independence, turned into a hospital. The bureaucrats of North and South Block, two symmetrical red hulks of buildings in a hybrid Mughal-European style which sweeps down Raisina Hill, still reign supreme – a tribute to the all-pervasive power of the Indian civil service.

Menon finally broke the silence. "What did you think of the prime minister's PPS? I found him sinister. The Skull didn't mince his words," Menon noted. *We want you to get rid of D-Company for bombing Mumbai. Do whatever it takes*. Certainly, lives up to his "Iron Man of South Block" reputation."

"There will be no tears shed by either of them if we can terminate the top tier of D-Company," said Massey.

"I hope that's not a condition for giving the green light to FLUENCY," said Menon.

"The prime minister is nobody's fool," Massey told him. "Getting rid of D-Company would certainly be popular with the voters. But I don't believe he's counting on it."

Menon, worried about his project, gazed out the window in sheer misery. After a while, Massey said, "I remember dining with the prime minister in his home when he was Chief Minister of his state in 2001. I was there to advise on security matters. During dinner the conversation turned to Indian prime ministers – it turned out he is fascinated with Indira Gandhi and Atal Bihari Vajpayee. I remember someone asking him why those two in particular. He replied that they were India's two greatest prime ministers. Then he said' – "Massey shut his eyes in an effort to recapture the scene" – he said, "In order to be a great Indian leader you have to be a courageous wartime leader. You have to be victorious in battle against China and Pakistan. He then went on to give further examples of Subhas Chandra Bose. Field Marshal Sam Manekshaw, and Jagjit Singh Aurora. Our prime minister is also fascinated by Israel's wartime leaders, men like Levi Eshkol who oversaw the Six-Day War in 1967." He opened his eyes and touched Menon on the forearm. "Our prime minister will go ahead with FLUENCY, mark my words. The only thing we need to do now is locate those weapons in Puntland. I think the time has come to visit my former mentor."

Massey had only one mentor. "Acharya Bhairava" said Menon softly.

"Yes, Acharyaji. I like the idea of my old mentor explaining the facts of life to the Compact," Massey announced, eying his colleagues over the top of his bifocals. "Coming from Acharya, the menace of reciprocity would almost certainly carry weight with the Chinese; Kai Ling knows Acharya doesn't play games." Massey pulled a cuff and glanced discreetly at his wristwatch. "I make it tiffin time. Write that up will you, I'll sign off on it."

12

Vir Vasant, Southwest Delhi

"Acharyaji, you look like something out of a Satyajit Ray film," said Massey when his former mentor at Lodhi Road opened the door personally. He had had called ahead so he was expected.

The Kashmiri spymaster lived in an old farmhouse surrounded by fields. A "farmhouse", in the modern Delhi vernacular, is a rich man's house in a walled compound on the outskirts of the city, built on what was once agricultural land. Originally, many of these farmhouses were second homes, built on the southern fringes of Delhi as weekend escapes. Acharya lived in a farmhouse surrounded by fields of mustard. There were acres and acres of spindly mustard plants, taller than a grown man; a gorgeous yellow carpet of flowers, swaying in the spring breeze, perfect for a Bollywood song-and-dance routine, or a secret assignation. "The mustard plant is loaded with symbolism you know," said Massey to his driver, a scarred veteran of the 1971 war. "Its yellow flowers are known as *Basanti*, the word for spring; and the flowering of the mustard plant marks the end of the cold season. The leaves are the main ingredient of Punjab's best-known dish, *sarson ka saag*. The seeds are used as a spice, and among poorer families, is the main source of cooking oil," he murmured. "It's also a useful mosquito repellent, a remedy for constipation, and Indian mothers have massaged their babies with mustard oil since ancient times."

Since his retirement he had retreated further into his faith and lived a simple life of austerity, meditation, and yoga. "I'm in the garden Masseyji." Acharya led his guest through an archway and into the largest and most beautiful garden Massey had seen. Immaculately maintained plots of herbs and flowers studded with metal sculptures. The back of the garden led into a tidy orchard. "The fruit trees – apples, peach, lychees, gooseberries, guava, apricot, and mangos - were planted by the British in the 1920s," said Acharya walking towards a wicker chair. Massey detected the hint of pride in his mentor's voice as spoke about his garden. He sat down heavily and pushed the chair back so that the sun wouldn't be in his eyes. "Had to happen eventually," he remarked in a feeble voice. "Far too much *hookah* for too many decades. The doctors want me to give up *feni* and smoking, but it is too late. Cancer, that's what they're telling me. Early stage. They have put me on painkillers that seem to work a bit less each day." He pushed his chair closer to his former protégé, who had taken off his jacket and pulled over an old wicker stool. "Odd thing is you get used to pain. Don't seem to remember what it was like without it." Acharya leaned back on his chair and stared for a moment at the neat plots of herbs and flowers. "I spend a lot of time out here," he went on. "The heat, the humidity, seem to help me forget."

"Forget what?" asked Massey.

"The pain. How much I miss Lodhi Road, and the Great Game played by the Wing. All the mistakes I made, and I made my share, as you no doubt know."

Massey let his eyes wander around the greenhouse set in the backyard of Acharya's sprawling bungalow. Clay pots. Glass jars, gardening tools, bamboo worktables, and wicker furniture everywhere. Half a dozen or so orchids in pots scattered around the floor. There were trays of saplings which occupied two tables.

"Nice of you to visit me," Acharya mumbled. "I don't see many former colleagues from Lodhi Road these days. Come to think of it, don't really see anyone much. Doubt if the new generation of officers even know who Acharya is."

"I think that's highly unlikely Acharyaji," said Massey. "Studying your operations and missions are mandatory reading at Gurgaon," he said mentioning the RAW training and language school that Acharya helped establish in the early 1970's.

"I suppose you're right.".

"I thought someone from the Wing ought to come out and brief you," said Massey.

"Brief me what?"

"I was summoned to South Block by the national security adviser," said Massey swatting away a bee. "I briefed the prime minister and his principal private secretary on an ongoing operation at Lodhi Road," he said.

Acharya squinted at the head of RAW across the bamboo table. He was familiar with Massey's pedigree – Agra University by way of Ajmer military school, a social scientist by training, an academic at heart, an officer and a gentleman by lineage, a risk-runner by instinct. It was the risk runner who had attracted the national security advisor's attention.

Massey absently caressed a flowering *Cymbidium erythraeum*, a species of orchid found in the foothills of the Himalayas. "Your reputation precedes you, Acharyaji," Massey shifted in his chair. "I've put together a task force. Which is the reason I've come to see you. I need your help again. I'll give you three guesses."

Acharya looked at Massey and gave a thin, watery smile. "Anything to do with the recent appointment of General Syed Musharad as Chairman of the Compact. I heard, also, a rumour that the prime minister's office is looking closely at D-Company. I hear that the Skull, in particular, wants to get even for the Mumbai bombings; not surprised though" said Acharya, suppressing a smoker's cough. "One more thing. A recent visitor to my garden, also from Lodhi Road, strangely enough, mentioned something casually about an operation called FLUENCY."

Massey nodded happily. "In time-honoured tradition, I see your eyes, ears, and spies are everywhere. The Skull has authorised me to develop a covert action capability against General Musharad and D-Company. The whole package goes under the code name FLUENCY."

Acharya puffed contentedly on his hookah. "What do you need from me, Masseyji? You know I'm finished with all that cloak-and-dagger side of things, besides I'm too retired and too tired to be of any use to you and the Wing."

Massey, pretending he hadn't heard what his mentor was saying, slipped around the table and unconsciously lowered his voice. "I want to put another arrow in your quiver, Acharyaji. I need help in setting up an offensive capability within the FLUENCY task force. Your first order of business will be to terminate the senior members of D-Company. The Skull wants the blood of the Pakistanis who spilt innocent Hindu blood in Mumbai and continue to do so from their safe havens in Pakistan and elsewhere."

A mobile phone rang inside Massey's jacket pocket. He pulled it out and listened for a few moments, then said "Put him through on the secure line." Wagging a finger in Acharya's direction to indicate he wouldn't be long. "Listen, Pafulji, the problem is I still have very little SIGNIT on Somalia and Yemen. I need NATRO to monitor everything in and out of Puntland. Everything, Parfulji, ...thank you *ji*....I know you will."

Massey flung the phone on the table. "You were the RAW point man with D-Company in Nepal during the running of CIT-X and CIT-J."

Acharya hiked his shoulders in a disgruntled shrug. "You can't judge a former Shaivite monk by the company he keeps if he works for the Wing in Lodhi Road."

"I want you to keep company with the Mumbai gangsters again. I want you to make contact with Chhota Rajan's gang."

Acharya leaned forward; his *kurta pyjama* sagged open revealing the ancient *tulshi* necklace around his neck. "You want Chhota Rajan's Hindu gang to go after D-Company's Islamist gang. Dog eat dog, eh Masseyji."

Massey smiled. "They've been known to do this sort of thing. And they have a reputation for being good at it. Also, for keeping their mouth mouths shut after the fact."

"What's the timeframe for FLUENCY?"

"I have to get something going within two months, probably much sooner. According to my sources, the Compact is moving fast. My informants tell me that bioweapons are involved. The weapons and explosives will be delivered into the Red Corridor, we think sometime in summer," he said opening the attaché case in his hand and extracting some folders. "It's all in here. All the files. What we have so far."

"Does the prime minister know about FLUENCY?"

"Only in the vaguest of terms."

"We currently have a coalition government, no? So, what guarantee do you have that he will authorise the operation?"

"We consider it unlikely he will back off from a paramilitary operation against Pakistan. So does his national security advisor. Particularly after the recent bombing, which the Home Minister witnessed. It would leave him open to all sorts of political flak. The Congress party and their allies would say he has no guts. All the regional parties will agree. Also, just before he passed away, his mentor, Vajpayee, gave his blessing to the operation."

Acharya stared out towards his beloved rose garden. The lure of the hunt never quite leaves, he thought as he contemplated Massey's offer. He turned back to Massey. "So, I accept," he said.

Massey was on his feet. "I'm delighted...."

"But on my terms."

"Name them."

"Thank you. Later. I need to be alone with those files. I will call you later and tell you what I need. I will work from here, so I need some gofers. Please have Mya Noori call on me."

Later that night, in a corner of his library and study, Acharya Bhairava pored over the classified files, cables red-flagged memos, and hazy photographs left by Massey.

Deeply inhaling the scented tobacco generously mixed with the dried leaves of *bhang*, he impatiently whisked ashes off the open folder with the back of his left hand. He reached again for the loupe and held it above one of the photographs. It had been taken with a powerful telephoto lens from a rooftop half a mile from the airport and enlarged several times in one of the dark rooms, leaving a grainy, image of a man emerging from the dark bowels of a *Xian MA60* that had landed at a heavily fortified Pakistani military airport outside Gwadar Port City. The man appeared to shrink away from the dazzling burst of sunshine that had struck him in the face. Speckles of light glanced off something metallic in his left wrist. But this was clearly no ordinary courier.

Acharya shuffled through a pile of cables and pulled one out. A long-time RAW asset in Islamabad had recently reported on a conversation overheard at a reception held at the Saudi embassy. A former chief of army staff, General Sawar Shah, had been describing a meeting in Libya with a Chinese philanthropist called Kai Ling. The *hookah* pipe glued to the end of Acharya's lower lip trembled at the possibility – at the likelihood even – that he was, after all these years, looking at a photograph, of his nemesis, Kai Ling of Macau, the psychopathic paedophile son of the man who created the Compact Accord. I should have killed the son along with his father in 1988.

Grabbing the half-empty bottle, Acharya poured himself a refill of the strong Goan *feni* and gulped down a large shot of the coconut liquor. The warm sensation in the back of his throat steadied his nerves; these days he needed more than the usual amount of *bhang* and *feni* in his system to function. Assuming, for the moment that the man in the photograph was Kai Ling of Macau, what was he doing in Balochistan? Acharya peered around his study, looking for the thread that would lead in the direction of answers. The *chaturanga* game he was playing with Golda two nights ago was still on the chess table. The ancient Indian strategy board game was a shared passion they discovered while serving under Ramji. Close to the Shaivite shrine, the soft light reflected off the statue of Shiva dancing as Nataraja. Acharya brought his focus back to the files. The only thing that would bring Kai Ling to Pakistan would be to deliver something that he didn't want to trust to other hands or send by cypher for fear that Indian cryptanalysts at NATRO would be able to intercept and read. Or to orchestrate something so secret that only the Eight Elders knew of its existence. If it was the latter, what was he orchestrating?

Acharya shifted the loupe to a second photograph. Like the first, it had been enlarged many times and was slightly out of focus. The all-powerful chief of staff of the Pakistani army could be seen shaking the hand of Kai Ling. The fact that the four-star Pakistani general who effectively ruled the country had personally come to the airport to greet the Chinaman reinforced the idea that the visitor, and the visit, must have been extraordinarily important. Agonising over the problem, he reflected once again on the central reality of espionage: everything and everyone connects in some way to everything else.

He opens yet another folder; this one containing the packet of photos included in Massey's brief. With the magnifying glass, Acharya studied each photograph. Chen Qiang nattily dressed in a cream suit exiting Djibouti-Ambouli International Airport, representing, Kai Ling; Haneef Hussaini, the mafia point man from the D-Company at a rally organised by Islam4GB at the Jameah Islamiyah School in Rotherfield, England; the Somali known as Salim, who appears to be acting as a quartermaster for the Compact, coming out of a *hammam* in Puntland frequented by sailors and stevedores. Acharya placed the photographs on his desk staring at them. What's the connection between them? And the all-important question: who to send into Puntland to infiltrate the pirate gang?

13

Heathrow Airport, London

"Whiskey. Double. No ice," she ordered glancing at her watch and ignoring the bartender's not-too-subtle glances at her cleavage. Normally she wouldn't mind but today she definitely wasn't in the mood. She had almost twenty minutes before her Air India flight to New Delhi and she needed a drink.

Mya Noori was angry and frustrated. Angry at Special Branch, the intelligence-gathering wing of Scotland Yard. Angry at MI5 and the Home Office, and angry at Whitehall. The reason why she was thoroughly pissed off was that she was convinced Britain had entered into a Faustian pact with Anjem Bakri Choudari, the notorious founder of Islam4GB, and allowed the huge redbrick building to become a recruiting agency for Islamic terrorist groups operating in Kashmir and elsewhere.

Choudari not only brainwashed vulnerable young British Muslims into a firebrand version of Islam, but he also acted as the recruiting officer for *Harakat-ul-Mujahideen* (HuJ) in Europe. The HuJ, which translates to the *Movement of Holy Warriors*, runs the notorious Mansehra training camp on a remote border of Kashmir. This was the reason why Mya Noori was in London, she had spent the last three months closely monitoring the activities of the mosque. Following the Mumbai bomb blasts one name kept surfacing during police interrogation of suspects: Anjemi Bakri Choudari. In late 2023, Mya Noori had been sent by the Wing to London to discover everything she could about the jihadist activist.

Arriving in London on a cold wet July morning she took a taxi to Sloane Square station in Chelsea where the Wing maintained one of a number of safe houses in the UK. This was the second time Mya

Noori had stayed at the London safe house. The first was during a familiarisation trip with her supervising officer. The small four-roomed apartment was located in a cul-de-sac near Sloane Square. "It was originally owned by a member of South India's Nayak dynasty of Madurai," said her supervisor as he showed Mya Noori around the four-roomed apartment. It was acquired by India in the 1950s as a safe house. "During the fifties and sixties this place became our base of operations for the training of India's covert military units by British special forces, mainly the Special Air Service and the Special Boat Squadron," he said. Prime Minister Nehru's spymaster, Bhola Nath Mullick, persuaded his boss to purchase the property because was located in the centre of British secret military operations, the Directorate of Special Forces. Located at the Duke of York's Barracks in Chelsea the DSF was responsible for SAS and SBS training operations around the world, mainly in former British colonies, and Persian Gulf States.

There were other reasons why the RAW kept the Sloane Square property. It was very close to an exclusive gentleman's club, tucked away behind Harrods. It was the place Robert Gage, the SIS station chief in New Delhi, more or less lived. "The Special Forces Club was the epicentre of Britain's thriving mercenary trade in the 1960's," explained Mya Noori's case officer during her briefing in Lodhi Road. "Robbie was very useful in supplying material and manpower during the early days of Independence. He obtained most of it from within a mile radius of this safe house. This area is littered with well-established mercenary suppliers, most of them trading as private security firms or so-called risk consultants," Acharya said. On that cold morning, Mya Noori began unpacking her bags and mentally acclimatising herself to her new home. She was going to be here for a while.

Mya Noori was tagged for recruitment into India's clandestine service at the wedding of a college friend who was marrying an officer in the Indian Navy. Among the wedding guests were several high-ranking members of the army and the civil service, including a large-boned man with a full Tagorean beard. During the traditional Hindu marriage feast, he engaged Mya Noori in polite conversation asking her the sort of questions all Indian elders ask the younger generation. Where did she study? What type of jobs she was applying for? Who her father was? When was she going to marry? What was her plan for the future? Captivated by this enigmatic man Mya Noori had said her only plan was to try to find a way to give something back to her Motherland, referring to India as "Bharat" and my family. A fortnight later she received a call from the wedding guest: he said he had been mulling over what they had spoken about and maybe there was a way for her to help. They met the following evening at the Delhi Gymkhana Club, and over a pleasant vegetarian meal she signed up with The Wing.

Acharya told her she would have to undergo a few preliminary tests and that he would be her supervising officer. During the next two months, she took a number of written tests and oral examinations in various safe houses around New Delhi and Mumbai. Her IQ – Mya Noori consistently registered 140 on these tests – her athletic background, general knowledge, and social and interpersonal skills made her an above-average recruit. At the end of her final written test, Acharya told her she was suitable for what he called "formal training at our schools in Gurgaon and Chakrata".

The night before she left for Gurgaon Mya Noori had a further one-to-one session with her case officer. He invited her to his home on the edge of Delhi and showed her his immaculately maintained orchards and garden. "I started this garden in 1962 and it still gives me the same joy," said the wily old spymaster. Over a frugal supper of dhal, spicy Kashmiri potatoes, mixed vegetable curry and boiled rice Acharya told her she was about to "enter a world which sociologists called a closed society. It is a world where you cannot share experiences with anyone, not even your beloved grandmother". In such a lonely place, she would feel vulnerable to what he called "the false and dangerous lure of trust." But she must trust no one except her colleagues. "And even with your colleagues you must be cautious" he said. She would be instructed in the art of deceit, taught to use methods that violated every sense of decency, integrity, and honour. "You must accept new ways of doing things" he said. "You will find some of these things highly unpleasant, but you must always put them in the context of your mission." Acharya leaned across the table and said there was still time to change her mind. "If you do change your mind there will be no recriminations and there should be no sense of failure on your part. None whatsoever" he said looking straight into her eyes. Mya Noori, without any hesitation, said she was fully prepared to undergo training at the RAW training and language school in Gurgaon.

For the next two years, Mya Noori was introduced to her new world. She learned how to draw a gun while sitting in a chair, to memorise as many names as possible as they flashed with increasing speed across a tiny screen. She was shown how to pack a Beretta handgun inside her sari, on the hip. She was sent on dummy training missions – breaking into an occupied hotel room and stealing documents from a locked office in a secure block. Her methods were analysed for hours by her instructors who reported back to Acharya. She was woken up from her bed in the middle of the night and sent on more exercises: picking up a foreign student in a nightclub and then disengaging herself outside his hotel. Every move she made was observed by her instructors.

Mya Noori was asked close questions about her sexual experiences. How many men had she had sexual relations with? Would she sleep with a stranger if her mission demanded it? She answered truthfully: she had slept with two men at university; and if she was absolutely certain that the success of a mission depended on it, then she would go to bed with a stranger. She learned how to use sex to coerce, seduce, and dominate. She became especially good at that. She was taught how to kill by firing a full clip of bullets into a moving target, and how to conceal and carry material wedged deep inside her vagina and anus. Her instructors taught her about the various sects of Islam and how to create a dead-letter box. She attended countless lectures on Maoism and Communism and learned about the Indian mafia. She became an expert on narcotrafficking. Mya Noori learned to disguise herself by inserting cotton wads in her cheeks to subtly alter the shape of her face. She became an expert at stealing cars, posing as a drunk, and chatting up men. She learned all this and more.

Towards the end of her training, Mya Noori's tradecraft classes started to taper off and she began the long, tedious process of creating two identical legends that she could slip in and out of at will. "This is more difficult than it sounds," cautioned Acharya "because every detail has to be compartmentalised in your brain so that you can never confuse the two identities." To help create Mya Noori's legend Acharya introduced her to the famous Gupta sisters. "It is of vital importance," the sister whose name was Shilpa told her as they set out two folders on the table, not to memorise a legend – "You must become the legend. This is essential for tradecraft and staying alive in the field."

Working from their folders, the sisters – both senior researchers in the Office of Special Operations, the department within the RAW that ran so-called illegals operating under deep cover in foreign countries – began to draw the outlines of what they called "the legend called Penni Patel." Penni had spent her childhood in Uganda before her parents immigrated in 1971 to Britain, settling in London, a city Mya Noori knows intimately. In each case, the sisters would use the addresses of buildings that had been demolished so that it would be difficult for the police to verify who had lived there. The foundation of the legend would be a birth certificate actually on record of an Indian woman whose body was never discovered by the authorities, Penni Patel.

"You must discard your real self," the other sister, whose name was Monica, explained, "the way a King Cobra sheds its scaly skin. You must settle into the identity of Penni Patel as if it were a new skin. This is important my dear, your life may depend on it one day."

On a bright March morning, she was summoned to Acharya's third-floor office in Gurgaon. He looked her up and down as if he were doing an inspection, checking off each item on a list in his head. Finally, he told her she had passed. A week later Mya Noori was assigned as a junior research officer – Indian intelligence operatives are called "research officers", not agents – at the Indian High Commission in London. Her specific role was to monitor the anti-India activities orchestrated by Pakistan in mainland Britain. She would receive an extensive briefing from the London Station chief, a veteran RAW hand. When she asked Acharya for any last-minute advice for her first posting the spymaster replied that she needed to find herself a "good infiltrator to gather information inside the jihadi groups. You must recruit someone good. Expendable, but very good."

"Is that OK?" the barman asked as he placed the tumbler of whiskey on the counter.

Mya Noori snapped out of her thoughts. She looked at the barman properly for the first time. He looked North African. Curly-haired and rangy. Long slender fingers. "Yes, yes thank you" she said with a faint smile, feeling guilty at having snapped at him earlier. "Sorry, I was a bit short with you earlier. Tough week. Please keep the change" she said handing him a ten-pound note.

The young bartender smiled broadly and thanked her. "Let me know if you need anything else," he said walking over to the other end of the bar where he was polishing glasses. Mya Noori took a long swallow of whiskey and gave a deep sigh when she felt the fiery liquor hit the spot. Sinking deeply into the soft armchair she luxuriated in the warmth that was spreading through her body. As she lifted the tumbler to her lips again her peripheral vision caught the barman looking at her. Half his face was masked in shadow. He looks a bit like Hassan thought Mya Noori. Yes, from this distance and with the shadows he definitely has more than a passing resemblance to Hassan.

Hassan was another reason Mya Noori was glad to be out of London. Without the help of the twenty-two-year-old Moroccan asylum seeker, she would have got nowhere with Islam4GB. One of Mya Noori's first tasks in London was to follow Acharya's advice and recruit a male infiltrator who would not attract attention from Choudari and the group of toughs who guarded him at all times. She decided early on her informer would have to be North African because the character of Finsbury Park and its surrounding areas was changing. The Bengali and Pakistani communities which had dominated the mosque and madrasa in its early days were moving out of the area, to be replaced by an influx of asylum seekers and refugees from North Africa and the Arab world who wanted sermons in Arabic, not Urdu. Younger worshippers, London-born and bred, wanted someone who could explain Islam to them in English. Mya

Noori's infiltrator was Hassan Rahmani, a young Moroccan student living in South London.

She met Hassan Rahmani in one of the many ethnic cafes dotted around Finsbury Park. Wearing the traditional *hijab*, the headdress of Muslim women, and carrying a leather satchel stuffed with books and papers Mya Noori had taken to strolling around the Finsbury Park area searching for a suitable male informer. In the esoteric language of Wing tradecraft, this was known as a "cold approach," suborning a foreign national. After two months of patient work, Mya Noori found him one early evening after Friday prayers in a busy coffee shop called *The Ottoman Cafe*.

Sipping his coffee Hassan tried to quieten his mind; he was disturbed by Anjem Bakri Choudri's sermon. Hassan had always been sceptical of religion. When he read the Quran at night on his bed alone, he suffered the same doubts about its promises of paradise as he did when he read the apostle's description of Christ rising from the dead. Yet he loved the Quran's exhortations that men should treat one another as brothers and give all they could to charity. The *umma*, the brotherhood, was very real to Hassan.

"*Salaam alaikum.*" Peace be with you. The voice was soft, gentle, and feminine.

"*Alaikum salaam,*" he said automatically.

"May I sit here and drink my coffee?"- Mya Noori asked quietly in Arabic.

An important part of the seemingly endless hours of instruction for junior intelligence officers at the RAW training school in Gurgaon was how to form relationships with innocent, unsuspecting people. Sipping her whiskey in the departure lounge of Heathrow Airport Mya Noori was under no illusion that one reason for her success with Hassan was lessons learned in those lectures. She remembered what her mentor, Acharya, always said to his students: "Everyone and anyone is your tool. You will be able to lie to them because truth is not part of your relationship with them. All that matters is using them for India's benefit. From the very start, you must learn this philosophy: Do what is right for the Wing and for India."

That Friday evening Mya Noori struck up a casual conversation with the young Moroccan. They spoke in pidgin English. They talked about family, friends, and food. Hassan told her about his life in Morocco and that he was in England to improve his English. Mya Noori noted the subtle but significant change in his body language as he lied about the reason for being in England. As they talked the door of the cafe opened and a group of heavy-set muscular youths sporting long beards walked in. Since taking over the little mosque Anjem Choudari surrounded himself with young muscular thugs who went by the name of Supporters of Shariah. "This place is getting a little crowded shall we go somewhere else" suggested Mya Noori quietly. These thugs made Hassan nervous thought the Indian intelligence officer. I wonder why? Hassan shook his head in agreement and the two quietly left the cafe.

"You seemed quite nervous back there" said Mya Noori glancing sideways at Hassan. "Yes, I find those big guys intimidating. I find the mosque weird, to be honest with you," he said with a nervous laugh. Mya Noori stopped walking and looked directly at Hassan. "I'm so glad you said that. I also find the whole mosque setup strange. That's why I'm here actually," she said. Mya Noori then gave Hassan her cover story which had been carefully prepared months earlier in Lodhi Road. "I'm a freelance journalist writing an article about Islamic terrorist groups using British mosques for fundraising" she said fluently. "I have reason to believe that the mosque is being used for criminal activities. The problem is that I don't have anyone on the inside to gather the information I need."

She handed Hassan a business card with her name, address and telephone number. She knew that if he tried to check the number, he would be greeted by a professional voice who would inform the caller that sadly Ms. Penni Patel was travelling in Europe covering a story.

"Let's go in here," said Hassan and led her to a nearby pub close to Finsbury Park tube station. "I think I need a whiskey". Mya Noori was a whiskey drinker and appreciated Hassan's choice on a personal level. But she also knew that a puritanical Islamist would not drink alcohol. That simple exchange broke the ice and forged a relationship between the Indian intelligence officer and the Moroccan student that would last until Mya Noori was recalled back to Delhi. "I hate fanatics," said Hassan gulping down whiskey to steady his nerves. His hands were shaking. "Fanatics are the reason I don't have a family anymore," he said sadly.

By the end of the week, Hassan agreed to help Mya Noori gather information on the activities inside mosque. They would meet in Notting Hill pubs where she explained the cartography of the different Islamist groups in London, the various factions and groups and leaders, all of them living in the city without any trouble from the police. "The British are infected with this irrational woke culture and do not see the threat from extremist Islamic groups," explained Mya Noori one evening. "They suffer from too much white colonial guilt."

If Hassan was to infiltrate the mosque, something needed to be done to give him credibility and legitimacy. Mya Noori suggested that Hassan use his background as a student journalist to his advantage. She suggested one evening that he writes and publish a pro-Islamist newsletter which could be sold inside the mosque. Hassan agreed and the *Liberation Kashmir Azad* appeared in print, with its front-line headline screaming "Jihad against India". There were colour photographs of bin Laden, Hamas leader Ismail Haniyeh, and al-Qaeda leader Saif al-Adel on the front. The content was anti-Indian, anti-American, anti-British, anti-Israel and full of florid praise for the mujahedeen and the struggle of the Muslim people around the world.

The newsletter helped Hassan have a free run of the mosque. Hassan became known for his passionate anti-India articles on the recent revocation by the BJP government of the special status of Jammu and Kashmir guaranteed under Article 370 of the Indian constitution. He quickly earned the respect and trust of his peers and mosque elders. He was able to come and go, picking up gossip, listening to Anjem Choudri preach and observing the expansion of extracurricular activities being conducted in corridors and office rooms inside the mosque. Hassan reported on the false documents being ordered and traded, stolen goods offered for sale, widespread Social Security benefit frauds organised and credit card cloning taking place on a cottage industry scale. He confirmed what Mya Noori already suspected: that much of the money had been funnelled to mujahedeen groups operating in Kashmir and elsewhere in the Indian subcontinent until the Israel-Hamas conflict. Since October 2023 most of the funds had been diverted to Hamas.

Every week Mya Noori would send a detailed report of what was happening in the mosque to her superiors in Lodhi Road. For nearly two months Mya Noori had waited for something to happen. She waited for the British authorities to take some kind of action against Choudhry and his Supporters of Shariah. She waited but still no action from the British. Initially, she thought her information was not being passed over to the British by Delhi. One early morning Mya Noori contacted her supervising officer in Lodhi Road and asked for clarifications, namely, why wasn't the Wing warning MI5 of what was going on in the Finsbury Park mosque? Trying to control her anger she explained patiently that the British authorities have enough evidence to begin an investigation into Choudri. Her supervising officer, a RAW veteran who made his bones in the 1980s infiltrating Sikh separatist groups that had been given safe havens in Canada, told her to calm down. He explained that every scrap of information she was sending was being forwarded to London. "London's not interested. They don't take Choudri seriously," he said. "They think he's a harmless Muslim clown; an insignificant camel fucker fiddling the welfare system. MI5 apparently have more serious concerns," he said before putting the phone down. Mya Noori was about to pick up the receiver when she received the call from Hassan.

"I have to meet you now Penni. Something has happened at the mosque. Something important," he said.

Mya Noori felt sick. The news Hassan had just delivered had shaken her. She wanted to get away so she could contact her supervisor at Lodhi Road. But she knew she couldn't. She had to get all the facts from Hassan before she contacted her supervisor.

"Are you okay Penni?" Hassan asked nervously. "You look ill."

"Hassan, I know you've already told me, but I want you to tell me again. I want to make sure I've got everything clear before I call my editor in Delhi," she said sticking carefully to her cover as a freelance investigative journalist.

By now Hassan was used to this routine. Mya Noori would often ask him to repeat something he had heard or seen several times over. "Sure, no problem at all..." he began.

Yesterday evening after Friday prayers Hassan, who was a well-known face at the mosque was invited to stay behind for dinner by Haroon Rashid Aswat, one of Choudri's most loyal aides at the mosque. "He asked me if I wanted to meet a guest who was coming to talk to the youngsters. Apparently, this guest had just arrived from Spain and wanted to talk with with us" said Hassan.

Mealtimes were chaotic at the mosque. Groups of volunteers took it in turns to cook in the cramped kitchen. The food was usually stewed or curried chicken with rice and vegetables, and everyone was supposed to contribute a pound into a collecting tin.

The group of about fifty volunteers that Friday night was a familiar mix of school dropouts, petty criminals who had served short spells in prison, the homeless, drug users, asylum seekers who had run away from their own conflicts, and enthusiastic teenagers at odds with their families. They came from various nationalities, "but all shared a feeling of alienation and anger" Hassan once remarked. "These young boys were almost all from immigrant backgrounds and felt cheated that their parent's hard work had not been rewarded since they came to Britain. These kids are ashamed that their parents have been too subservient. This generation was not going to stomach what they regarded as third-class treatment, or the racist taunts and beating from white gangs who wanted to drive them from their inner-city communities" he observed.

Hassan was helping a group of volunteers clean away the remnants of the evening meal when Choudri joined his followers sprawled around the first-floor prayer room. "It was unusual to find him at the mosque so late," said Hassan. "Normally he's driven back to his huge house in Shepherds Bush, leaving a couple of his henchmen to keep an eye on the squatters."

"Tell me why Choudri was at the mosque so late" asked Mya Noori. She always tried not to rush Hassan who liked to tell things in the typical Arab way with all its finery.

Hassan told her the reason for his presence that evening was that an honoured guest wanted to address them. "He's like a circus ringmaster," said Hassan. He described how Choudri warmed up his young audience, drawing them into his world by teasing them about the surprises to follow. He held up both his arms and, in an act familiar to Hassan, cast his gaze to the floor and complained that his age meant he could no longer fight, so his gift to Allah was to encourage those who could. "He stared into my eyes" said Hassan "and then turned to look at each of the faces around him." "I was so mesmerised by his performance that I didn't notice a man enter the room. He was wearing dark glasses and was dressed in a grey, loose-fitting *shalwar kameez*. He looked like a rich man, a man used to wealth and good food."

"Tell me about him," Mya Noori said softly. "Let me know everything you can remember Hassan. This is important. I need the details. Please, it's really important." Hassan had never seen Mya Noori so agitated. He continued with his report of what happened.

Members of Choudri's entourage rushed to embrace the guest, who greeted them warmly. Choudri introduced the guest as Sir Ibrahim Ali. He explained to the group how Ali had proved himself a true Muslim by establishing many charities for young people and the needy. "For this, he has been greatly honoured by the British government and the Queen," Choudri had said to the group.

For the next four hours, Ali recounted his experiences in Pakistan and experiences of impoverished immigrant life in Portsmouth, lacing his tales of war with verses from the Koran. Afterwards, Choudri gave an impromptu sermon where he asked for volunteers to help Sir Ibrahim in his charitable works. "The greatest thing you can offer Allah is your sweat and blood. Faith without works is dead," he said to the group. "Give Allah your bodies and our brother Sir Ibrahim will give you the means to better yourself." Towards the end of the meeting, a shower of hands was raised when the cry went out for volunteers.

"Do you know who he is?" asked Hassan in a worried voice. In the all the time he had known Mya Noori he had never seen her so shaken.

Mya Noori certainly knew all about Sir Ibrahim Ali. The former Pakistani intelligence officer had been on the RAW radar since the early 1990s when he helped train the Taliban in explosives and mine warfare at Miranshah. As Hassan spoke Mya Noori tried to recall everything she knew about Ali. She wasn't worried about missing anything important Hassan might say, it all be picked up by the concealed recorder in her bag.

Mya Noori tried to recall all she knew about the Pakistani criminal. Ali first came to the attention of the RAW station commander in Islamabad. He reported that following the decision of Pakistan's Chief of Army Staff to support the Taliban regime "at all costs" a Karachi-based intelligence officer had been appointed to oversee the operation. That officer was Ibrahim Ali. Throughout 1994-95 Lodhi Road received regular updates from Islamabad station that Ali had recruited around twenty thousand from the army, in particular from the Frontier Corp. The reports detailed how Ali had recruited "around eight thousand from *madrassas* around the country and a further four thousand recruits from overseas mosques." Ibrahim Ali was described as "a Pakistani national and former ISI officer with extensive links to Islamic terrorist groups and criminal syndicates."

In Delhi, the RAW expanded its operations in the region by giving support to Ahmed Shah Massoud, the charismatic and fearless leader of the Northern Alliance. Massoud was admired by the Indian public as a modern-day Che Guevara figure. Lionised by his men Massoud was a devout Sunni Muslim who always carried with him a book of poetry written by Ghazali, the celebrated Sufi mystic.

Mya Noori sent detailed reports to Lodhi Road about Ali resurfacing in England. There were no replies from Delhi. Mya Noori's frustration was reaching an all-time high when she received the message from her supervising officer, Anita "Golda" Kinnar, to return to Lodhi Road. As she swallowed the last of her whiskey, she heard her Air India flight to Delhi being called. As she gathered her things a short nervous-looking man approached her. He looked vaguely familiar. "Excuse me Miss Noori but I'm from OTG" he stammered. "We received an urgent message from Shivraj," he said. Shivraj was the cryptonym for Acharya. "He said you are to meet him at the safe house," he whispered.

The identity of Hassan was a closely guarded secret known only to her and the operational technical group. The OTG was a small multi-functional team working out of a nondescript office close to the Indian High Commission in Aldwych. It was responsible for providing logistical and technical support to RAW operatives working in the UK. Should anyone bother to check the phone number on Mya Noori's business card the person answering will be from OTG. The OTG was responsible for writing Hassan's newsletter every month. They can also provide forged documents should Mya Noori require them. In the event Hassan needs urgent assistance it will be the OTG team that will exfiltrate him from the mosque.

"Which safe house are you referring to?" she asked the little man.

"'Madanpura" he replied referring to the beautiful apartment the RAW maintained next to an old Shia mosque in the heart of the city's Muslim community.

"Thank you" she said. "Please look after Hassan for me while I'm gone."

14

Science & Technology Directorate, Lodhi Road

Established in 1968 on the orders of the founder-director of the Wing, the Science & Technology Directorate was located underground in the Santanam Bunkers, as they were known in-house. The entire division was housed in the former Indian branch of the Combined Services Detailed Interrogation Centre, a sealed-off warren of underground tunnels beneath Lodhi Gardens. The CSDIC were facilities established by the British War Office between 1942 and 1947 and staffed by MI5 and MI9 officers. Anyone suspected of working for Nazi Germany and Japan found themselves in the CSDIC. Its most famous inmate was the Indian nationalist Subhas Chandra Bose.

The only entrance, guarded around the clock by armed *4 Vikas* soldiers, was hermetically sealed with a red hazard pictogram of skull and crossbones embossed on the door. Many of the rooms and labs were carefully temperature-controlled to encourage the germination of spores in petri dishes.

The elegant, silver-haired woman who led the division, Priyanka Bannerji, a highly accomplished professor of biotechnology at the Hindu College in Delhi University, was a member of the Indian Council of Medical Research and a principal scientific advisor at the Ministry of Defence. Her most recent achievement had been the development of the toxin-sprayed garland of marigolds that the Wing had delivered to Kailash Mirchi Rajput, the Indian narcotics trafficker hiding in London. Rajput had been on the wanted list of India's Narcotics Control Board since 2013.

"It's an honour to meet you again, Acharyaji," Professor Bannerji told the spymaster when he turned up in her office. "I am guessing you are here to discuss the report I sent to Secretary Massey, no?"

Acharya looked around the room. The walls were lined with metal shelves filled with specimen jars carefully labelled in red and black ink: Botulinum toxin, Bubonic plague, Ebola virus. "Yes, professor, I am here to talk about your report."

"What can I do for you, Acharyaji?"

"You can tell me about the Chinese biological weapons program. I know you covered this in your excellent report, but I want to hear it from you personally."

"Well, as I said in my report, we have been aware of China weaponizing very large quantities of these," she said pointing to the jars of toxins on the shelves. "Not just these but during the Cold War they mass produced ricin, anthrax, cholera, and tularemia."

"How do we know this?" Acharya enquired, tugging his left earlobe.

"Delhi first became aware in October 1960 after the Chinese launched Operation Chamdo. This was a full invasion of Lhasa, the Tibetan capital."

"I was under the impression that we were involved with the American CIA Tibetan program well before 1960."

"That is correct, Acharayaji," replied Bannerji adopting the same professorial tone she uses when engaging with her doctoral students. "Nehru's intelligence chief, Bhola Nath Mullick, was instrumental in facilitating the CIA Tibetan program in India and Nepal but we only knew the details of the Chinese use of biological weapons against the Tibetans after the Dalai Lama fled Tibet and entered into India on 30the March 1959. Mullick's Intelligence Bureau officers interviewing the refugees were the first to hear reports of Chinese scientists using Tibetan monks and civilians as human guinea pigs during biochemical experiments similar to the ones used by the Nazis and the Japanese."

"How real is the threat to India from China's biological weapons programme, Professor?"

"As I have said in my report to Secretary Massey the threat is very real," said Bannerji emphatically. "Beijing continues with its Cold War policy of engaging in biological weapons activities with dual-use applications. I believe that Beijing possesses capabilities in biological warfare and bioterrorism that pose a clear and present threat to India, her allies, and QUAD partners."

"You write in your report, Professor Bannerji, that you strongly suspect China has or is developing an ethnic bioweapon to be used against India. Please can you amplify and clarify that statement for me using layman's terms."

"Certainly. An ethnic bioweapon is a type of biogenetic weapon that targets people of specific ethnicities or people with specific genotypes."

"In other words, it's a biological weapon which could theoretically be tailored to wipe out, say Tibetans, or used to genocide the Uyghur people of Xinjiang," Acharya said.

"Absolutely correct," said Bannerji. "An ethnic bioweapon could also be tailored for the genocide of the entire Northeast of India. The weapon could be genetically programmed to wipe out the specific genotypes of, say, the Assamese people. Or the Nishi, the Bodo people, the Bengali people of the Barak Valley, the Meitei community of Manipur, the Tripuri people, the Mizo, the Khasi people of Meghalaya, the ancient Naga people, and the entire Sikkimese population."

"I agree with you, Professor, that the Northeast is one of our most vulnerable regions when it comes to dealing with the Chinese.

Okay, now, the most important question: what biological weapons have the Compact been storing in Somalia?"

"Based on my research and understanding of the Chinese biological weapons program, my study of the Science of Military Strategy published by the China National Security Studies Centre, the People's Liberation Army National Defence University, and the Nanjing Political College I have concluded the following likely scenarios. The Compact has stored quantities of botulinum toxin, bubonic plague, and Ebola virus in Somalia to be used against India. I base this on the pathogenicity of the agents, the incubation period required to cause harm after exposure, the lethality of the agents, transmissibility of the disease, and the treatments and cures available."

Acharya uncapped a fountain pen and jotted something down a pad. "What would be the method of delivery of the biological agents into the civilian population along the Red Corridor?"

"Aerosols," Bannerji replied without hesitation. "Tiny particles that will be suspended in the air and inhaled by people will be the best method for infecting an entire population."

"How is the Compact stockpiling the bioweapons in Somalia?"

"I would say they are using a process known as microencapsulation," Bannerji said. "Let me explain. Biological weapons can be stored for many decades if correctly stored. However, because bioweapons are living organisms they will decay and die if exposed to adverse environmental conditions. Unless an agent is used shortly after its production it will need to be stabilised in order to withstand the stresses of storage, transportation, and changing temperatures."

"How exactly would the Compact stabilise these bioweapons during transit?"

"The simplest methods involve freezing and dehydration in order to slow the metabolic rate of the biological agents. However, I believe the Compact is using microencapsulation which involves applying a coat of protective material to the bioweapons which slows their metabolism by forming dormant spores."

"Why are you so certain that the Compact is using this method, Professor?"

"Because I have been following closely the career of Dr. Chen Quanguo. He is the only member of the Chinese Politburo who has served as committee secretary of Tibet and the Xinjiang Uyghur region. He was responsible for running the prisons and labour camps in Tibet and the concentration camps in Xinjiang where the Uyghur Muslims are imprisoned in internment camps."

"What are saying, Professor?" Acharya asked with a certain amount of discomfort.

"I have read reports of Tibetans and Uyghur Muslims being subjected to medical experiments. They are used as human guinea pigs. This includes pregnant women and children. The Chinese Ministry of State Security is using the process of microencapsulation and experimenting using anthrax, botulism, plague, tularemia, smallpox, and Ebola on the Tibetan and Uyghur people. They are now extremely proficient in the use of these agents."

Acharya looked around the room as he absorbed what Professor Bannerji was saying. Images of the Rayerbazar killings fields in Bangladesh flashed through his mind. The Bangladesh Liberation War of 1971. He saw the piles of rotting bodies piled high during the ethnic cleansing of Bengali Hindus. Teachers, doctors, and public intellectuals lined up against a wall on the campus of Dhaka University and killed by napalm using American M2 flamethrowers.

Mustard gas used against protesting students. The Pakistan army called it Operation Searchlight. "It can never happen again," he said looking at the shelves of jars containing some of the deadliest microbes known to humans. "Tell me, Professor," Acharya asked, his eyes burning into Bannerji, "how does the Wing neutralise these biological weapons?"

"Agni," replied Bannerji. *Fire.*

"I thought you would say that" replied Acharya. "Fire it is then. I have one more request to make of you, Professor."

"What is the request, Acharyaji?"

The veteran spymaster spoke for another twenty minutes describing in detail what he wanted from Bannerji. "Can this be done?"

Professor Bannerji finished scratching notes on her pad. "May I ask if you are working on a tight schedule?"

"Let's just say I am hurrying without indecision or haste."

"I see." Professor Bannerji rose to her feet and looked up at Acharya. "If you come and see me again in, say, three days, I will probably have what you need. I will need to speak to our ETS arm and also the NATRO but I think we can work something up."

Acharya nodded. The ETS was the electronic warfare division of the Wing and NATRO was the country's principal technical intelligence agency. "I thought you might. Thank you for your time, Professorji," Acharya said walking towards the door. "I have to go to Old Delhi now. No rest for the wicked as the Britishers like to say."

15

Mandurana Safe House, Old Delhi

Acharya sat knee to knee with Mya Noori on the ancient Persian carpet in the middle of the secret room situated within one of the three domes of the Shia mosque, known as the *Qubba*. Above them hung a large calligraphic frieze and a cartouche from Iran. The calligraphic inscriptions were quotations from the Qur'an. The safe house was frequently used by Acharya to brief his agents; the imam of the mosque was the father of an Intelligence Bureau officer and had a long history with the Wing. In the ornate *sahn* courtyard below, he could hear members of the congregation chatting while performing their ablutions in the fountains before prayers.

Mya Noori looked miserable. Miserable and angry. She was nursing three fingers of whiskey, talking in undertones. There was a hint of desperation in her leaden voice. "I stumbled across a British SIS report describing how the KGB dealt with a religious cleric in Kabul during the Soviet occupation," she said. "The imam and his brothers was recruiting young men from the city to become suicide bombers – a bit like Anjem Bakri Choudri is doing in Finsbury Park. The KGB in 1981 didn't sit on their hands, agonising over what they could do about it. They abducted the imam's older brother and sent his body back with his testicles stuffed in his mouth and a note nailed – nailed, for God's sake – to the back of his skull warning that the mosque leaders and their sons would suffer the same fate if they didn't behave themselves. Suicide bombings stopped for a long time in Kabul." Mya Noori leaned forward and lowered her voice. "Sir, we've identified Anjem Choudri as a recruiter for terrorist groups operating here in India – Choudri has family in Pakistan and Bangladesh".

There was an embarrassed silence. Acharya studied very carefully the interior decoration of the Qubba. It was a symbolic representation of the vault of heaven. The intricate artwork beautifully emphasised this symbolism, using floral motifs of desert plants, stellate, and other geometric patterns designed to create a sense of awe, inspiration, and devotion to Allah. "The RAW is not and never will be like the KGB, Miss Noori," he said finally. "I very much doubt if Massey, the prime minister, his NSA, or our parliamentary overlords would let us get away with using similar methods."

"We wouldn't have to do it ourselves," Mya Noori persisted. "We could farm it out – the Israelis would know what to do, especially as Choudri threatens them as well. Choudri and his followers are pathologically anti-Semitic. They would send one of their lethal *kidon* teams to the mosque."

"Absolutely not Miss Noori," snapped Acharya irritably. "I know how disappointed you must be at the lack of action from the British end. But this is a non-starter. Do I make myself clear?"

"I'm sorry sir, I was just letting off a little anger and frustration."

"Perfectly understandable in the circumstances," muttered Acharya embarrassed by his momentary loss of control. "Now, forget about Choudri and Sir Ibrahim Ali for the moment, let the Britishers deal with them. I need you to run an errand for me in Thailand," he said.

"Who?" said Mya Noori still embarrassed for her earlier outburst.

"The Guru, as he's known. Our political masters in South Block want the blood of the Muslims who bombed Mumbai, so we're getting into bed with the Hindu mafia." Acharya explained that FLUENCY had a general and offensive capability side to it, namely, weakening the threat to India from organised crime. "The Pakistanis supply the Muslim mafia with arms and explosives, so we will be working with the Hindu gangs," he said.

"What exactly do you want me to do in Thailand?" asked Mya Noori.

"I need you to call on an old friend of mine who goes by the name Guru and give him a message from me," explained Acharya.

"And what is your message to the Guruji, Sir?"

For the next three hours, she listened carefully as Acharya explained what he wanted done.

16

The Red Corridor, Jharkhand

The battered Tata truck had been climbing a steep mountain track for the better part of three hours. At first light the driver, downshifting and veering to avoid shell holes filled with rainwater, steered the vehicle onto a level clearing and killed the engine. The unfastened plastic was flung back, the tailboard was removed, and the crates unloaded. The crates contained neat rows of Chinese Type 56 assault rifles and rounds of ammunition. They were in some sort of a guerrilla encampment high in the Chota Nagpur Plateau. Layers of blue-grey mountain ridges fell away to a cinereous horizon stained with veins of tarnished silver.

Around the encampment bearded men, some with blankets over their shoulders, others wearing surplus army coats, were loading arms and ammunition onto mules. Nearby, yelping Indian pariah dogs brawled over a bone. Next to a long low mud-brick shack, a bearded rebel wearing a woollen cap read aloud from Mao Zedong's *On Protracted War* to a circle of men sitting cross-legged in the dirt. At the edge of the clearing, a teenage boy dragged over a wheelbarrow and began to collect woodfire.

Its spluttering engine straining, thick black exhaust fumes streaming from the tailpipe, a second truck came up the mountain track and pulled to a stop nearby. A lean and graceful figure emerged from the passenger seat signalling to his driver, a huge turbaned figure, to remain in the truck. Chen Qiang was wearing the new type 07 uniform of pine green with the open-collar design adopted by the People's Liberation Army Ground Force. He had the dark intense eyes of a jungle hunter, with shadowy hollows under them that didn't come from lack of sleep.

"I'm here to meet Ganapathy Rao of the Maoist Front," he explained loudly. "His people bear the brunt of the fighting against the Indians while the other dozen or so resistance groups spend a lot of their time fighting each other."

"Who are you?" shouted a grizzly-looking bearded fighter.

"Tell him Chen Qiang brings greetings from Beijing and also gifts of weapons and clothes for our cause."

Ganapathy, a thin, bearded man with a direct gaze and cruel face, came out of a tent to greet Qiang. "Major," he said shaking his hand firmly. He gestured toward the rugs scattered on the ground. They made small talk for an hour – Ganapathy brought Qiang up to date on the shifting front lines inside the Red Corridor and gave the names of those killed in the last three months since they last met. At dusk, wood-burning stoves were lighted around the camps and a sooty darkness settled over the area. Qiang accepted a cup of sickly-sweet *chai* from a boy as he got down to business. "It is this way, Major," he began. "The modern weapons which the Pakistanis receive from the Americans finish up in the hands of the Pakistani army, which then passes its old hardware to us. We go into battle against the Indians at a great disadvantage. The situation has gotten worse in the last months because the Indians are starting to use their Swarm Drones to direct the firepower of their helicopters."

"I will see if I can get some portable radar that can detect the helicopters."

Ganapathy shook his head vigorously. "We have been attacked by their DRDO Ghatak drones. They fly silently through the valleys tree-high and pounce on us without warning. Our anti-aircraft guns, our machine guns are of no use against their armour-plating. I have lost a lot of men in this way," he said. "No Major *saab*, the radar will not improve our situation. Heat-seeking Stinger missiles, on the other hand…." Ganapathy was referring to the shoulder-fired ground-to-air missile that could bring down a plane or helicopter at a distance of over three miles.

Qiang cut him off. "Stingers are out of the question. I can't give you any because the Americans have taken most of them back," he explained. During Operation Cyclone, the name given to the training and arming of tribal groups resisting the Soviet invasion of Afghanistan, the CIA supplied around a thousand Stingers in September 1986 to the Mujahedeen. By the time the Soviets withdrew in 1989, the CIA realised the dangers of giving away the Stingers. They attempted to buy back the Stingers with a seventy-million-dollars fund. "The Americans are afraid that Pakistan is going to become a haven for extremists and terrorists – they're afraid the Stingers will fall into the hand of Islamic fundamentalists and attack Israel."

"Give them to me Major, and the Indians are defeated." Ganapathy leaned forward. "The group which defeats the Indians will decide the future outcome of the border skirmishes between Delhi and Beijing – if China wants Asia, you must help me."

"What you are asking is impossible. You know as well as I do that the Americans won't give Pakistan any high-tech weaponry because they know it will fall into the hands of extremist groups, like al-Qaeda, the Haqqani Network, and the Pakistani Taliban."

"If not Stingers," Ganapathy pleaded, "then the MG FF Cannon – it has the firepower fire to bring down the Indian helicopters."

"These are wrong weapons for this sort of low-intensity guerrilla war. We have discussed this already. Many times, we have discussed this. The armour-piercing ammunition is expensive; the guns are very sophisticated and require complicated maintenance. Our people in Islamabad agree that blowback operated cannons wouldn't be operational. Beijing agrees with this assessment."

"So, what is left?" asked Ganapathy.

"Conventional weapons," said Qiang passing over a piece of paper. "Just make sure your men are combat-ready."

Ganapathy stared at the long list Qiang had handed him. "What are these?" he asked pointing to the biological weapons typed on the long list. "I do not understand."

"Biological weapons will give us a strategic and tactical advantage over India," explained Qiang. "Let me explain." He spoke for the next three hours.

Ganapathy smiled without humour. "If you supply my men with even half of what's on this list, we can bring Mao's original formulation of the military strategy of a people's war in India."

"You will have the weapons shortly," promised Qiang.

17

7, Lok Kalyan Marg, New Delhi

One night every two weeks Mya Noori reported for the Delhi dawn shift at Lodhi Road. She started at four in the morning as the RAW representative to the team producing the daily intelligence briefing earmarked for the prime minister and the Cabinet Committee on Security. For the next three hours, she and the others sifted through the overnight cables from RAW stations and culled the items that ought to be brought to the prime minister's attention. The end document was known as a national security briefing document. The NSBD was a twenty-page briefing arranged in a pamphlet format and marked "For the Prime Minister's Office Only" It was delivered by armed guards from Lodhi Road to the prime minister's official residence at 7, Lok Kalyan Marg every morning in time for him to read it over his breakfast of toast and fresh seasonal fruits.

One morning the officer who was supposed to deliver the NSBD got a call to say his young daughter had been admitted to hospital. The research officer asked Mya Noori to stand in for him while he attended to his injured child. Mya Noori's official credentials were checked at the gates of the residence. A Black Cat security officer led her through the vast building into the prime minister's living quarters. Mya Noori recognised the head gardener carrying a basket of flowers he'd cut from the garden. She settled onto a chair in the corridor to wait. After a while, the door to the private dining room opened a crack and the familiar figure of the prime minister wearing a sleek cream-coloured Nehru jacket and trousers gestured for her to come on in. Flustered to be in the company of the prime minister himself, Mya Noori followed him into the room. To her surprise, she saw the national security advisor sitting at the breakfast table.

"I see Golda's girls are everywhere these days," the NSA growled, his forehead wrinkling in amusement.

"You two know each other, *yaa*?" the prime minister enquired in a soft-spoken voice.

"Research Officer Mya Noori works closely with my colleague, Golda, on the FLUENCY taskforce," said the NSA with a smile. "First time we talked she grilled me about our Balochi strategy. She gave me ten reasons why we should be doing more in that region."

The prime minister looked at Mya Noori. "I admire a woman with *shakti*," a little bit of mettle in her, like my mother was. "What reply did you get about our Balochi strategy?"

"I cannot recall the incident. I'm sorry, sir, but I seem to have forgotten."

"Excellent!" he said beaming. "I'm a great admirer of discretion, also."

The prime minister took out a pen, uncapped it and started to underline items in the NSBD. "When you get back to Lodhi Road please ask Masseyji to prepare an update on the situation in Somalia. I consider this to be a priority national security issue." He scribbled cryptic questions in the margin as he talked. "I want to know who these pirates are. Where do they come from? What are their demands? What kind of support do they have in Somalia? I need further details of how Operation Prosperity Guardian and our own Operation Sankalp which is taking place in the Red Sea will impact FLUENCY. Most importantly, what kind of contingency plans are you in Lodi Road preparing if the pirates harm our people? I understand we are sending in a young journalist, no? Brave *beta*. He clearly has the heart of Hanuman. I would like to meet him after this business is concluded."

The prime minister closed the Lion of Ashoka cover and handed the briefing book to his national security advisor. "Thank you for your service, Mya Noori, on the FLUENCY taskforce," he said. "Golda is a fine officer. I know her personally. She has briefed me many times."

From the table, the NSA observed in a not-unkind tone. "Looks like Lodhi Road has a little operation in Somalia to assemble."

18

Sir Robert's bungalow, Chanakyapuri, New Delhi

Dressed in a light-coloured shirt, chinos, and wearing Birkenstock sandals Hari Vandra walked up the path leading to the bungalow complex where his godfather, Sir Robert, lived following his retirement from the British Foreign Office. At the walled entrance, a Black Cat armed policewoman stepped out of the booth and crisply demanded Hari's passport. The complex in Chanakyapuri had been set aside for high-ranking members of India's bureaucracy and senior foreign diplomats and was guarded around the clock by members of India's National Security Guard counter-terrorism unit known as Black Cats. The star resident, so Robbie had boasted drunkenly on the phone, was none other than India's indomitable national security advisor. The policewoman examined the photograph in the passport and glancing up, carefully matched it against Hari's face, then ran a finger down the long list on her clipboard until she came to the name Hari Krsna Vandra. "You are expected," she announced in the mechanical tones of the police the world over and pointed toward the building. There were two more Black Cat policemen inside the complex and a third operating from inside a security booth. They all watched Hari until Sir Robert answered Hari's ring and signalled that he recognised his guest.

"I say, that's an excellent outfit you're wearing, dear Hari. You look most dashing, as usual. Please do come in." the retired English diplomat in the doorway was wearing a baggy blue and white striped blazer with tarnished gold buttons and an ascot around his neck. His rheumy eyes had the puffy look of someone who consumed a great deal of alcohol. Ushering Hari inside the bungalow, he remarked in an off-hand way, "You really shouldn't have bothered, Hari; I'm absolutely fine. I have no idea what Padre said to you but please stop looking so bloody worried. I'm as fit as a fiddle. You should be with your boy, Jago, or chasing that story of yours instead of fretting about me. The last thing you want is to let that story go cold." A nervous tic of a smile appeared on his flushed face. "To tell the truth, I'm just taking a few days' rest. I'll be back to work soon." Sir Robert drew his godson into the air-conditioned apartment and embraced him tightly, planting a scratchy kiss on each cheek. "I hope you don't mind, Hari, but I've invited a friend, and my friend brought along a friend of his. He gave Hari a mysterious grin. "I think you may find my friend interesting."

Hari caught a whiff of whiskey on Sir Robert's breath. "Jago is absolutely fine. He's busy learning the fine art of being a thespian," replied Hari. "Padre said you had a serious heart attack, Robbie. Is that true?" through the double door of the vast living room, Hari caught a glimpse of the picture window with its breathtaking view of the carefully cultivated Mughal gardens sprawling beyond it. "Here, I've got you this," and handed a tattered copy of *If Israel Lost the War*. "I found it in Brighton's Amnesty International bookshop. It's utterly riveting," Hari said watching his beloved godfather flick through the book. "One of the authors is Robert Littell, one of my personal literary heroes. A brilliant writer. I just wish I could write like him. It's an alternate history novel of what would have happened if the Arabs conquered Israel in the Six-Day War. I read it in one sitting." Sir Robert's longtime manservant, a lean elderly man from Patna, was serving plates of hot snacks to the two guests near the window. A sound of pure joy and happiness escaped his lips when he saw Hari. Rushing over, he cried out to him in his native tongue, Magahi, as he pulled Hari's head down, and planted kisses on his forehead and both shoulders.

"Namaste to you, Bilal," said Hari. "So good to see you again. I've brought you a selection of Brighton rock candy; I haven't forgotten about your sweet tooth."

"Bilal practically raised Hari when his parents and I were posted in Nepal," Sir Robert explained to his guests.

"In 1962, I spent several months in Kathmandu during the war with China," the older of the two remarked. "My memory is that it was a chaotic city."

Hari noticed that the guest spoke English with an accent he took to be Russian. "It was my dream to be allowed to live in the city and roam the streets," he said, "but Nepal in those days was a centre of espionage and international intrigue – there were daily kidnappings and murders – and I was forced to remain in Kathmandu with Robbieji and Bilal for safety's sake."

Sir Robert made the introductions. "Hari, may I present to you my friend and colleague, Ajit Massey. Masseyji, please meet my godson I told you about. He's a rather talented crime reporter from Brighton. And this is Acharya Bhairava, a great friend of mine whom I've known longer than I care to remember."

Hari shook hands with both men, then flung an arm over the shoulder of Bilal as he inspected Sir Roberts's guests. Ajit Massey was on the short side, stocky, in his early fifties with the washed-out complexion of a lifelong bureaucrat. An office monkey, as Jago would say. He was dressed in the manner of a typical Delhi office *wallah*. Acharya was a tall, large-boned man who looked like he had stepped out of another century and was uncomfortable with modern India. He stood there smoking a cigarette. His age was impossible to guess, he had the long flowing beard of a *swami* and dark brooding eyes that narrowed slightly and fixed on you with an intensity that was unnerving. What struck Hari was the man's uncanny resemblance to Rabindranath Tagore, the Bengali polymath who in 1913 became the first non-European to win the Nobel Prize in Literature. He was dressed in a spotless white *kurta*, a loose collarless tunic that traces its roots to central Asian nomadic garments.

Acharya, puffing on a Wills Navy Cut cigarette, eyed his host's godson. "Contrary to outward appearances, I do not live in the Raj-era," he said flatly.

"That alone sets you apart from the rest of Delhi's political elite and many of its public intellectuals," Hari said, "India's greatest enemies are not the Chinese or Pakistanis but its treacherous public intellectuals." He helped himself to a vegetable samosa. "Acharya was what the students and disciples called the philosopher Chanakya. I believe it means an expert or a scholar in a subject, doesn't it? How did you come to be called by such a name?"

Sir Robert quickly answered for him. "In the case of Chanakya, it was because he was so much older and wiser than his contemporaries when he was writing the *Arthashastra* in the second century. In Acharya's case, it was because he talked like Chanakya long before he let his Tagorean beard grow."

Hari, who had acquired the Brightonian gift for casualness when addressing his elders, asked with an insolent grin, "So, what do you talk about when you talk like Chanakya?"

Sir Robert tried to divert the conversation. "How are you getting on with your story about that crime syndicate on the Costa del Sol, Hari? I heard from Padre that things are rather bad out there."

Acharya affectionately waved off his host. "No harm done, Robbieji. No harm done, *yaa*. I prefer young men who have a strong sense of curiosity and inquiry to those who, at twenty-six, know all there is to know about God's world."

He turned a guarded smirk on Hari for the first time; Hari recognised it for what it was – the enigmatic expression of someone who viewed life as an intricate game of chess. Another member of the band of brothers who, like Robbie, had climbed over the warm bodies of his colleagues to get things done.

Acharya spits out a spoiled Monkey nut onto the palm of hand. "What I talk about to my students and disciples," he told Hari, articulating his words carefully and slowly, "is a state secret of Bharat, what you in the West refer to as the Indian Republic."

Later, over dinner, Acharya steered the subject to the ongoing Israel-Hamas war in Gaza, the Red Sea crisis, and China-American relations. He asked Hari for his impressions. Did he believe tensions in the Middle East would lead to an uprising among members of the Organisation of Islamic Cooperation? Hari, who was beginning feel the onset of jetlag, replied by saying that he hadn't been to any of those countries – that he lived in Brighton, a quaint shopping district in England populated by members of the international privileged classes who could afford tuition or the occasional underprivileged kid who aspired to join the privileged class by adopting the so-called woke culture. "As for America," he added, "the business of America is business. Always has been. Always will be. Anything else is just conversation filler."

The conversation then drifted to the latest developments in the Israel-Hamas war with Acharya declaring that the assault by Hamas was tantamount to genocide. "Delhi must increase its assistance to Israel," he declared, "after all, Israel stood by India in every conflict we have been involved in with the Islamists since 1947." As he listened carefully to the unfolding conversation Hari's eyes widened slightly. How was it that Robbie's friend knew so much about the intricacies of the conflict? Was Acharya connected with India's clandestine service? Hari glanced at his godfather – he had always assumed that Robbie had some sort of relationship with spies. After all, the British Secret Intelligence Service was answerable to the Foreign Office and diplomats abroad were expected to keep a close eye on people and report back to their handlers. What was the nature of Robbie's relationship with this Acharya fellow?

There was another puzzle that intrigued Hari: who was the quiet bureaucrat who went by the name Massey? And why did he defer to Acharya in such a way?

Later, waiting for the cars to arrive to take the guests home, Hari noticed Acharya huddled in a corner with Sir Robert. They had been there for some time and were whispering furiously like a married couple. As the front door opened Acharya turned back towards Hari and casually offered him a small calling card. "I invite you to join me for *chai*," he murmured. "Perhaps I will tell you what I talk about when I talk like Chanakya."

It was then that Hari understood that dinner had been a strange test of sorts and that he had passed. Against his will he found himself drawn to this enigmatic man who – judging from his bearing; judging, too, from the deference with which Robbie and Massey had treated him – clearly outranked an English knight and a senior Indian bureaucrat. And much to his surprise he heard himself say, "I would consider it a privilege to take tea with you, Sir."

"Tomorrow at three for tiffin." Acharya wasn't requesting, he was informed. Leave word with Robbieji where you will be, and I will send a Maruti for you. "I look forward to seeing you at the Irani Cafe."

"Where is that?" Hari asked, but Acharya had disappeared through the door into the night.

Later in the night in the spare bedroom, Hari settled down behind an ancient desk and stared for a long time at the ceiling fan. He opened his hand luggage and took out his laptop. There was an email from Jago. It was written in his usual style. "Hari, my itinerant boyfriend and future husband," it began. "Thanks for your voice notes. Sorry for the snail-slow response from me but I've been busy trying to mend my broken little heart and addressing my abandonment issues. I'm also making progress with my daddy issues; you'll be pleased to know. I want you to know how sorry I am for the things I said that night. I was trippin big time and you just happened to be there. I was being a selfish little cunt and I'm sorry I hurt you, Hari. I've decided to take your advice and have attended my second Marijuana Anonymous meeting in two days. Nothing changes if nothing changes, and I need to change. I don't want to end up like my dad. I've met a woman in MA called Allegra Cavendish. An elegant old bird who dresses in vintage clothes and was a ravishing beauty in her time. She likes to be called Poppy and I'm thinking of asking her to be my sponsor. There's not much I can tell you about Poppy, or The Twelve Steps, sponsorship, or MA because (as we say in the fellowship) it's anonymous and you, darling man, don't need to know. The only thing you need to know is that I love you, always have, and always will. What else is happening in the life of your boy, JJ? I've got an agent (finally!) who says she believes in me and can guarantee me a bit part in a TV commercial for life insurance. She says that because all British commercials must now have a black or brown person, an LGBTQ angle, an interracial relationship, and no white, straight men I should do well. She says that if I play the game well, I will profit from woke culture and our diversity, inclusion, and equality (DIE) industry. She's promised to help me be a player in the industry to use what she calls "the White Peoples Guilt Complex". It's a good time to be a black actor, Hari, because according to my agent, Britain is undergoing reverse colonisation. I'm more than willing to follow her salty advice and guidance. This bitch knows how to hustle! Anyway, all this is a new experience for me. Call me when you can. I hope Robbie is feeling better. Say, I said hello. I love you, man."

There was a postscript added to the email. "Came across someone hanging out in *Chocolate Bar*. Not the usual tired-looking St Jame's Street dinge queen on the lookout for hung dreadlocked niggas, roadmen and rough trade. I recognised him because you pointed him out once. I'm pretty certain he's one of the Skinny Skoda Boys. He looked like he was scouting the joint for bait. I'll keep my eyes and ears open for you. I know you're working on that Portsmouth drugs story (I read your notes when you weren't looking!). I like the idea of Jago being one of your confidential informers!"

19

The Irani Cafe, Old Delhi

They arranged to meet at an upmarket Irani cafe in Old Delhi. Acharya had arrived first and ordered *paani kam chai*, *akuri*, and *Duke's Mangola*. He was carrying an ancient attaché case and astonished Hari by citing with complete accuracy his school grades, his Natwest and American Express bank balances, his recent published articles, and his family history including the circumstances of his parent's death in Bristol. Perhaps sensing his outrage at having his privacy violated, he explained how he accessed all the information.

    Acharya gulped some tea. "I propose that we speak as if we have known each other as long as I have known your grandfather." Hari's grandfather, a retired academic who spent his entire life teaching history at the University of Allahabad, had passed away many years ago. Acharya continued after he nodded his assent. "You come from a distinguished Hindu family with a long history of service to Bharat, the Indian state. In the thirties, during our fight for freedom, your grandfather was Gandhi's gatherer of secret information. Your grandmother's brother was a liaison officer between Subash Chandra Bose and Hitler's Nazis – ah, I see you were not aware of that. Let me tell you more about the family you don't know. Your grandfather was the personal tutor of Ram Nath Kao who studied at Allahabad University. Kao was a great friend of mine who, in 1968, created India's foreign intelligence agency the Research & Analysis Wing. The RAW is the equivalent of your MI6."

    "I was told that he was a travel photographer and that he worked for.... but it doesn't matter what I was told... how do you know this?" said Hari staring at Acharya. He was stunned by these revelations. He was finding it difficult to articulate his words properly.

"Your grandfather, my friend, was at the heart of India's intelligence community," Acharya corrected, "and your father...."

"My father? I'm sorry I don't understand," he said confused.

"Your father – one of my oldest friends, we met in Banaras, worked for Indian intelligence for years while he held various diplomatic posts overseas, the most recent of which, as you know, was a deputy secretary-general at the Commonwealth Secretariat in London. Since he began to work for us, I have been his conducting officer, so I can personally attest to his enormous contribution to our work in keeping India safe protected and free. Now tell me, how long were you in Europe for?"

"My father began working at Marlborough House in 1979 after graduating from Edinburgh University. This means I've lived in Europe for a total of fourteen years, first in England at Brighton College. I studied in Paris, Rome, and Dublin and thanks to the strings my father pulled I also......"

Acharya had pulled out a folder from the attaché case. He held the folder so he could see the cover. The folder was navy blue with the official seal of India's Lion Capital of Ashoka on the cover. His name "HARI KRSNA VANDRA" was written across it, with a fine notation: "Secret restricted information. No distribution." He pulled the folder and yanked out a sheet of paper filled with spidery handwritten notes. "Your father was not the one who pulled the strings for you. It was me, working through your grandfather. The people I work for are always looking for people with language skills and your grandfather had told me that you had an ear for European languages." Acharya paused to take a long sip of tea. "You obviously have no memory of it, but you and I have met before, Hari *beta*. It was at your grandfather's college study. You were not quite seven and attending the British Embassy School. You were eager, bright, with an ear for languages; you already spoke French, Portuguese, and Spanish well enough to converse with your grandmother – it was, I remember, your secret languages so that your parents would not understand what you were talking about."

Hari smiled at the memory and wiped away a tear thinking about his grandparents and parents. He still had difficulties accepting his parents were really gone. Talking with Acharya, he understood what it must be like to confess to a priest; he felt an overwhelming urge to tell him things he wouldn't normally reveal to a stranger. In many ways Acharya reminded him of Padre. "For obvious reasons, it was not something that was spoken of but my grandfather broke tradition and married a non-Hindu. My maternal grandmother was Spanish and Portuguese and a devout Roman Catholic. She loved all things European, and adored shopping in Madrid and Lisbon. She had studied painting in Madrid and Barcelona before teaching in Delhi."

"Your grandparents and parents were servants of the Indian state. Your father especially believed passionately in our country and our way of life. He believed in Bharat. He also very much wanted you to join his work. He was going to take you away for a weekend break so he could tell you all about his secret work and ask if you would join him. Sadly, my friend died before he could have that talk with you. Before he died, I gave him my pledge that I would have this conversation with you, Hari."

"Why are you so sure I will join the Indian intelligence community?"

"I was not, but I was willing to take the risk for your grandfather's sake. And then.... then there was something about you Hari, a lust lurking in the pupils of your green eyes when I first met you. You wanted to believe – in a cause, in a mission, in a person even as a boy." Acharya's eyes narrowed. "You were like your grandfather in so many ways. That is why the Wing invested time and money in you."

"What do you mean?"

"It was me who arranged for you to study at those top European schools. It was I who arranged for your grandfather's book – *Perspectives on the Gurukula Model of Education in Ancient India* – to be published by a friendly left-wing publishing house I am familiar with; they have offices all over the developing world and socialist countries. It was I who made sure the book sold enough copies so he could afford your tuition fees."

Hari said, in a soft muffled voice choked with emotion, "What you are telling me stuns me. I'm blown away. I had no idea about any of this."

Acharya suddenly sprang to his feet and came round the table and gazed down at Hari. "Have I misjudged you, Hari Vandra?" he demanded. "Have I misjudged your hidden courage and your conscience? Your command of European languages, your knowledge of Europe, your years of studying European history and politics. Your reputation as an investigative crime reporter. All this gives you the possibility of making a unique contribution to the life of our nation. You, young man, know only what you have read in the books; I promise to instruct you in things you will never read in the history books. Will you enlist with the Wing and work with the dreamers, visionaries, and the mavericks of Lodhi Road?"

"Yes, I will" said Hari Vandra without hesitation.

"You asked me what I speak of when I talk like the philosopher, Chanakya. Do you remember?"

"Yes, I do," replied Hari, "you said that you spoke of state secrets. Secrets belonging to Bharat."

"That is correct, *beta*. Well, remembered," Acharya reached over and clasped Hari's hands with both his large hands. His lips curled into the enigmatic smile. "There are many rites of passage into the shadow world I have lived in my entire life, Hari, but by far the greatest – the strongest – is to demonstrate to you how much I trust you – with the secret lives of my agents, with secrets of Bharat, with my secrets. Now I will tell you a story. I have already told of the secret lives of your parents and grandparents and forefathers. But this is a state secret of the highest order – so high that even your father did not know of it. Once you hear the story there will be no turning back for you. Or for me. Do you understand what I have just said to you, *beta*?"

"Tell me this secret. I want to hear it."

"It concerns Robbie's father, Sir Jasper Vincent Gage," he began in a hoarse whisper. "He was a spy for India. He began spying for us – Acharya's eyes burned into Hari's - during the Partition when our Motherland was dismembered by Britain. Yes, the great English diplomat Sir Jasper was a spy working for Sardar Patel, Nehru's deputy and confident. Robbie's father was an Indian agent from the early 1930's. During this period, we encouraged Sir Jasper to become the British interlocutor dealing with the Muslim League and thus gain access to Muhammad Ali Jinnah's inner circle in London. Jinnah confided everything in Sir Jasper, including his discussions with the military. On the eve of independence in 1947, Sir Jasper betrayed Jinnah's military strategy to Patel. Based on his intelligence, India was prepared for the 1948 war with Pakistan. He told us about the war preparedness of the Pakistani battalions, he told us how much ammunition they had, he told us that their air force did not have enough fuel for their engines. From the time of Partition, Sir Jasper was instrumental in pushing Jinnah, over the objections of the generals, to make irrational decisions. It was through Jasper that Patel became one of the few to know that Jinnah was dying of tuberculosis. And during all this time my father was Sir Jasper's handler."

"But Sir Jasper was one of England's most ardent imperialists. He more of an imperialist than Churchill ever was," Hari said. "He believed passionately in the righteousness of the British Raj. He wrote books on the topic."

"Yes, my father encouraged him to do so," said Acharya. "After Patel assigned him to be his case officer, he told Sir Jasper to seek membership in the gentlemen's clubs in Pall Mall which he did. The intelligence he picked up from eavesdropping at the Travellers Club and the Special Forces Club in particular was pure gold. My father was awarded the Kirti Chakra for his efforts."

Hari finally asked the question that was reverberating in his mind. "Is Robbie one of your agents?"

"Yes, he is, *beta*. Robbie, like you, is his father's son, and began working for the Wing in September nineteen-forty-eight during Operation Polo."

Acharya released Hari's hand and returned to his seat. "Now," he said in a quiet and triumphant voice, "we will, together, take the first steps in a long journey."

20

Patpong, Bang Rak District, Kingdom of Thailand

Mya Noori had spent the day wandering around the infamous Silom and Surawong roads which make up Patpong, one of the biggest red-light districts in Bangkok. She wanted to make sure she wasn't tailed. She checked her watch. The dossier said that Chhota Rajan's consigliere, the man known throughout India's underworld as the Guru was a stickler for punctuality.

Mya Noori ignored the obvious tourist traps of the infamous Patpong area. All expensive froth and no action; or, as someone once put it put it, "All mouth and no sequins." The skimpy, drugged-up masseuses offering foreign men a card with the words *"Follow Me For Blowjob & Boy Body Massage,"* the Chinese-owned brothels with their special bathrooms designed for water sports, scat, anal fisting, and oil wrestling were doing brisk trade, as were the pimps specialising in the quick blowjobs in the parks with child prostitutes. In the area close to Soi Thaniya, zoophilia was available. The most commonplace were canine sessions but there were also specialist studios with donkeys, horses, pigs, and monkeys. Most of these enterprises made their profit through selling videos of the action, mostly to Germans, Japanese, and Austrians. Finally, close to the appointed hour, Mya Noori quickly entered a teakwood house called the Klong Guest House.

Walking toward the lift, Mya Noori pulled the grille open and thumbed the ivory button with the Roman numeral four on it. Somewhere deep in the dark bowels of the building, a motor groaned. The lift jerked several times in aborted attempts, then started with infinitesimal slowness to rise. Two men were waiting on the fourth floor. One of them opened the grille. The other frisked

Mya Noori very professionally, checking the tailored pants, the small of her back and her ankles, as well as the creases in her blazer jacket. Satisfied, he nodded to his colleague, who pulled a latchkey from a pocket and opened the armour-plated door.

Mya Noori entered a spacious, brightly lit room decorated in teakwood and rattan furniture; stainless steel chrome stools were gathered around a glass-topped table. Two lean men with alert black eyes slouched against a back wall. A short, elegantly robed man with fine white hair stood from one of the chairs and brought his hands together in the traditional *anjali* greeting of Hindus and Buddhists. His eyes, only half open, fixed themselves intently on his visitor. "Welcome Miss Penni," he said using Mya Noori's usual cover name. "Our mutual friend, Acharyaji, has told me nothing about you. People like me do not get to meet someone like you every day. If you please," he said, nodding toward the chair. "Can I offer you some tea, perhaps?"

Mya Noori settled into one of the wicker armchairs and discovered it was very comfortable. "Thank you, just some mineral water, if you have it." The Patpong Museum was clearly visible through one window, as was the Foodland supermarket and the Black Pagoda.

The sexagenarian Guru mumbled something in a strange guttural accent and nodded toward one of the men. Mya Noori noticed that in place of a hand, he had a steel hook attached to his right forearm. It reminded her of Abu Hamza, the former imam of Finsbury Park Mosque now serving life in a maximum prison in Colorado. One of the guards along the wall sprang to attention and threw open the doors of the drink's cabinet crammed with liquor bottles and glasses. He bought a bottle of mineral water and a glass with a slice of lemon in it. The Guru, with his disfigured hand buried in the folds of his robe, returned to his place at the head of the table. "Any friend of Acharyaji...." he said, waving his good hand to show there was no need to finish the sentence. "Now Miss Penni, what is it that I can do for you?"

Although he hadn't formally introduced himself Mya Noori knew his identity. She had carefully read his dossier held at the central registry in Lodhi Road. Known as 'Guru,' he was the most powerful member of N-Company after Chhota Rajan. The Guru, like his boss, started out as a small-time thief and bootlegger working around the Chembur neighbourhood of Mumbai.

Mya Noori glanced at the bodyguards along the wall. The Guru pursed his lips, a gesture which made him appear gnome-like. "My protectors are Kafir Kalash, Miss Penni," he informed her. "They are non-Muslim Pakistanis believed to be descendants of the mercenaries who fought for Alexander the Great in his invasion of India in 327 BC. "Because they are non-Muslims they are known as black infidels and hated and hunted by the Pakistani military who use them for target practice. They speak only Kalasha-mun. You may speak freely."

Mya Noori said, "I can see you helping my boss – our mutual friend - in arranging to kill eight to twelve people in the service of Bharat."

The Guru didn't flinch. "I admire your frankness, normally we Indians tend to equivocate. So: the going price to have someone killed is between ten and twenty-five thousand US dollars, depending."

"Depending on what, Guruji?"

"On how important he is within D-Company; his closeness to the Big Boss, which in turn indicates the type of close-quarter protection he is likely to have."

Mya Noori was having difficulty getting a handle on the man. How could such an obviously genteel, refined, and cultured a man become a top-tier *goonda* in the Mumbai underworld? She decided it would help if she knew more about her host. "They had a go at you at some point; the Dawood mob, I mean," she remarked. "I noticed your hand."

"Actually," what you saw was the absence of my entire forearm. They used a machete just below my elbow. The Guru started to elaborate, then gestured with his good hand; again, the sentence didn't need to be finished. "On to our business then: you will surely have a hit list of the targets."

Mya Noori produced a picture postcard of Delhi's Red Fort. One of the bodyguards carried it around the table and set it before his boss. The Guru looked at the photograph, then turned the card over and squinted at the names written on the back. "Acharya is a serious man with a serious project," he said mumbling to himself. "Permit me to pose a few questions."

"Please go ahead Guruji," said Mya Noori. "I am here to answer any and all questions you may have."

"Must the people on this list be killed simultaneously or would results spread over a period of days or weeks be acceptable?"

"The results could be safely spread over a period of days. Maximum."

"I see, I see."

"What do you see Guruji? Would you care to elaborate for me?"

"I see that all the people on your list are connected to each other in a way that I can only guess at."

"Please, guess away."

"They are most likely associates in a secret plan. You want to avoid a situation where the targeted killing of one alerts the others to the danger of assassination."

"You read many things from a simple list of names."

"I read even more, Miss Penni. This one for example achieved notoriety in Afghanistan because of his addiction to *bacha bazi* boys. He used to chain those children to his bed and rape them before going to sleep." He pointed to a name on the postcard. "Filthy Muslim pig."

"Since you come to me, as opposed to another person of influence, and since you arrived with the blessing of Acharyaji, it must mean that this secret plan in question is one that will be inconvenient to the prime minister and his national security advisor. The single thing that would be inconvenient to Delhi at this moment in time would be the arming of Maoist groups operating in the Red Corridor, which would leave the Hindu state at a permanent economic disadvantage vis-a-vis its huge and dangerous Chinese neighbour. The Naxalites and Maoist insurgents are India's greatest internal security threat. Your national security advisor has said so and the prime minister agrees."

"All that from one tiny list," said Mya Noori. "You are remarkable, Guruji."

"I have only touched the surface, *beti*. Since the Naxalite and Maoist insurgency has been pacified in recent years, and according to my information is now restricted to areas around Bihar and West Bengal, this insidious complot must be aimed at the destruction of India's eastern and central regions. In short, what we have here Ms Penni is a coup against India's strategic and financial interests, and an attempt by the RAW and her allies to nip it in the bud with a series of surgical assassinations of these ringleaders," said the Guru softly. "In any case, Delhi needs to get even for what those Muslim pigs did to Mumbai in 2008. Your national security advisor has staked his reputation on it. Systematically degrading terror networks is his top priority."

"At this point Guruji, I think you know more than I do."

The Guru motioned his good hand again; Mya Noori's comment was so absurd it did not to be denied. "A last question: do you require that the deaths be made to appear suicides or accidents?"

"Neither" said Mya Noori evenly. "The deaths need to be sensational and public, give the papers something to write about. This is important."

"I am beginning to see you in a new light, Miss Penni" he said to Mya Noori. "Given the names involved, given the requirement for publicity and sensationalism, the normal cost per head will be close to one hundred thousand dollars. There are two, even three names that will still be more expensive, something like a quarter of a million dollars, perhaps."

Mya Noori pursed her lips. Half-jokingly she asked, "You're a devout Hindu, me being a friend of our mutual friend Acharya – doesn't that get me a discount?"

"The money is used to buy those people who could not care less that I am a Hindu and that you are Acharya's pert, pretty and persuasive little messenger," the Guru said quietly. "When it comes to calculating our fee, I will deal directly with Acharyaji. We have known each other since 1976." The Guru rose to his feet and Mya Noori followed suit. "Take it for granted, Miss Penni, that when I give Acharyaji my word my boys will deliver the bodies. Come follow me."

He led them through a door leading to a flight of stairs. "Chhota Rajan *bhai* knows you are here," said Guru. "He asked me to apologise for his absence. He said you are to wait here, and he will call to speak to you on the telephone" he said. "Can I offer you some coffee or more water? Something stronger, perhaps?"

He's obviously not taking chances following his narrow escape in Bangkok thought Mya Noori. "Some coffee would be nice, thank you" she said watching him disappear into an antechamber.

As she watched Guru across the room, she remembered Acharya's words in the safe house. "He's first-class organiser of criminal enterprises. Watch him carefully. It was Guru who was responsible for Chhota Rajan's rise to power in Mumbai. It was Guru who helped forge the relationship between the Muslim Dawood Ibrahim and the Hindu Chhota Rajan," said the veteran spymaster. "And it was Guru who convinced Chhota Rajan to leave D-Company after the Mumbai bombings and create the criminal syndicate which he named N-Company. It was Guruji who contacted the Intelligence Bureau to pass on information about D-Company. He's a priceless asset."

The Guru's mobile phone rang as he handed Mya Noori a glass of steaming espresso. He quickly answers. "*Ji, bhai. Ji, bhai,*" he says softly into the phone.

"She is standing in front of me" he says softly. Guru hands the phone over to Mya Noori, and Chhota Rajan comes on the line.

The Hindu Don immediately brings to her attention his reason for speaking to her, "I do not like the police" he says softly, "I am only doing this because I love my Motherland" he states. Mya Noori can hear the latest Bollywood song, *Laal Peeli Aichiyaan*, in the background. He speaks in chaste Hindi; obviously, his years in Malaysia and Thailand have changed his Bambaiyya Hindi through Mya Noori. Throughout the telephone conversation, the don is very respectful, relaxed, and confident. He never hesitates; it's a voice used to give orders. There is not the merest hint of anger in the don's voice, just suggestions he expects to be obeyed. Many of his answers are roundabout, like those of India's politicians.

"I miss my beloved India. My Bharat. I miss Bombay. There is no city like it in the whole world. I miss my people, my land; that air, that sky; those known faces, those relatives," says one of India's most notorious gangsters. Mya Noori sensed that the don was trying to convey, in Hindi, his great love for India in some poetic form. "It's like a dish which, once tasted, is never forgotten. I miss my whole family, but apart from that I was born there. A man never forgets where he was born. A man never forgets his childhood, his school, his neighbourhood. A man loves this very much. To go on long picnics with his school friends....to see films" he says in the manner of an actor explaining himself in a Bollywood movie.

"I have a letter from my boss for you" said Mya Noori careful not to use Acharya's name in front of the don's men. "He said I was to deliver it to you personally."

"I know what the letter says, and I know your boss, he is a good Hindu who also loves his Motherland like I do." In the background, she could hear the roll call in Tihar Jail where he was currently serving a life sentence for the murder of a journalist. He's somewhere in the Mandoli complex thought Mya Noori. "I admire your boss. We both have the same agenda. We both want to protect and serve our beloved Motherland" said Chhota Rajan. "My intention was to become a military officer, and at school, I wrote a composition on it. I wanted to die for my Motherland. The feeling a man has for his country – some people think about it, some people do it. I had a desire to do it, but the circumstances and conditions took such a turn that I became a lieutenant in the D-Company." He certainly knows who to pin the blame for his inability to serve his country thought Mya Noori. "The bastard police in India have a hand in my life being spoiled. The father of that bastard dog, Dawood Ibrahim, was a head constable. Then I became involved in this line and the result is in front of you."

"My boss says you can help us deal with those involved in the 1993 Mumbai bombings. He says you know where they are hiding" says Mya Noori bringing him back to the matter at hand.

Chhota Rajan considers this carefully before speaking. "Leave it with Guruji. You can trust him with the letter. He is my mentor and my lifelong trusted advisor. I trust him with my life," said Rajan. "These boys are my lieutenants in my war with that pig, Dawood, and his D-Company. I am at war with Dawood because he has declared war on my beloved India" says the don. "When D-Company bombed the city where I was born, he became a dirty swine. A dog. I do not want to share the same air we breathe. I have already told your boss I will hunt down the Mumbai bombers for him. My intention is to always do what I can for my Motherland. Tell him not to worry. Tell him Rajan *bhai* is a man of his word. We both have the same agenda. We are both Hindus – children of Manu – and we are both patriots. We are brothers," said Chhota Rajan. "Together we will destroy these Muslim dogs."

"Thank you," said Mya Noori. "My boss said your assistance in this matter will not go unnoticed."

"I ask for nothing from my Motherland. Everything I do is for Hindustan. Leave the letter with my boys and let the game begin" said the don using the ubiquitous cricket analogy common to Indian crime. Much of gangster language is borrowed from cricket: the lookouts are called "fielding"; they watch for the police while the shooters "play the game' of the victim" or "take a wicket." Indian mafia men like Chhota Rajan love cricket; they spend a lot of time watching it and bring cricketers over to the countries where they are hiding. They regularly bribe players to throw the matches and make enormous amounts of money betting against them.

Mya Noori handed the phone back to Guru. "I believe you have something for me" he said. "I will ensure Chhota *bhai* receives it." Mya Noori hesitated before taking Acharya's letter out of her jacket pocket and handing it to Chhota Rajan's second-in-command.

"Thank you" said Mya Noori before walking towards the door and letting herself out into the corridor.

Inside the apartment the man known as The Guru opened and read Acharya's letter once quickly, then a second time, this time slowly. After he finished reading, he used his mobile phone and dialled a number in Mumbai. It was answered after the third ring. A deep voice answered. "Yes, Guruji."

"I have work for you," said The Guru. "You will go to London to make a courtesy call on a man who lives in Carlton Terrace House. You will receive instructions through the normal channels."

The turf war between N-Company and D-Company had begun. Blood will be spilled.

21

Science & Technology Directorate, Lodhi Road

Sitting behind her desk, Professor Bannerji opened a drawer took out a metal box and placed it on the blotter. Producing a key from the pocket of her lab jacket, she inserted it into the magnetic lock on the side and opened the box. Fitted into a bed of foam was an ornately decorated silver tube. Professor Bannerji removed the item and set it on the desk. "This is a *ta'awidh*. An amulet crafted from silver," she said. "You said you wanted something that would be instantly recognised in Somalia and treated with respect and deference. Well, this is it. The lettering you see are the names of Allah and prophetic supplications."

"It is beautifully made," Acharya said.

"Yes, we asked the Wing station chief in Riyadh to find the best Bedouin jeweller for the job. And he did. It would be a brave Muslim who would contemplate desecrating a *ta'awidh* crafted in Mecca, by a family that has been serving hajj pilgrims since the founding of the Wahhabi movement."

"But will it do the job?"

"We believe it will," Bannerji replied. "There are always risks but we believe it will do the job perfectly. The GPS tracker is embedded inside the amulet. It will emit signals that will be picked up by our vessels in the Gulf of Aden and relayed back to Lodhi Road via NavIC" She unscrewed the amulet and separated the pieces with the tip of her pen. "There can you see? Small, no?"

"NavIC?" Acharya asked picking up one of the pieces on the blotter.

"It's the Indian Regional Navigation Satellite System," explained Bannerji. "It's our own GPS covering India and an area of about one and a half thousand kilometres around it. Our space agency, ISRO, is planning on extending its range, apparently. They're very gung-ho after the Chandrayaan-3 moon mission last year."

"Thank you, Professorji."

"Before you, there are several things you should take note of. The amulet should not be placed in a hot, steamy place – I'm thinking of a spa. I would highly recommend that this little ornament be used within a year. Anything longer and the electronics inside risk becoming unstable, which would be most undesirable for your man."

"As usual you have done an excellent job," Acharya said. He carefully placed the metal box into his attaché case.

22

Karachi, Province of Sindh, Pakistan

Maverick One. *Jaldi jaldi!*
With those words, the eight-member *4 Vikas* hit team moved like black jaguars through the stillness of the dawn. Based at the Sarsawa Air Force Station in Uttar Pradesh, the *4 Vikas* team were a special forces unit of the RAW and responsible for covert and paramilitary operations. Dressed in identical black trousers and turtleneck sweaters, they assaulted the villa outside Karachi. Three of the troopers cut the telephone lines and electricity cables, then came over the high wall, dropped lightly down onto the lawn and entered the guardhouse. Using aerosol cans filled with an updated version of the experimental nerve gas manufactured by Mossad scientists for the targeted killing of Hamas leader Khaled Mashal in 1997, they subdued the two sentry guards sleeping on woven *charpai* beds before the alarm could be raised. Two other troopers silently cut the glass out of a ground-floor window and slipped through. Making their way to the servant's quarters in the basement, they bound and gagged the housekeeper and her husband in their beds. The Sikh team leader moved up the stairs to the second floor, jimmied open the lock, and slipped through the frame, tiptoeing into a room filled with imported German and Italian furniture. The guard on duty was dozing in a chair. He was neutralised with nerve gas and lowered onto the floor. Gripping their IWI Masada semi-automatic pistols fitted with silencers, the troopers pushed through a door into a large bedroom that reeked of stale cigarettes. Startled out of a deep slumber, a heavy-set moustachioed man wearing silk pyjamas sat upright in bed to find himself looking at three flashlights and the nozzle of a gun.

"*Ullu ka patha!* What duh fuck…." The man was groggy from sex, alcohol, and cocaine.

A young Lollywood starlet slid naked from the sheets and cowered in a corner, shielding her body with a pillow. One of the troopers gestured towards the bathroom door. The waif teenager, grateful to escape, fled from the room and locked herself in the bathroom.

From the bed, the man croaked, "Who sent you?"

The troop leader produced plastic handcuffs and began tying the man's wrists and ankles to the four bedposts. The second trooper kept a flashlight and pistol trained on the mafia boss's face.

"You are making a big mistake. You do not know who I am? Do you know who my fucking *bhai* is? Dawood Ibrahim. That is my boss!"

The last restraint was slipped over his ankle and pulled tight against the bedpost. The spread-eagled man on the bed began to panic.

"Stop, wait, wait. Listen to me. Whatever they are paying you, I'll pay you triple." In desperation, he twisted his head and neck towards the door. "Isa, where are you?" He turned back to his captors. "Why don't you say something? Why are you staring at me?"

The Sikh troop leader removed the cover from a pillow. "*Antam Sansar*," he murmured softly.

"What are you saying? I don't understand you. What tongue are you speaking? Speak Urdu, you fucker!"

"I'm reciting the Sikh prayer for the dead," the troop leader told the D-Company underboss. "I am reminding you that life is about living with the choices we make. When you chose to bomb Mumbai, you signed your own death warrant. Your death warrant was signed in Lodhi Road. We have been sent by the Wing to execute that warrant."

"You're spies from Lodhi Road. You're going to end me," screamed Mushtaq Memon, the gangster and mastermind of the 1993 Mumbai bombings. The once powerful lieutenant of D-Company boss, Dawood Ibrahim, had soiled his pyjamas. "*Inna lillahi wa….*"

The team leader of *4 Vikas* slowly placed the pillow cover over the terrorist's face. Shaking his head from side to side, pulling hard on the restraints until the plastic cuffs bit hard into his skin, the mafia man spat out stifled words. "for the love of Allah…. please don't……mercy on…..have eight children…..wife Shabana….please…..*innas ilayhi raji,un….*"

On command from the Sikh officer, the second trooper pressed the tip of the silencer attached to his Masada semi-automatic pistol deep into the eye of the D-Company mobster and fired five 9mm bullets into the gangster's face.

In Delhi, Acharya took a call from the Guru. "D-Company's number two is zero. He took the bullet an hour ago."

"*Dhanyavad shukriyah,*" Acharya murmured before ending the call.

23

McGregor's Club, Safdarjung Road, New Delhi

"I get the feeling Jago may be willing to forgive me for, as he put it, abandoning him again," said Hari, sipping his Desi Daru vodka on the rocks.

Acharya drained the last of his *feni* and signalled a passing waiter for another. "Young love," he said chuckling under his breath. He and Hari were enjoying a tiffin lunch at a corner table in a private dining room of McGregor's Club, an establishment reserved exclusively for senior members of the clandestine services and their guests. "Ah, our tiffin is ready. It's your lucky day, Hari *beta*," Acharya said as he nibbled on delicate slices of home-smoked mackerel wrapped in little pouches of banana leaves. "Alfonzo, our resident Goan chef is in the kitchen today. Very good, our little kitchen."

Two little palate-cleansing bowls of spicy seafood broth known as *tomyupkung* and a plate of steamed mussels in garlic, cumin, and wine sauce appeared within minutes of their arrival. "This place is rather impressive," said Hari chewing on a piece of Portuguese bread, "nothing like I've ever seen before."

On arriving Acharya had given him a tour of the club which was housed in a traditional *haveli* that once belonged to a minor royal house. "McGregor's has a long-standing tradition of inviting allies and friendly nations to decorate one of the rooms with memorabilia." He showed Hari the various rooms marked with individual plaques: the Brezhnev Reading Room, created during the golden-era of Soviet-India cooperation of 1964. Decorated with rare caricatures and political cartoons of Leonid Brezhnev's Politburo and first editions of Russian literature, the room was dominated by a huge portrait of Brezhnev and his wife, Viktoria. The Alexandre de Marenches master bedroom, donated by the French SDECE in 1973 was beautifully decorated with Expressionist art from the School of Paris. The interior design was classically French: ornate crown moulding, gold mirrors, parquet flooring, dark wood furniture, and nature-inspired patterns. The Oman Room, donated by the House of Al Said, in 1965 was decorated with eleven different types of daggers, including a priceless silver *khanjar* with a handle studded with precious stones. The Maurice Oldfield bedroom, donated by the British SIS in 1977, was adorned by a huge oil painting of a stern-looking gentleman of the Elizabethan-era: Sir Francis Walsingham, spymaster and principal secretary to Queen Elizabeth I. The Chiyoda Room was exquisitely decorated with Japanese watercolours, prints, and old manuscripts.

  The mobile phone on the table started to beep. Acharya snatched it up, listened for a moment, then said, "Put him on the line." Motioning with his finger in Hari's direction to indicate he wouldn't be long and that he should continue eating, he listened intently. Hari helped himself to tiny crisp-crusted vegetable samosas and a slice of *apa de camarao*, a type of Goan pie with a golden rice crust over a succulent mix of whole prawns cooked in savoury coconut milk. "Listen Masseyji, I need the Radio Research Centre to work with NATRO for once. Remind them, especially that bastard at the RRC, that we are on the same side. I cannot have the usual turf wars with the Puntland plan because we are on a tight schedule. I need better signals intelligence. Much better and I need it yesterday," Acharya said with irritation. "Yes, I know this. Call me when you have the intercepts. Yes, yes, I'm with Hari now."

  They were eating in the Nkrumah Dining Room. The chamber was decorated with furniture and memorabilia from Ghana, including rare tribal artworks depicting the Great War of the Golden

Stool. The centrepiece was an enormous oil painting of Kwame Nkrumah dressed in traditional Ashanti costume. "After Ghana achieved independence our prime minister, Nehru, sent Ramji to Accra to set up their intelligence service in the late fifties," remarked Acharya. When the drinks arrived, Acharya looking more worried and drawn than Hari remembered, tapped him on the forearm. "Now, where were we? Ah, yes, you were telling me about your love interest. To Jago and young love," he said, clinking glasses with Hari. "How is Robbieji?"

"I find it very hard to read him these days." Hari shook his head in dismay. "We used to be so close. Sometimes I feel there's an invisible barrier between us. I think he suspects something happened during our meeting. He's become withdrawn and is drinking a lot."

"Having second thoughts about the choice you made?" A waiter arrived with a platter of *Pomfret Recheiado*, a whole fish filled with a rich pungent stuffing of sour red masala and grilled until the skin crackled like cornflakes when cut.

"No, I'm not, Sir. There's a war on. A war my grandparents and parents took part in. The same war Robbie is still fighting in. It's the never-ending war to protect India and everything the Motherland stands for against her enemies. It's a war I was born to fight in," Hari declared, tossing off his vodka.

"Sounds like you're ready for some action," said Acharya.

"Really?"

"Yes. Do you still speak Bengali, Hari? I know you have an ear for languages. Came in use infiltrating that Bangladeshi grooming gang in Portsmouth, so Robbieji tells me," recalled Acharya. "I've actually visited Portsmouth you know. A long time ago, but I still remember the city. I was visiting a friend who was a senior instructor at the MI6 training school which I believe is still running from Fort Monckton in Gosport."

Hari hiked his shoulders in a disgruntled shrug. "You can't judge a journalist by the company he keeps if he's investigating an insidious Muslim grooming gang and child rapists. And yes, I do speak the language a little," admitted Hari. "I picked up the Sylheti dialect investigating those child grooming gangs on the Albert Road a few years back."

"Yes, I recall Robbieji showing me your articles and features," said Acharya, eying Hari closely. "You did an excellent job exposing those miscreants. There were quite a few of them; interesting characters if memory serves. A Bangladeshi police sergeant taking hush money from local Bangladeshi restaurants and kebab shop owners pimping out little white English girls for *desi* workers," he recalled with obvious distaste. "Filthy swine with filthy habits."

"The Rotherham child sexual exploitation scandal that was uncovered by Andrew Norfolk of *The Times* is the story of broken Britain. The whistleblower, Jayne Senior, definitely deserved her MBE. The recent spate of Muslim child grooming gangs in Britain is a sad symptom of what's happening in Europe," said Hari sombrely, "but the truth always prevails in the end. Its why I do what I do."

"Exactly. Which brings me to the subject matter of this luncheon. I'm offering you an assignment, Hari. I want you to keep company with filth. Jihadists. Members of a group called Al Shabaab to be precise. Oh, and pirates; Somali pirates. And Houthis," Acharya said, removing a fish bone, "here, try this *khatkhate* curry made with five types of vegetables. It's the best in town."

Hari absorbed the information. "Offering suggests I can refuse."

"You'll have to volunteer for the job. It'll be dangerous, very dangerous," warned Acharya. "If you nibble at the bait, I'm dangling I'll reveal more to you."

Hari leaned across the glass-topped table. "I'm nibbling, Sir."

"Thought you might, Hari *beta*. I knew you were made of the right stuff, just like your parents. I want you to go into Somalia," said Acharya wiping the corner of his moth with a napkin, "to a place called Puntland."

Hari whistled softly under his breath. "Somalia! It's run by pirates and warring clans from what I've read. Doesn't the Wing have assets there already – under diplomatic cover, in the embassy? Isn't that how these things work?"

Acharya looked towards the door. "This is our dilemma. All our embassy people were tailed by Al Shababb, who are on the payroll of the Pakistanis and their Chinese paymasters. This is when we had an embassy in Somalia. We have not had an embassy in that country since 1991. The entire country is infested with various jihadist groups." Acharya turned back to Hari. "I need to send in a new face, Hari."

"Why me?"

"Good question. First off, you have extensive crime reporting experience. Your recent articles exposing the child grooming gangs operating in Portsmouth have been published all over Europe and the Commonwealth. Yours is a well-known face in far-flung places. In our business there's no substitute for experience," Acharya explained carefully. "Finally, you're a bona fide journalist, which means Lodhi Road can work up a watertight cover story that gives you a solid reason to be in Somalia. You also have a large following on social media, so I'm told."

"True, but not quite as large as our prime minister," Hari said with a mixture of pride and envy. "Apparently he has over ninety million Instagram followers."

Acharya stopped talking when a waiter arrived with the food and laid out a platter of vegetarian dishes, rice, pickles, sambal, and paratha bread. "Thank you, Karim. This looks and smells excellent."

"Look Hari *beta*, here is the deal: there's a delegation going to Somalia from our foreign aid agency in a week's time to negotiate the amount of humanitarian assistance the Somalis need. They will be visiting various colleges to let the Somalis know that they are eligible for scholarships under the Indian Technical and Economic Cooperation Programme. The idea is for you to join them for a couple of days to establish a cover story. If anybody wants to check you out, Lodhi Road will backstop you with a solid cover story."

"You have yet to tell me what my real mission is," Hari noted.

Acharya glanced at the ornate colonial-era clock on the wall; Hari noticed a slight twitch in his eyes. "Golda specifically said she wanted to brief you herself."

"Golda?" asked Hari quizzically. "Who the hell is Golda?"

"One of our finest," Acharya said with obvious pride. "She was of the people Ramji recruited shortly after the RAW was established in 1968. In the run-up to the 1971 war with Pakistan, he sent her into Pakistan under deep cover to set up a *Hijra* dancing school in Rawalpindi in the same district where General Yahya Khan lived. You will remember from your studies at Kings that he was the one responsible for orchestrating the genocidal Operation Searchlight, the plan to wipe out the Bengali people in East Pakistan."

Hari listened in silence. He was very familiar with the Bangladesh genocide having spent hours reading up on the subject as part of his undergraduate degree in the War Studies department of Kings College London.

"Golda made sure there was either a RAW operative or an informer inside every Pakistani air base and army barracks. There were no fewer than five in the army headquarters at Chaklala. To each informer in place, she had given the same instruction: get me the big picture and the small details. How far did a PAF pilot have to walk from his barracks to the mess for his meals? How long was a staff officer held up in the city traffic jams? Did any of the key planners have a mistress? All of this was passed to Lodhi Road." Acharya paused to sample a *Katori chaat* and declared it to be delicious. "I remember one of Golda's agents managed to get himself a job as a waiter in the officer's mess in a frontline fighter base. Every day he passed details of aircraft readiness and the lifestyle of pilots and technicians. Their flying skills, whether they had achieved their rank through ability or nepotism, their drinking habits, narcotics, and sexual habits were all secretly radioed to Lodi Road for Ramji. He in turn passed the information to Sam Manekshaw who was our chief of army staff at the time."

"The year 1971 was also the year Ramji established the Wing's Psychological Operations & Warfare Division, which he euphemistically called the Information Division. He staffed it with media professionals from the Ministry of Information & Broadcasting who were given the task of ensuring the world's attention was kept focused on the genocide committed by the Pakistanis in Dhaka." He paused for a while before resuming. "On my advice, Pakistani families of servicemen began to receive anonymous letters posted in Rawalpindi giving explicit details of their loved one's sexual activities. Golda's informers reported back to Lodhi Road details of family conflicts leading to aircrew going on sick leave. Staff officers in Rawalpindi and Lahore received anonymous phone calls giving details about their colleague's private life. I remember a case where the headteacher of Army Burn Hall College in Abbottabad was called by a sympathetic-sounding Golda to be told that the only reason a pupil was doing badly was because her father, a senior planning officer on the staff of Yahya Khan, had a secret male lover; the call led to the officer shooting himself on the parade ground. Golda's relentless campaign caused dissension and chaos within the Pakistani military. Morale was at an all-time low. Without her the outcome of the 1971 war could have been very different."

"What does she do these days?" asked a captivated Hari. The more he learned about the Wing the more he wanted to know. "I'm beginning to see why my father signed up to work for Lodhi Road."

"These days Golda heads the Directorate General of Security and is responsible for the Wing's air arm, the Aviation Research Centre and the Special Services Bureau which is tasked with undertaking covert paramilitary operations. For our purposes Golda is one of the senior planners of the Puntland mission; your assignment," Acharya explained as he picked his teeth using a *miswak* stick. "She made her bones during the 1971 war with Pakistan when, like me, she was young. With age, she's become for lethal." Acharya stopped talking. Images of mutilated bodies flashed before his eyes as he recalled vividly the genocide perpetrated against the Bengali people of East Pakistan.

"She sounds extraordinary," Hari exclaimed. "What does *Hijra* mean? I'm not familiar with the word."

"Hirja means transgender," said Acharya in a matter-of-fact manner. "She is a practising devotee of the goddess Bachuchara Mata."

"Now I know I've made the right decision," Hari said, wiping the corners of his mouth with a napkin. "You were you so confident I'd accept. Why?"

"It's because you're very much your father's son, Hari. I see so much of him in you. Now, I think you're ready to meet Anita "Golda" Kinnar," said Acharya getting up from the table. "She is downstairs waiting for us. It is advisable not to keep this lady waiting."

Her eyes glinting behind her trademark ivory lorgnette, Golda was regaling the group of awestruck men gathered around her at the bar. She was a matronly woman with a deeply lined face, heavily rouged lips, and painted eyebrows. A velvet choker was tied around her neck; heavy gold Rajasthani earrings hung from her lobes and an elongated red *tilaka* mark was etched between her eyebrows. "It happened in Kathmandu in the run-up to the 1962 war with China. Ramji had sent me to advise King Mahendra of Nepal," she was saying while rearranging her intricate *dupatta* shawl cloaked around her elegant *madisar* sari. "One of our people told me a man was waiting to see me in my office at the embassy, but I decided the hell with him and went to the cinema instead to watch Raj Kapoor in *Aashiq* and to listen to Roshan. This is how I missed meeting Moshe Dyan, one of Israel's greatest military strategists. It was he who compared me to his friend Golda Meir, who was foreign minister at that time. It's how I acquired my nickname of Golda you see."

Spotting Acharya and Hari entering the bar, Golda pushed through the crowd and steered them into a beautifully decorated anteroom that she often commandeered for private meetings. Known as the Bush Room, it was decorated with memorabilia donated by former director of the CIA, George W.H Bush. A portrait of William "Wild Bill" Donovan, the founder of the Office of Strategic Services, the precursor to the CIA, dominated the west wall of the room. Acharya introduced Hari and then took a back seat; he knew from long experience that Golda relished breaking in a new recruit on the operations side of the Wing's work. It was one of her many talents.

"So, you are Hari, Robbieji's boy," Gold said, gesturing her guest towards a peacock chair, settling into another so close to him that their knees were scrapping. Puffing away on a cigarillo, she walked Hari through his curriculum vitae; she wanted to know details of the British schools overseas he had attended until his enrolment at Brighton College; she wanted to know what subjects he had studied at the Department of War Studies at Kings College London; what undergraduates clubs and societies he'd belonged to; his experiences editing Strand magazine; why he chose the Brighton Institute of Journalism; how he ended up working as a freelancer; the details of how he exposed a notorious child grooming gang operating on the Albert Road in Southsea in Hampshire; and why he chose to publish his work in those particular outlets. Then, suddenly, she changed the subject. "Acharyaji informs me you have volunteered for the Puntland assignment," she said. "Do you have an idea why we're sending you to Puntland?"

"I was hoping you could tell me," Hari replied. He was utterly fascinated by Golda's unique sub-Garbo appearance.

"Take a guess, *beta*. Take a guess."

"I've been doing some thinking," Hari admitted. "Somalia is a failed state run by various warring clans and factions. The place has become a safe haven for al-Qaeda jihadists and pirates. Neighbouring Djibouti is virtually a Chinese satellite state, the People's Liberation Army base in Balbala more or less runs the country; the place is crawling with Chinese military contractors and mercenaries. The entire region is seething with unrest and insurrection. I assume you want me to infiltrate some dissident network and gather information for you," said Hari looking around for the drink's cabinet. "Or you want me to light the fuse. Or both."

Golda, who was cordial in social situations, but icily shrewd and calculating in private looked at Hari carefully, taking in the emerald green of his eyes. Her eyes narrowing, she briefly glanced at Acharya, then looked at Hari again. "You are clever, *beta*. Excellent analysis. You are very much your father's son, I see, but you are wrong."

"You knew my father. How did you know my father……."

Golda cut him off. "As your father would say, "Time to get down to business." Leaning forward, her voice low, Golda said, "We strongly believe the Chinese and Pakistanis are storing a huge weapons cache somewhere in Puntland in Somalia…." and went on to explain to Hari about TUPAC II. She spoke for over ninety minutes without referring to any notes.

When Golda finished Hari sank back into his chair. He was sweating despite the air condition. "What you're describing is satanic. Those biochemical weapons released in the Red Corridor….my God. I still remember reading about the Tokyo subway sarin attack at university." He desperately needed a drink. "Could I…" He nodded his head in the direction of the drink's cabinet.

"Please help yourself, *beta*. That's what it's there for. In this room, it's only American beers and spirits," said Golda, "for obvious reasons. You'll find beer in the fridge over there."

Hari grasped a bottle of Tito's vodka and helped himself to four fingers of the distilled yellow corn alcohol. He dropped in an ice cube, and stirred it with a bamboo stick, tinkling the cube against the side of the glass. Then he drained off two finger's worth in one long swig.

"You're a vodka man, see," observed Golda. "Your father was, of course, a whiskey man. We always made sure we had a few bottles of his favourite Amrut single malt whenever he was in Delhi."

Hari felt the alcohol hit the spot. "You want them infiltrated so they can lead you to this Coptic monastery where the weapons, including the dirty bombs, are stored. Am I correct?"

Golda smiled thinly. "Precisely, *beta*. You've been known to engage in this sort of activity. And you have a reputation for being very good at it. I understand you have been shortlisted several times for true crime awards and for your investigative journalism work into British Asian gangs."

"What time frame do you have in mind for me?"

"The national security advisor, who is chummy with our boss at Lodhi Road has already given us the green light."

"Does the prime minister know about the operation?" asked Hari. "What guarantees do you have he'll sign off on the day? He no longer has a clear majority in parliament and his is a coalition government. It's my arse on the line after all."

"You're asking the right questions, Hari. I agree with my boss at Lodhi Road. We think it highly unlikely a BJP prime minister, particularly this prime minister will back off from a paramilitary operation initiated by his former mentor, Vajpayee. It would leave him open to political ridicule by the Congress party. The Nehru family would say he had no spine and was a threat to national security."

Hari tugged a handkerchief from a jacket pocket and mopped his brow. Now that he had asked questions, he felt he knew Acharya and the Wing better. He got up from the chair and ambled over to the window and stared out at what he could see of Delhi. He turned around to face Golda and Acharya. "I have a question for you?"

"Ask away, *beta*. Ask away. Anything you like?"

"Was it not risky opening a Hijra dancing school in Pakistan during the eve of the 1971 war? From what I've read Pakistan is not exactly a safe haven for sexual and religious minorities."

"No, not at all risky, it was the perfect cover for us," said Golda unfazed by the question. "In fact, it was Robbieji who suggested it to me. You see, Hari, the position of the Hijra is explained by the collision of two traditions, Islamic and Hindu," she explained, lighting another cigarillo. "In ancient India, castration was seen as a degrading act, and we were relegated to the very lowest of the low in society. This is all recorded in the *Vedas*, written in the second millennium. By the time the *Mahabharata* was written, a thousand years later, our position had changed very little. To be a Hijra was still a curse; even the mere sight of us was defiling to a Brahmin," Golda said quietly. "As a solitary concession, we were allowed to dance. In this field we excel, is that not so Acharyaji?"

"Yes indeed," Acharya agreed. "The position of the Hijra in Islam was always different, *beta*. Although the Prophet Mohammad prohibited castrations, eunuchs were always common in Muslim society and because of their sterility were thought to be free from the taint of sexuality. Muslim rulers used them to guard sacred relics, artefacts, and religious sanctuaries. The shirt and weapons of Prophet Mohammad in Cairo were guarded by eunuchs, as was the Great Mosque in Mecca. Pilgrims would kiss the eunuch's hands on their way to see the Ka'ba, Islam's holiest shrine."

"It is for this reason, that we decided to go with a Hijra dancing school," Golda said blowing smoke towards the ceiling. "My girls danced many times for the Pakistani corps commanders when they gathered for their regular briefings. General Zia and Yahya Khan were notable patrons of my school. As was Tikka Khan, *The Butcher of Bengal* who murdered over four-hundred-thousand Bengalis during the 1971 war."

"So, what say you, Hari Vandra? Time is of the essence," Acharya said glancing at the classic Seth Thomas clock mounted on the wall.

"So, I accept the Puntland assignment," Hari said without hesitation.

Golda was on her feet. "I'm delighted by your decision…."

"But on my terms."

"Name them, Hari *beta*," said Acharya softly.

"I write the story after it's all over," said Hari.

"As far as the Wing is concerned you can write about the operation all you like, subject to certain security restrictions of course. We will provide you with all the material you need to write your articles or even books if you so wish."

"I will find this monastery for you, but I don't want any other government agency to know about me. The Indian government leaks information like a colander, so Robbie tells me. And inside Lodhi Road, everything needs to be done by word of mouth."

"No paper trail," Golda agreed. "I forgot to mention that you won't have to start from scratch. We have someone in Puntland waiting for you. He's a Wing asset."

"Really?"

"Your contact in Somali is an Al Jazeera correspondent called Jabir Khanfari. Now refresh your drink. Pour me a large rum, and a glass of *feni* for Acharayaji and then sit down. I am going to walk you through the paramilitary concept of the Puntland plan," Golda said, pulling out a navy-blue folder from her handbag that Hari had failed to notice.

"We will not be leaving this room until you have memorised the entirety of your assignment, *beta*," said Acharya.

Sir Robert had drunk more than usual ration of booze by the time Hari returned to the Chanakyapuri bungalow. The English knight, a lonely and skeletal figure of a man at the bitter end of a long and illustrious career with British intelligence, slowly pushed himself to his feet and lost his balance, falling back onto his armchair.

"Here, let me," Hari said walking towards the drink's cabinet. He poured a measure of Amrut single malt for Robbie and fixed a Cherrapunji gin and tonic for himself.

"I've been thinking about my boy, Vivek, quite a bit; I cannot help it," Sir Robert mumbled. He raised one palm to his forehead and began massaging the migraine lurking behind the eyeballs. "I've never told you the entire story, Hari. I have a need to tell you now." Avoiding eye contact with his godson, he continued slowly. "The Wing knew by 1977 that the nuclear physicist Abdul Qadeer Khan had stolen nuclear secrets from a Dutch company called Verenigde Machine Fabrieken and was engaged in the production of weapons-grade uranium in a place called Kahuta but we had no actual proof. That was the problem, you see; we had no bloody proof."

"Listen, Robbie, are you sure you want to talk about Vive......"

Sir Robert appeared not to hear. To Hari he seemed to be in a near trance-like state. "The Wing decided to get the proof. Ingenious really if you think about it. They came up with a plan to collect hair samples from the floor of local barber shops around Kahuta Research Laboratories. The hair samples were sent to Trombay for testing. We soon discovered that Pakistan had developed a way to enrich uranium to weapons-grade level."

It was clear to Hari that his maudlin godfather was talking to himself and needed to rest. "Robbie, it's getting late; I think we should both get some sleep."

"Promise you'll be careful in Somali, Hari, it's a very dangerous place." Sir Robert looked intently at Hari in a manner that unnerved him. "I cannot lose you, *beta*, like I lost my Vivek."

"Don't be silly, you're not losing me. I'll be fine, Robbie," Hari said uneasily. He had never seen his godfather so distraught.

"I don't know if I ever told you, but it was Vivek who volunteered for the mission to enter Pakistan and collect the radioactive hair samples. My boy was caught and murdered by their wetwork specialists trained by my employers, MI6 and our so-called cousins, the CIA."

Hari knew that wetwork referred to torture and targeted killings, but he was confused. "Sorry Robbie, I don't follow what you're saying…what do you mean MI6?"

"It was the start of the Soviet-Afghan War, you see Hari. The CIA's Operation Cyclone was a program to arm and finance the mujahideen in Afghanistan. The Americans chose Zia of Pakistan to distribute the funds among militant Islamic groups, including groups with strong jihadist ties. Zia was a true believer, you see. We called him the Godfather of Jihad. The Cyclone operation was the longest and most expensive ever undertaken by the CIA. Everything else played second fiddle to the Americans, including Pakistan's nuclear weapons program which Washington turned a blind eye to. Vivek was collateral damage. He was sacrificed by the Wing. And by me, Hari *beta*," Sir Robert murmured, "I gave him my blessing to go on that mission and he was caught by their dreaded Inter-Services Intelligence people. Zia's men posted me the video of their work. They sent it to my office at the British embassy. I can never forget that day. I can never be rid of those appalling images." Sir Robert downed his whiskey and gestured for a refill. "They tortured him to death using the Palestinian hanging method, a favourite torture method of the Pakistani's. I can see you've never heard of it." He was silent for a while as the images of the torture played out in his mind. "They tied Vivek's hands behind his back and suspended him by a rope attached to his wrists until his shoulders dislocated," he said very quietly, "I hear that awful sound of his bones being pulled out of their sockets every night, Hari *beta*. Its unbearable. They added weights to his body to intensify the pain. God, I can still see the terror in his eyes……"

"You cannot blame yourself," Hari said softly. His brow was pleated in pain. He hated seeing his godfather like this. He hated feeling so powerless to help him in his grief.

"I want you to listen to me very carefully, Hari," Sir Robert said urgently. "Don't interrupt me until I have finished. Please! I know you've already accepted the Puntland assignment. I know about the dinners with Acharya and Golda at McGregor's. I know all about it, my boy. This is why I must tell you what I'm about to tell you."

"I'm listening Robbie."

Speaking like someone stone cold sober, Sir Robert continued, "Vivek was murdered by an organisation known as the Compact Accord. This organisation was created by an almost mythical Chinese officer, a protégé of Chairman Mao's spymaster Kang Sheng. Today, the activities of the Compact are directed by his equally loathsome son, Kai Ling of Macau. The Compact has one goal, Hari; to orchestrate the cold war between Beijing and Delhi. The Compact was the foreign hand responsible was murdering the Indian nuclear physicist Homi J. Bhabha in 1966 by planting a bomb in the Air India flight carrying him over Mount Blanc in the Alps. The Compact was desperate to paralyse India's nuclear weapons program, you see. Thirteen days later the Compact struck again. This time by murdering India's prime minister, Lal Bahadur Shastri, in Uzbekistan one day after signing the Tashkent Declaration on 10 January 1966 to resolve the Indo-Pakistani War of 1965. I remember that day well, Hari, because I was there with him as a Commonwealth observer. The Compact killed him using poison from one of the Chinese labs. The Indian government remains silent to this day about the murder of prime minister Shastri."

Hari could see Bilal standing in the doorway glancing uneasily at Sir Robert. Hari, who was accustomed to his godfather's occasional drunken ramblings didn't have the heart to interrupt him. He was also fascinated by what he was hearing.

Shaking himself out of a psychotic-like trance, Sir Robert opened his eyes and began to speak more rapidly, as if he was running out of time. "Be under no illusions, Hari, that the Compact is very real. It's a subject I only discuss with Acharya because very few in Delhi understand this diabolical Sino-inspired chimera. Also, because Acharya and I go way back. I trust him implicitly, as I trust you. The foreign hand of the Compact was, of course, evident in the murder of the five Ghandhi's." Sir Robert scoured his bone-dry lips with the back of his hand. "I am of course referring to the assassination of Mohandas Gandhi, the Mahatma, in 1948 by Nathuram Godse. One day Hari I will tell you how the Compact created a front organisation called the Hindu Rashtra Dal for Godse and his followers to carry out their treasonous activities."

"Hang on Robbie, I thought Mahatma Gandhi was murdered by the Hindu militants," Hari said mixing another gin and tonic for himself.

"No Hari, the Compact has twisted the evidence and caused generations of scholars to overlook the facts," Sir Robert said morosely. "The Compact worked hard to kill India's first prime minister, Nehru, but failed largely due to Ramji who was his bodyguard. So, it changed tactics and started killing members of Nehru's family. The poisoning of his alcoholic son-in-law Feroze Gandhi in 1960 and the murder of Nehru's grandson, Sanjay Gandhi, by sabotaging his plane in 1980. The assassination of Nehru's daughter Indira Gandhi by her Sikh bodyguards in 1984 and the murder of her son Rajiv Gandhi by using Tamil militants in 1991. The Compact has been the cause of the downfall of Nehru's family." Sir

Robert paused in his monologue and took a big gulp of whiskey. "I have studied all these targeted killing in detail and am convinced that they are the handiwork of the Compact. Which brings me to the current plot – the one designed to bring biological weapons for distribution among the Maoist insurgents all over India's Red Corridor. The assignment you have volunteered for, Hari. You will be facing the Compact in Somalia. It was important for me that I tell you this, my boy so that you are under no illusion about what you're up against. The tentacle of the Compact is global." His voice faltered as he settled heavily into his chair. "It was important for me to tell you I believe in you, that you're doing the right thing. Do what you need to do, Hari; destroy these monsters so we don't have to share the same air." Sir Robert stood up and said, very quietly, "Be careful, my boy. Don't let them take you. For the love of God don't allow them to take you. Believe me when I say I speak from experience that anyone can be broken in a matter of hours. Anyone, including my Vivek." An indescribably sad expression had settled on Sir Robert's face. "It's not the pain that breaks you, Hari, but the fear. My Vivek died because the Pakistanis managed to instil fear into him. So, I'm going to say this just one time to you and I beg you never to forget it. For the love of God, never, never get caught. I beg this of you. You're all I have left." A watery rheum seeped from his nostrils onto his upper lip. He flicked it away with the back of his hand. "Thank you for listening to me, Hari." Looking relieved, he walked unsteadily towards Bilal who helped him make his way to his bedroom.

    Before going to bed, Hari checked for emails and found one sent a few hours earlier from Stax. It was written in his usual manner: to the point and without any preamble. "Thanks for your help, Hari. Inspector Charles von Strett came through with the information we needed to help Swarnjeet in her recovery. I've asked

Gizmo and Grace to look into this for me. Gizmo has already uncovered a fair amount on the bent Bangladeshi copper in charge of the Southsea plod squad; the one taking hush money from the child grooming gangs. They've also confirmed that the Skinny Skoda Boys are in bed with the Yardie gangs working the Hampshire turf. We now know the Yardies are the muscle in the ever-expanding crack ghettos of Portsmouth. These gangs are single-minded and quick to use ruthless violence in protecting their assets. Charles von Strett tells me that over forty-per-cent of all crimes in Hampshire are violent and gang-related, and that violent crime is at one-hundred-and-twenty-per-cent of the national crime rate. The Skinny Skoda Boys and Yardie-men have quickly carved a niche in the Portsmouth area at the expense of the Central European gangs, including the notorious Albanians. Apparently, local drug dealers are being picked off by the Yardie posses, who very quickly establish their own ghetto bases in the local sink estates. Cuckooing is rampant." Hari reflected on Stax's message as he undressed for bed. He was familiar with the practice of cuckooing, where drug dealers take over the home of a vulnerable person in order to exploit them. He had written an article for the *Hove Herald* on how a county-lines drug gang lead by two brothers known as Flamez and Fyre were targeting vulnerable young adults with learning disabilities in Brighton, getting them addicted to drugs, and forcing them into sex work. The gangs use the property to deal, store and take drugs, and also for sex work. "I'm concerned Hari. A few members of the Skinny Skoda Boys have been seen prowling around Brighton. The Aces think they're trying to find Swarnjeet Agarwal. I agree with them. Skeezy and Squeaky also reported seeing a few Portsmouth taxis belong to Pompey Cars & Valeting Service. I don't need to tell you that this is worrying news, Hari." Pompey Cars & Valeting Service was a taxi company managed by two *desi* underlings, Kunti Goshall and Nuzul Haji Akash. "Two very shifty little characters who have their filthy little fingers in many *harami* pies. Gizmo managed to get some video footage showing Kunti Goshall dumping car batteries into the Wallington River and the River Hamble. Grace has located the curryhouse owned by Nuzul Haji Akash where Swarnjeet was groomed and raped. It's a fuck flat," wrote Stax with obvious distaste. In reality the taxi firm is owned by Sir Ibrahim Ali. Hari discovered early on in his investigation into the Muslim grooming gang operating in Portsmouth that taxis were used to transport drugs and children. It was only when Swarnjeet began talking about her ordeal from the safety of Blayney Parke that the various bits of the puzzle began to fit. Hari went back to the email. "Shortly after you left for India, Swarjeet managed to get back to the Parke. I don't want to go into it right now, but she was abducted by the Skinny Skoda Boys who took her back to Portsmouth. They pumped her full of drugs again ready to be pimped out for Sir Ibrahim Ali's men She managed to escape. She is being looked after by Padre and Sister Ananda. But they will want Swarnjeet back. She's too much of a looker, stunning, as you know. Also, she knows too much about their outfit. She was always kept for servicing Ibrahim Ali's top lieutenants. She was special. They're not going to let her go without a fight. Also, Swarnjeet knows the names of the bent coppers and council officials on Ibrahim Ali's payroll. She knows the names of all those who have been paid off." From the hallway, the sound of the hauntingly beautiful sound of the *shehnai*, a reeded woodwind instrument filled the room. As was his habit before retiring, Sir Robert would always play the music of Ustad Bismillah Khan from the 1959 film, *Goonj Uthi Shehnai* staring Rajendra Kumar. "I've placed the Aces on full alert. Gizmo has increased the surveillance around the Parke and Grace will be holding safeguarding workshops for everyone. Swarnjeet will remain within the Parke until things settle. These are dangerous people, Hari. I don't need to tell you this. Unlike Chinese, and Albanian groups, Jamaican posses are divided and unstable, doubly dangerous because of their spontaneous, almost natural violence towards one another as much as to outsiders. Once they take hold, they control street dealing in cocaine and crack through extreme brutality and cruelty. This extends to sexual violence towards their women and baby mama's. They have no code of ethics and virtually no ties of internal alliances. The posses fight within themselves and then split to form further factions which quickly turn on the original one. It's like the fucking Hydra. Enough from me. I miss you, Hari Vandra and need you here beside me. The Aces are saying that we need to prepare for some serious shit (to quote Grace). You're an Ace. We need you. Hope all is well in Delhi and please give my best to Robbie. I know he's been in touch with Padre regarding Q cottage. Tell him not to worry. By the time he gets back to the Parke, his cottage and beehives will be ready for his retirement. As for you, hurry up and get your arse here, where it belongs. Affectionately, Stax. *Ad maiorem Dei gloriam.*"

With email still open on the laptop, his eyes fell on the packed Matein backpack near the door. It contained everything a backpack reporter like him needed to do his job: his customised laptop, satellite phone, and digital camera with plenty of room for paper documents. He could feel a magnetic energy pulling him toward his quest on the African continent. Accepting his destiny – or as Acharya described it, his *pratityasamutpada* – with a grudging smile, Hari sat down on the bed for in preparation for a long voyage.

24

National Security Council Secretariat, Sardar Patel Bhawan

"Am I correct?" the national security advisor asked Massey after the RAW director finished bringing the NSA and the council up to date on the Puntland operation. "We're using a British journalist of Indian heritage as bait in order to locate the monastery where you believe the Compact is storing bioweapons destined for the Red Corridor. This journalist will be working with the last sleeper agent the Wing has in Somalia, a man by the name of Khanfari. Is this what we're doing, Masseyji?"

Secretary Massey, glancing at the notes he had scribbled on a memo pad, nodded. "That's broadly the idea, Sir. The journalist in question is by all accounts quite a remarkable and resourceful fellow. He comes from a Hindu family with a long tradition of service to India," said Massey, cleaning his reading glasses with a tissue. "I am confident that Hari Vandra will not fail us, Sir."

The NSA, a professional intelligence officer and former head of the Intelligence Bureau sat in silence. In a career that began in 1968, he had run many such operations. His eyes wrinkled at the corners with tension, his forehead and brow furrowing in concentration, he slowly shook his head. "I have read your memo carefully on Hari Vandra and his family and in the circumstances, I agree that he is our best chance in convincing this Lazarus fellow to tell us the location of the Coptic monastery and stopping those weapons from landing on Indian soil. Does anyone have any comments?"

"The idea that we can plausibly deny Indian involvement in bombing a foreign country will be comprised from the start," said the Foreign Secretary, the country's top diplomat and administrative head of the Ministry of External Affairs. "The African Union will be outraged. All the work done to include Africa in the G20 will be undone in a matter of minutes."

Dressed in his habitual dark suit and tie, the NSA presided from the head of a long Raj-era oval table cluttered with cups, glasses, and files. A huge oil painting of Sardar Vallabhbhai Patel dominated the room. The NSA had attended a meeting of the Cabinet Committee on Security in the morning. Chaired by the prime minister and attended by the ministers of defence, home affairs, finance, and external affairs the CCS has the final word on all matters relating to national security.

"Sir, if I may," said Massey. "It's clear that the key to the operation is to obtain the location of the monastery. And the key to obtaining that information is the skill of the agent in getting that piece of intelligence for us. As I have noted in my report, I have complete faith that the agent – Hari Vandra – will not fail us."

"What concerns me is that Mr Vandra is a foreigner. He is not a member of the Wing. The second thing is that he is a journalist who is clearly chasing a story. In my career, I, too, have used many journalists to infiltrate networks and they always want to write about it afterwards."

Massey decided to play his trump card. "Sir, Hari Vandra was recruited for this mission by Acharya Bhairava on the recommendation of Sir Robert Gage," Massey said softly. "Sir Robert is Hari's godfather."

The NSA looked at Massey for a long time. "You failed to mention this in your report, Masseyji. Your report went into considerable detail about Hari Vandra's parents and grandparents, but you neglected to mention this," he said flatly. "To be chosen for a mission by my former mentor, Acharya, is a great honour indeed. He was with the Directorate General of Security when he recruited me personally into the Intelligence Bureau. And if Sir Robert is his godfather, I can see why his godson would jump at this opportunity."

Noticing the perceptible change in the NSA at the mention of Acharya's name, the people around the table started firing questions at Massey. Which special forces unit will be used for the mission? Do we know the number of Houthi rebels in Somalia being trained by the Pakistanis to use Chinese weapons? Are we notifying our QUAD partners? Do we know which groups in the Red Corridor the weapons were destined for? "What's the actual threat level from the Chinese, Iranians, North Koreans, and the Pakistanis?"

Massey handled all the questions with his usual consummate professionalism. A team of the Special Frontier Force commandos had been chosen for the Puntland mission and were readying themselves at their Chakrata Barracks for deployment to the Gulf of Aden where they will remain onboard *INS Indira Gandhi* until D-day. The Wing has been unable to obtain reliable figures for the number of al-Qaeda jihadists, Al-Shabaab, or Houthi rebels camping in Somalia. "This question is very difficult for us to answer at this time because the Red Sea crisis is intrinsically linked to the Israel-Hamas war, the ongoing Iranian-Israeli proxy conflict, the Iranian-American proxy war, and the crisis in Yemen. The water is very muddy. And in muddy waters, Pakistan is always there to pimp out its army to the highest bidders." Massey confirmed that the intelligence agencies of India's QUAD partners, namely the USA, Japan, and Australia would be notified through the usual back channels of Operation FLUENCY. The latest RAW intelligence report that had been distributed to council members earlier that morning has recommended that Israel and the United Arab Emirates also be told of the operation. "They will be informed during the final stages of the operation," he said looking directly at the NSA.

From the far end of the table, Vice Admiral Kuldeep Singh, a deputy national security advisor and coordinator of national maritime security, asked what would happen if Hari Vandra was taken hostage or killed. The NSA caught Massey's eye and made a grim expression. Massey admitted that the Wing would have a logistical problem. "Everything would then depend on Khanfari who is also not trained in fieldcraft. Hari Vandra is also not trained in fieldcraft but is entering Somalia carrying technology with which we will track his movement inch by inch. That is not the case with Khanfari."

The NSA said, "I need to move this on. I'm seeing the prime minister in forty-five minutes. I would like to go around the table – I need to hear what everyone is thinking." He looked across the table at Vinay Chandi, the veteran Africa specialist at the Ministry of External Affairs who began speaking aloud a pros and cons list. "Chandiji, I am waiting for you to vote. Vote please," snapped the NSA irritably.

Chandi formally declared, "I vote yes, Sir."

The Foreign Secretary, who had been on every planning of operations since the Kargil War, was not convinced that the Wing's operation would succeed but he felt that the Ministry of External Affairs had to support the NSA and the prime minister, and he did so with a lukewarm endorsement of the operation. The Defence Secretary and all five deputy NSAs voted in favour of green-lighting FLUENCY. The Chief of Defence Staff and the Director General of the Defence Intelligence Agency voiced serious concerns about the suitability of an untrained foreign journalist to carry out the mission. However, when pressed by the NSA and Massey, both conceded that Acharya and the Wing were better judges of this aspect of the operation than the military.

"Good, thank you, everyone. What is the timeframe for my decision?"

Massey said, "Our special forces and naval vessels are operational. *INS Indira Gandhi* is already in the Gulf of Aden. We currently have forty-six warships as part of Operation Sankalp." Launched on 19th June 2019, Operation Sankalp was the Indian navy's initiative aimed at ensuring maritime security and protection of India's merchant ships in the Red Sea, Gulf of Aden, Arabian Sea, and the Indian Ocean. It was the perfect cover for the Puntland operation.

The NSA's eyes narrowed into slits and focused through his glasses on an object in the distance. He looked completely alone in the crowded room. "Four days."

25

Carlton House Terrace, Westminster, London

Hassan Aga Abedi, the Pakistani banker and *hawala* trader, tumbled to death from his top-floor apartment in the St James's district of Westminster. The banker had recently been questioned by regulators and the Serious Organised Crime Agency. His passport had been withdrawn and he was confined to his residence after SOCA discovered he was involved in large-scale fraud, and money laundering for the Irish criminal syndicate, the Kinahan Cartel and the Canadian Khalistan movement involved in narcotrafficking. He had worked for Pakistan's spy agency, Inter-Services Intelligence since July 1991. Hassan Abedi was wanted by India for the financing of the Mumbai bombings of 1993 and 2008.

Back in New Delhi, the Wing initiated the second stage of the operation to neutralise D-Company. From the third-floor office of Lodhi Road, the Psychological Operations & Warfare Division began coordinating the meticulously planned disinformation campaign. The division had built up a global network of media contacts over the decades and used them with great skill. The death of Hassan Aga Abedi will produce numerous calls to news organisation contacts with "background information" that was of sufficient interest to be worked into a story, giving it the necessary spin Acharya wanted. The same unit also created information for press attaches at Indian embassies, consulates, and High Commissions to pass on to journalists over a drink or dinner, when a 'secret' could be quietly shared, and reputations discreetly tarnished. Within hours of Abedi's death, Acharya would convene a meeting with the Wing's disinformation experts, a group that was collectively known in-house as the Chennai Shadow Brokers, to discuss plans for feeding stories to selected journalists and broadcasters all over South Asia and the rest of the world.

Days after Abedi's death news-hungry editors in American, Britain, the Commonwealth, and the European Union will start printing stories pointing the finger at the Pakistani intelligence agency, Inter-Services Intelligence, as the prime suspect in Abedi's death. Papers will report that Ashraf Marwan, the Egyptian billionaire, who worked as a spy for Egypt and Israel was Abedi's neighbour. His apartment was a few doors along the corridor. Marwan, who was given the codename "Angel" in May 1971 by then Mossad chief Zvi Zamir, also fell to his death in similar circumstances on 27th June 2007. Was there a connection between the two deaths? Was Marwan moonlighting for the Pakistanis? Did Pakistan infiltrate the Israeli intelligence community? Or the Egyptian Mukhabarat? If so, how? They will hint darkly that the banker and *hawala* trader had upset Islamabad with his reckless money laundering operations for the Kinahan Cartel and Canadian Khalistan movement and that he had to be removed. European and American journalists will point out that only a week before Abedi's death the British government had declared publicly that strong action would be taken to clean up London's reputation as the money laundering capital of the world. Their readers will be told that the Foreign Secretary took the extraordinary step of summoning the Pakistani High Commissioner and informing him that they had credible evidence of ISI involvement in Abedi's criminal activities.

At the same time, the Wing will feed information to Russian and Chinese journalists around the world who will write stories accusing America, Canada, and Britain of orchestrating the murder of Abedi. Chinese and Russian news agencies will vividly describe how the CIA and MI6 became alarmed when Abedi began diverting American-supplied weapons to the Kinahan Cartel in Dublin. These editors will point to Britain's increasing levels of anxiety about British Pakistani and Sikh involvement in drug trafficking and money laundering operations. British editors will print a leaked MI5 memo briefing the Cabinet Office on the opium cultivated by farmers on 40,000 hectares of land owned by the Pakistani army and destined for European markets.

In Pakistan and India, newspapers and magazines will speculate whether Abedi was removed by a powerful faction within the Pakistani Army. They will point out Pakistan's ISI has a long history of funding their operations through drug trafficking and that Abedi was the chief financial officer for such operations in Europe, America, and Canada. The editors will point out that Abedi was on the board of all the conglomerates that managed the thirty-billion-dollar business interests of the Pakistani armed forces.

Acharya will also plant the story that the private contact details of Hardeep Singh Nijjar, a Canadian Sikh militant leader shot dead outside a *gurdwara* in British Columbia in 2022, was discovered by the police while searching the apartment building. The police also found a letter purportedly written by Nijjar on Abedi's desk. In that letter, Abedi was told that Nijjar wanted him to meet a delegation from Surrey in British Columbia because he needed his advice on "a matter of utmost importance."

In London, an elderly cleaner working in the offices of Ernest Oppenheimer Mining opposite the apartment later told the Metropolitan Police that he had seen five men on the balcony before he heard the scream. He said he saw them look down and then go back inside the apartment. The cleaner, an illegal immigrant from Eritrea, was questioned and when searched, marijuana was discovered in his possession. Following a thorough medical screening he was found to be suffering from a number of mental health conditions including psychotic depression. Shortly afterwards the Coroner's Court for the City of Westminster discounted the cleaner's testimony and ruled the death to be an accident.

26

Al Ahmer Hotel, Puntland, Somalia

"If you're not doing anything later, would you like to join me in the *Old Mukalla Hamman*," Yusuf enquired pouring more mint tea while staring intently into Hari's eyes. "I'm sure you'll enjoy the experience. It's the perfect way to end the day in this part of the world," added the Somali university student.

The instructions from Golda were very clear. After landing in Garowe Airport via Doha, Hari was to take a taxi to the Al-Ahmer hotel, near the port, where a room had been booked in his name. He was to wait for Jabir Khanfari at the hotel. Golda didn't say when Khanfari would show.

The Al-Ahmer Hotel turned out to be a rambling old three-storey building run by twin brothers. "This hotel has been in my family since the time of the Italian Somaliland. King Victor Emmanuel III stayed here in November 1934," said Pasha Nassa proudly, one of the Egyptians manning the small reception desk. "I will have someone take your bags."

Hari was given room 04 on the first floor. It was a typical Third World hostel. Nearly everything was of Chinese manufacture. The soft close toilet seat, made of thin, pink-coloured plastic, refused to stay upright unless Hari blocked it using his knee. The once transparent shower curtain had blackened with a thick film of scum. Balanced on the chipped sink was the tiniest bar of "best Chinese sulphur soap" Hari had ever seen. The taps on the sink and bathtub worked but what emerged, with an alien-sounding gurgle, was a faeces-coloured liquid that bore only a passing resemblance to water. In the bedroom, the under sheet was stained and not large enough to tuck beneath the woefully thin mattress. There was a television set that tuned in to a strange psychedelic screen that hummed loudly when Hari switched it on. There was an electric insect killer with a tray full of cremated insects. An empty wardrobe stood in one corner with not a single hanger in it. The room contained no hooks or selves of any kind. Against one wall, next to a desk with mildew in the drawers, stood a small Haier refrigerator with a very large and very dead Goliath beetle inside. Hari, crawling on all fours, was unable to locate anything resembling a socket for his laptop and mobile phone. On the back of the door to his room were instructions in Arabic, Chinese, and the local Somali language about what to do in case of fire, a series of red arrows showing how the guest of room 04 might navigate through the maze of burning corridors to a fire door.

Hari was still digesting his first impressions as he walked down the stairs to see if he could a place that served decent food. He was pleased to see the canteen was still open; he hadn't eaten since Doha. He was led to the dining area. It was a large airy room with potted shrubs and frescoes on the wall. "Menu please sir!" said the waiter – another teenage boy; this one was wearing tracksuit bottoms and football boots - thrusting a laminated menu towards Hari. "Thank you," he said sitting down at one of the tables. He looked at the menu and noticed that it was written in the Somali language and what he took to be Arabic.

"I recommend the *mandi*" said a voice from the shadows. Hari strained to see who was speaking before a figure emerged. "Forgive me if I scared you but it looked like you couldn't read the menu." He was a curly-haired slim Arab around his age. The man was wearing faded jeans and a chequered shirt. "My name is Yusuf" he said holding out his hand. The Arab looked at Hari in a way he instantly recognised. Yusuf's gaze was not only lingering but visually probing as he searched Hari's face for recognition. The look he gave comes from a special gift of insight which Hari instantly recognised anywhere in the world.

Hari said he was glad of the company and invited Yusuf to join him for a bite to eat. They both ordered the *mandi* and mint tea. As they sipped tea Yusuf told him he was studying English literature at the local UNISO university and hoped to find work as a translator for the United Nations. "I find studying boring. I mean, what is the point?" Yusuf explained that people like him were fed up with the dictatorship of the Somali warlords. "These sick dogs have been in power since 1978. Different clothing but same beasts." Since that time Somalia acquired an appalling reputation for human rights abuses. Somali warlords ensured that the secret police received the best Chinese, Iranian, and Pakistani training money could buy. "My friends and I have to keep a low profile," said Yusuf lowering his voice unnecessarily in the empty dining room.

"Why? What do you get up to?" asked Hari listening intently. His reporter's instinct detected a possible story. Yusuf explained he was a part of an underground movement in Somalia which wanted to see change in the country. "We are a loose group of student activists working under the banner of Coalition for Democratic Change," he explained. "I myself chose the name" he said smiling proudly. "We're just people who are sick of the unemployment and corruption in our country. We all want to see change in Somalia," he said taking a sip of tea. "We are sick of being tied to the Chinese and Iranians. We don't want to become another Chinese satellite state like Djibouti. We want elections" he said. "When the time comes you will watch on your BBC in London as thousands of Somali students – my friends, all of them - take to the streets of Mogadishu and in Puntland," he said breaking a piece of flatbread with his right hand. One of the hotel brothers came over and placed a huge plate of rice and meat on the table. "This is *mandi*' said Yusuf helping himself to rice. To Hari, it looked like a kind of Indian *biryani* with layers of tender meat and lightly spiced rice. Yusuf waited until Hari had tasted a piece of meat and pronounced it delicious before eating."

"Would you mind if I made some notes while you talk – sorry, but it's a working habit," said Hari taking out his Moleskin pad and pen. Yusuf made it clear he didn't mind at all. In fact, he said he was pleased as punch that a British journalist was taking an interest in his story.

Talking as he ate, Yusuf explained that he doesn't get time to do any study. "Most of my time is spent writing emails to other activists," he said between mouthfuls of rice. He carried on a huge correspondence with angry students all over Africa and the Arab world. "We have supporters on campuses in Egypt, Libya, Bahrain, and Syria. Our Egyptian and Libyan brothers are particularly strong," he said. "We want to bring down the strong-man regimes." He mentioned that he receives funding for his work from small groups in Algeria, Iraq, Mauritania, and Saudi Arabia. Hari ate steadily, listening intently to Yusuf talk about his hopes for Somalia. Privately he thought it was going to take a long time before Yusuf and his chums rid Africa, the Middle East, and the Arab world of absolute monarchies and dictatorial regimes.

"So, Hari, what brings you to the graveyard of Africa; our sick, sad, sorry Somalia?" he said looking at the journalist closely. Yusuf was bewitched by Hari's green eyes. He was a frequent visitor to the port and a regular at the Al-Ahmer Hotel. Yusuf had arranged to meet someone – a French sailor who was bringing him some material from a Paris-based human rights organisation – who hadn't turned up. It sometimes happened and he wasn't unduly alarmed. He was a little disappointed though because after they concluded their business of passing information, he always took the handsome

Frenchman to a nearby *hammam* where they spent a couple of hours relaxing in one of the steamy darkrooms. Yusuf had a preference for foreign men and would regularly pick up sailors – usually Europeans and Slavs - and take them to the *hammam*. Realising his Frenchman had bailed out on him, Yusuf was about to leave when he saw Hari walk into the canteen. He hesitated for a second before deciding to approach the handsome stranger with green eyes.

"I'm working on a story for a news magazine – it's on piracy off the coast of Somalia and the going Red Sea crisis with the Houthi movement in Yemen," he said. "I'm actually waiting for my guide and translator." Hari saw no reason to tell the activist student he was meeting a pirate named Lazarus.

"I can tell you a lot about Somali pirates and Houthi rebels being trained in Puntland," said Yusuf, chewing thoughtfully. He suddenly looked at Hari directly. "Would you like to go to a *hammam* after we finish eating? You could interview me there; it's very relaxing and discreet. I will also point out a pirate or two."

Hari knew that since antiquity the *hammam* has been a feature of Arab culture. "Okay then, lead the way."

Pasha Nassa watched as the British journalist, Hari Vandra, and Yusuf left the canteen before making his way through the maze of alleyways of the Sheba Bazar to the shop owned by the Pakistani pharmacist. He went inside and sat down in the ancient dentist's chair in the far corner of the room, which was illuminated by a single naked electric bulb dangling from a piece of wire attached to the ceiling. The floor was stained with slimy green spittle from the *paan*, small balls of chewing tobacco, limes, and aromatic spices, that the Pakistanis chew incessantly. Pasha Nassa glanced at the ancient 1960's British GPO 746 telephone. Thirteen minutes after his arrival the phone rang. Nassa snatched it off the cradle. A voice on the other end of the line said, in heavily accented English, "The English journalist arrives. He is not alone."

Nassa muttered, "I understand," and cut the connection with a thumb. He dialled the number of the duty officer in the Chinese embassy in Djibouti City. "This is STORK," he said abruptly, giving his cryptonym assigned to him by his Chinese handler. "Send this following coded message to Chen Qiang in Beijing."

27

Old Mukalla Hammam, Puntland

Yusuf led Hari through a maze of small dusty lanes before they finally reached the *hammam*. Even at this late hour, the port city was humming with life. People were strolling and traders still doing brisk trade. A small discrete wooden sign marked the entrance to the *Old Mukalla Hammam*. "It's over four hundred years old and still popular with the sailors and stevedores working in the port," declared Yusuf pushing open the ancient wooden doors. Inside they stood under a high domed roof beside a murmuring fountain that bubbled up from the tiled basin. Yusuf took Hari into a room where a coffee-coloured youth gave them a towel each and took their clothes for safekeeping. A fat Arab, a soggy sheet wrapped around the lower half of his corpulent body, was sitting on a wooden bench. A young attendant was flaying his back with a leafy branch. Yusuf was obviously well known to the staff because he noticed a knowing smile pass between him and the towel boys. They walked over to a stone slab and lay on their sides soaking up the intense heat. Yusuf peeled off the sheet and pulled Hari into a steam room. An ancient Brannan thermometer on the wall read eighty-seven centigrade and the heavily scented steam scalded Hari's throat when he tried to inhale. "This is definitely not my cup of tea – not sure how long I'll be able to stand this."

Yusuf, his face flushed, splashed a wooden ladle of water onto the hot stones. A haze of scented vapour sizzled into the damp air. "Relax Hari, you will become used to it," he whispered huskily. As they talked quietly, soaking up the heat, a muscular black man in his late thirties walked slowly across the back wall, his curved dick swaying from side to side. He was circumcised and his pubic region closely shaved. The man had an intricate tribal tattoo on his left shoulder blade. Hari noticed he had a distinct military bearing with a ramrod-straight back. He had obviously just come from the hot room because his aubergine-coloured skin was slick with oil and sweat. He was heading towards the dark rooms to cool down. A few moments later a slender Chinese youth scuttled after him.

"I see him – the one with the tattoo, I mean - in here quite a lot," said Yusuf speaking quietly. "I saw him the other day at the Al-Ahmer hotel talking to an important-looking Chinese man. I think I heard the name Chen Qiang mentioned. They seemed to be having an argument. Later on, I saw him in here taking out his anger on a skinny white sailor. The pirate fucked him senseless. I think he likes boyish men." Yusuf giggled coquettishly as he remembered the scene. "They say he's a soldier-turned-pirate, that he and his gang of Somalis and Houthis are responsible for the recent hijacking of ships and fishing vessels in the Gulf of Aden and more recently in the Red Sea." Hari silently digested this piece of information, his eyes glued to the man's magnificent physique. Yusuf said the pirates were lionised by the Somali clans in Puntland and the Houthis of Yemen. "You mean they support criminals" asked Hari innocently.

"It's a bit more complicated than that, Hari." He explained that Yemen has longstanding ties with Somalia which were as old as the hills. "During the civil war in Somalia it was Yemen who opened its borders to Somali refugees'," he said solemnly, "we Somalis can never forget this fact." Very quickly, there were over a hundred thousand Somali refugees in Yemen. "They all receive news from family still in Somalia. Piracy is a big topic of community gossip in both countries," said Yusuf. He told Hari that the pirates spend a lot of money in the local community around Puntland. "Most of the street vendors, shops, and restaurants in Puntland survive on pirate money. They have a big stake in the local economy."

Yusuf got up from the bench. "I'm going for a shower. There's a dark room just around the corner. I'll meet you there," he said. "This is your first visit to Somalia – you should enjoy everything we have to offer, and we have a lot to offer". He laughed and headed to shower.

After a few minutes, Hari walked across the floor towards the showers. As he passed the dark room where the pirate had entered, he paused to peer inside. It took a few seconds for his eyes to adjust to the dim light inside the hot steamed room. The Somali had the Chinese youth bent forward and had spread him out on a worn, foot-thick table topped with a stone slab. Hari watched the pirate's long cock curving and buckling with anticipation as the youth waited with a greedy expression on his face. Suddenly the boy yelped as the Somali's hand came down with wild, hard slaps on his buttocks. Again, the pirate swung his well-muscled arm and slapped the youth's upturned buttocks with a loud crack. The Chinese sailor gasped loudly as the sharp pain lanced across his arse. Fascinated, Hari watched as the pirate straddled the sailor from behind and expertly positioned himself, holding the youth tightly by the waist. Gripping him tight and without warning, the pirate slammed his cock deep inside the sailor. The pirate held the Chinese youth firmly in place, forcing him to relax his anal muscles and accommodate the entirety of the pirate's cock inside him. He fucked with thrilling leisured violence, giving each long stroke, when it was deep into the balls, a final hard shunt that left the youth gurgling with pleasure and grunting with exquisite pain. The Somali was finished quickly, and he slowly pulled out of the youth's slick hole before slapping him hard one last time. He turned his face and looked in Hari's direction, smiled and motioned him to enter the room.

He heard Yusuf. "There you are, Hari, come on……."

The next morning Hari was woken by a sharp knock on the door. He smiled at the memory of the previous night; it had been fun with Yusuf. The knock on the door grew louder. Hari dragged himself out of the bed.

"There's a man waiting to see you downstairs," said Pasha Nassa, handing him a cup of hot sweet coffee.

"*Mashallah*," said Hari. "Did he give a name?"

"Yes. He said his name was Jabir Khanfari."

28

Puntland, Somalia

So much dust and fine sand had been kicked up next to the sprawling United Nations and African Union refugee camps that it was hard to make out the individual players players. "We Somalis love football," explained Jabir Khanfari, glancing at Hari's eyes. He had to shout into Hari's ear to be heard over the clamour and loud cheers of the crowd.

A skinny twenty-three-year-old with open, slim features and a mop of soft curly black hair typical of Somali men, Jabir Khanfari gazed across the makeshift football pitch at the scores of young men sitting on a low wooden fence, passing marijuana joints, and chewing *khat*, a mild narcotic popular in the region. Beyond the playing field, Hari could make out a mass of cylindrical and mud huts stretching back as far as the eye could see. Back in Delhi, Acharya had mentioned that so many refugees were created during the Somali Civil War the aid agencies had given up trying to count them.

Khanfari must have noticed the expression on Hari's face. "Somali culture shock is completely curable," he observed. "In a few days, all this chaos will seem perfectly ordinary to you."

"That's what I'm worried about," replied Hari. "Those football players don't look like Somalis."

"That's because they are not. They are all Yemenis," explained Khanfari. "Members of the Houthi tribe in Yemen. They're mostly Zaidi *Shias* who follow the teachings of a man called Hussein al-Houthi. The usual anti-American, anti-Israeli, anti-West rabble-rousers. Not much changes around these parts."

"What are they doing here?" asked Hari.

"The Houthis, Hamas, Hezbollah and all the others come here to be fed, watered, clothed and sheltered by the humanitarian aid agencies."

"What do you mean?"

"This will be an eye-opening experience, a real fucking awful experience," said Khanfari vehemently spitting on the ground. "The refugee camps in Somalia are heaving, and the aid workers are at the mercy of warlords. The sad truth is that the noble Red Crescent rules are unenforceable in these parts. In Somalia, Yemen, or Gaza, expecting those animals from the clans or Hamas to respect humanitarian principles is like calling on a gang of armed muggers to fight by your aristocratic Queensbury Rules of boxing; it's not just laughable, it's irrelevant. See him, he's a known pirate." He was pointing to a handsome, muscular, tough-looking man watching the game. Was he the same man in the hammam? Hari studied the man carefully as he listened to his companion, fascinated by Khanfari's words.

Hari, listening intently, asked if Khanfari thought aid agencies should continue providing aid, knowing that much of it is going to end up in the hands of the warlords which prolongs conflicts and suffering? Or should the agencies leave? "Which option, in the long run, is crueller?"

"I don't know, Hari," he said staring at the football pitch. "A lot of the European and American aid workers sent to Africa and elsewhere give fuck all thought to the ethics of the aid agencies. To them, it is a career in the marketplace for good works, and its big business. The salaries, *per diems* and danger-and-discomfort bonuses on offer make working in the aid sector very lucrative; very lucrative indeed."

"What do you mean? Explain?"

"These refugee camps act as a magnet to jihadists. We call them refugee warriors. The jihadists, pirates, warlords, and warriors use a common military tactic of simply concealing themselves among genuine displaced civilians. The aid workers haven't a clue who's who. And the problem, Hari, is that since aid agencies have neither the power nor the resources to prevent abuse, they ignore or keep quiet about the problem."

Hari said, "So you're saying that aid agencies are feeding, clothing, and sheltering jihadists."

"Exactly that! These fucking agencies in Somalia, Gaza, and Yemen are in the grip of contract fever," Khanfari said, his voice rising ever so slightly. "So much of the talk between aid workers and their headquarters and field offices is about contracts to implement their donor's projects, securing them, maintaining them, and increasing them. It was always about more contracts! How many contracts do we have? When were the contacts up? What were the chances contracts would be renewed? Were there any competitors in the moral economy? All aid agencies operate in the moral economy."

Hari said nothing. He knew when someone needed to vent. This is definitely a moment to keep quiet. Besides, he was getting good background material for his story. He could see many spin-off articles coming out of this Puntland assignment.

"The international humanitarian aid industry – and it is an industry – looks like one big, concerned family dedicated to easing human suffering, but what I find in Somalia and Gaza is that the most powerful link between all the aid agencies is corporate competition. The Somali clan wars, like other conflicts including the ongoing war in Gaza and Yemen, attract these garish agencies, each with their own corporate agendas, religious affiliations, commercial policies, and institutional survival tactics. I discovered that the top management of these aid agencies working in Africa and the Middle East was made up of graduates trained in non-profit management and economics. They're all experts in product positioning, proposal development and corporate-client relationships...."

"Listen, Khanf......."

"They all dress in sharp business suits, Hari! Can you believe that? These fucking people! And there's no sign of donor fatigue; the budgets of donor governments and contributions from businesses and ordinary people grow every year, as does the number of aid agencies wanting to spend those donated billions," Khanfari exclaimed. "And the competition between these agencies just grows and grows. They call it the moral economy."

A roar went up from the crowd as a player wearing a torn Liverpool vest and a Lakers baseball cap scored a goal. With a whoop, the opposing team tore after him in hot pursuit. Once again, the playing field was lost in the dust billowing from the desert. One of Khanfari's minders, a bearded clansman wearing a sweat-stained vest and soiled jeans with a Soviet AKM bayonet knife in his leather belt and an RPK machine gun under one arm, pointed to his watch. Khanfari led Hari away from the wooden benches and the pair made their way to the truck stop and petrol station. The second bodyguard, a giant of a man with a dusty black turban around his head, brought up the rear. Khanfari's driver, slouched behind the wheel of an old Soviet jeep, chewing *khat* came awake. "Where to, coachman Big Boss?" he asked.

"Baqaar Market," Khanfari ordered as he and Hari settled into the back seat. One of the guards slid in next to Khanfari, the other man rode shotgun up front.

"Where'd you find these chaps?" Hari asked under his breath. "Psycho city?"

"They're both members of the minority Bantu tribes, which is the clan that controls Baqaar Market," Khanfari explained, glancing behind his back. He was clearly on edge. "Don't worry they're Lazarus's people. The one with the Russian knife used to slit the throats of Siad Barre's soldiers the way Muslims slaughter cows for *Eid*."

Baqaar Market, a warren of shack-like stalls and huts topped with corrugated iron roofs selling everything under the sun, was swarming with clansmen. The ravages of war were everywhere Hari looked: old turbaned men hobbled on makeshift wooden crutches, a horribly disfigured teenage girl with the stump of an arm, jeeps and trucks crammed with skinny youths brandishing weapons, and makeshift ambulances. In an empty lot between shacks, Pakistani and Iranian gun merchants had spread their wares on rugs and plastic sheets. There were neat rows of Uzis and American M-1s and Chinese and Russian versions of the AK-47, and every kind of pistol manufactured.

The jeep turned suddenly onto a pitted side lane and bumped its way down it to a shop belonging to a Goan dentist with a colourful sign out front that read, "Teeth & Gum Problems." Inside, a squat woman dressed in a shroud-like costume worked the bellows, heating the kettles suspended above the paraffin stoves. In an alcove off to one side, an itinerant Indian dentist was drilling into the tooth of a Somali fighter. A teenage boy pedalling a bicycle bolted into a metal frame ran the lathe that turned the drill in the dentist's fist. "Don't get a toothache in Somalia," warned Khanfari. "The dentist will fill the cavities with molten shotgun pellets."

After waiting for a signal from the woman, Khanfari led Hari down a long flight of concrete steps, passing a narrow wooden door on the landing. The Al Jazeera correspondent glanced back nervously. Seeing no one behind them, he stepped quickly to the door, yanked it open, pulled Hari through, and jammed it shut behind him. "We were followed when we arrived at the market," Khanfari informed him. "I saw them at the football game – members of Al Shabaab. There seemed to be an entire gang spread out behind us – two truckloads, a least ten-foot soldiers.

Khanfari started down a wooden staircase no wider than his body and lit by dim light bulbs on every landing. At the bottom, he pushed open another door and stuck his head through. Seeing the coast was clear, he nodded for Hari to follow. They made their way across the cement floor of a vast storage room filled with paintings, icons, and Christian relics to a door locked and bolted on the inside.

He fixed his dark eyes on Hari. "We have to be very careful here, Hari. The Al Shabaab cells are well trained by al-Qaeda and its allies." Producing a large skeleton key from a pocket, he threw the bolt on the door. As they emerged from the basement into a sunken patio he locked the door behind them, then led the way up a flight of wooden steps to a door in the high iron fence, which he unlocked with a second skeleton key and locked again when they passed through it. Crossing the street, he led the way down a narrow dirt track to an ancient two-door Fiat parked in a shed. Khanfari unlocked the door, slid behind the wheel, and then reached across to unlock the passenger door. Gunning the motor, he set off down the alley and melted into the traffic on the main road.

Khanfari piloted the tiny car through the crowded streets of Ely with total concentration. After a while Hari broke the silence. "Where are you taking me?"

"Lazarus and his people are waiting for you in the Las Anond apartment that serves as their underground church." Khanfari spoke without taking his eyes off the road.

"Underground church?" asked Hari. "Curiouser and curiouser."

The corner apartment on the top floor of the house was lost in the labyrinth streets of Las Anond. When Hari appeared at the door, a heavyset man in his late forties, with a mane of prematurely grey hair and flat forehead and a broken nose, strode across the room to greet him. He was wearing the traditional Somali dress of a *Malawi*, a sarong-like garment worn by men around their waist and a large cloth draped around the upper part of his well-built body. His head was covered with an intricately embroidered skullcap known as a *koofiyad*." I welcome you with all my heart to Puntland," he declared, burying the visitor's hand in both of his hands, minutely examining him with dark, restless eyes.

"This is Brother Lazarus," Khanfari murmured.

"It is an honour to meet you," Hari said. He noticed that Lazarus had a single-decade rosary wrapped around his left hand.

Lazarus turned away to hold a hurried conversation in his native Osmanya mother tongue with Khanfari and the two young men sitting at the edge of a table. Hari took in the room: there was an enormous 1960s Italian Mivar radio on a side table, wooden beams overhead, and on the walls hung numerous pictures and posters of leading Jesuit exponents of liberation theology. Hari recognised many from the Jesuitical discourses with Padre during their long walks in the Parke: Rubem Alves of Brazil, Jose Miguez Bonino of Argentina, and James Hal Cone of America. The portrait which took centre stage showed Gustavo Gutierrez holding his defining book, *A Theology of Liberation*, in his right hand. Heavy rug-like drapes were drawn across the windows, a fireplace stuffed with kindling waiting to be burned, a bucket of coal, and a small mountain of Bibles stacked against a wall. Khanfari glanced back at Hari. "Excuse me for a moment – I'm just telling Brother Lazarus about the Al Shabaab gang who were following you. He wants to be sure they did not follow us to the church."

Lazarus switched off the overhead light and went to a window, where he parted the heavy drapes with the width of two fingers and surveyed the street below. "I do not think you were followed," he announced, speaking slowly. "In any case I have my people watching the street from another building. They are trusted members of our congregation and will alert us if there is any sign of danger." Lazarus motioned for Hari to take the empty chair at the table. He nodded towards the two other men and purposely introduced them by their first names only. "Meet please, Yusuf; meet, also, his brother, Osman," he said. "They are members of our black liberation church and the resistance movement against Al Shabaab."

Yusuf gave no sign of recognising Hari from the day before. Or the time they spent together in the *hammam*. Hari after a flicker of hesitation immediately regained control of himself and reached to shake the hand of each man – Yusuf was wearing the distinctive short jacket of a UNISO university student; Osman, the vest and detachable-collar shirt and steel-rimmed glasses of an office worker – and then sat down in the empty chair. Khanfari settled onto an ancient Vittorio Bertazzoni couch beneath a painting of the Christian missionary Frumentius, ready to translate for the Somalis if required.

Lazarus filled a glass with a cloudy liquid and pushed it across the table to his guest. "Are you familiar with our *Chang'aa*? Ah, I did not think so. It is a home-brewed spirit fermented from sorghum, very popular in Kenya," he said filling to the brim his own glass. "My mentor and confessor, Father Abraham Umtali dispatches a few cases each month from Nairobi. He says it's good for the spirit; cleanses the soul of the worst of sinners. I agree with him."

"For the greater glory of God," the two men at the table echoed, saluting Hari with raised glasses.

"For the greater glory of God," repeated Hari, instantly recognising the famous motto of the Jesuits. He thought of Padre, the Five Aces, and his beloved Blaney Parke.

They downed their shots. The spirit scalded Hari's throat. He opened his mouth wide and exhaled and pulled a face. The others, including Khanfari, smiled.

"If you please," Lazarus said with great formality, "what would you like to know? Our good friend, Jabir, tells me you are a celebrated crime journalist who is interested in writing about what is happening here, in Puntland."

"I bring you the good wishes of my editor who has commissioned me to write a feature on the Coast Guards of Puntland and the issue of piracy in the Gulf of Aden…."

Lazarus's palm came down on the table so hard Hari was astonished it didn't splinter under the blow. Yusuf said something in Osmanya and Lazarus answered him irritably. From the couch, Khanfari said something in soft tones and when he persisted, Lazarus nodded reluctantly. He glanced back at Hari. "Forgive me, I am not a diplomat or politician," he said gruffly, refilling his glass before passing the bottle to Hari. "I am a simple fisherman concerned about the future of our community. My friends and I do not need the good wishes of your British editors. Nor do we need their sympathy or their respect. We do not need the pity of English people. We need you, Hari Vandra, to tell the world the truth about what is happening here."

"I apologise if I have offended you…." said Hari.

"You have offended me, Hari," Lazarus said. "You have offended me greatly by describing my coastguard brothers and sisters of Puntland as pirates. We are not pirates. We are servants of God who humbly follow the teachings of liberation theology, specifically black liberation theology. We do this to free Somalis from the evil that is engulfing our country."

"Then please tell me," Said Hari recognising the pain, passion, and religious fervour of Lazarus. "This is why I'm here: to interview the man who created the Coastguards of Puntland that inspired a Hollywood movie to be made."

"If you are referring to that *Captain Phillips* rubbish, it is yet another way Hollywood exploits the plight of us Africans to make more money for themselves," said Yusuf with a faint smile. "We are definitely not pirates, Hari. Captain Jack Sparrow is a pirate," said the university student. "We are, or were, coastguards. Coastguards are very different to pirates."

"Let me explain why we created the Coastguards of Puntland," said Lazarus. "It's simple really. It was to prevent illegal fishing in our waters. Somalia has been plagued by civil war and clan conflicts for more years than I care to remember. We do not have a navy to protect the people and our marine resources."

"British, European, and American companies steal around one and a half billion dollars of Somali money through illegal fishing," said Osman, wiping his eyeglasses. "That is a lot of money."

"You British are stealing food from the mouths and bellies of Somali children. That is what your editors do not write in their papers and magazines. This is what we are hoping you will do, Hari."

"That is what I'm here to do but I need background information for the story," Hari explained, "So, how do you go about hijacking someone's boat? I mean what's the basic operation?'

"For a simple operation – taking a medium-sized cargo ship for instance – I need a minimum of eight to twelve of my crew prepared to stay at sea for long periods" said Lazarus staring towards the window. "The team takes a minimum of two attacks skiffs, weapons and ammunition, ladders, food, and fuel with them. I insist at this stage of the operation the cost is paid by the investor."

"The investor?"

"Very often shipping and insurance companies pay us to do things. Many of them are based in London. The real cutthroat pirates of the world all wear business suits and work in the City of London."

"I see I have a lot to learn about piracy in Somalia," admitted Hari. "How many men in your team?"

"There are six of us who started the piracy operation in Puntland. I've known the boys since I was a boy. We're all from the same clan. There's Salim who gets me the volunteers, the fresh bodies from Puntland. These areas have no work so there are lots of people doing nothing and earning nothing. He's a former member of the elite *Duub Cas* and has contacts with local militiamen who supply us the muscle recruited from the refugee camps." Hari quietly absorbed that bit of information. The *Duub Cas* was an elite security detail which surrounded Siad Barre during his presidency. "As well as hiring the local muscle, Salim works out what each volunteer receives as a share of profits," said Lazarus. "Osman here is responsible for organising the land-based operations and hiring locals to provide food, supplies, and shelter. Yusuf is in charge of liaison and communication matters. Mustapha who you will meet later is the youngest – he's only twenty-two and has a computing degree from UNISO – and provides the technical know-how." Lazarus squinted in Hari's direction. "We don't kill hostages Hari. They are well-fed, and we have a local Indian doctor on standby for medical emergencies. We release them when the ransom has been paid."

"How do you divide the loot?" Hari asked, bringing the conversation back to the piracy operation.

"It is not loot; it is colonial taxation. It is our due," Osman said quietly.

"Most of the business side of things is done by my cousin Aaden, who I've known longest. We're the two ex-fishermen, the others are ex-military or college educated," said Lazarus. He explained that generally financiers and investors get thirty per cent of the ransom. Local clan elders receive five to ten per cent of what he called anchoring rights. Militiamen and technicians get so-called class B shares, roughly sixteen thousand dollars. The remaining sum – the profit – is divided between Lazarus and his brothers.

"Do you get much resistance from your victims?" asked Hari.

Lazarus laughed. "You make me sound like a monster; a wild African savage," he said. "We have no trouble with most of the boats we hijack. People are usually smart when staring into the barrel of a gun. The crew know the drill. We wait for the boat owner to pay the ransom money."

"How do you take payment?" Hari asked.

"Uncut diamonds," said Lazarus. "Also, emeralds, sapphires, rubies, and alexandrite gemstones. Easy to carry, easy to sell."

"Who do you sell the diamonds to?"

Lazarus laughed. "We have a friend in South Africa who knows about diamonds and precious stones. Now, no more questions Mr Reporter, I'm exhausted. I am not so young anymore. I promise to answer all your questions on our coastguard operations by the time you leave Puntland. Our operations were so we could defend our fishing rights and feed our families."

"You describe the coastguards in the past tense," noted Hari. "What has happened to them?"

"My brother-in-law, Salim, is what happened," Lazarus said bitterly. "He betrayed our family, his clan to join those filthy flea-infested Al Shabaab dogs that roam freely in Puntland today. Salim turned the coastguards into a bunch of thugs that indiscriminately hijacked ships for profit. He became seduced by his love money and power."

"Salim and his Al Shabaab cell have turned Puntland into a land sick with the dreaded doorknock fever," said Yusuf.

"Doorknock fever?" enquired Hari, looking first at Lazarus and then Khanfari for a translation.

"Yes, yes. Doorknock fever. Everyone waits for the Al Shabaab gangs to knock at midnight and drag him and his family away for question or torture. I myself have been taken five times in the battles and wars so far. Twice by the Islamic Jihad who control the refugee camps and the southern part of Puntland, and three times by Al Shabaab with the help of Salim. I live in hiding now." Sinking back onto his chair, Lazarus sucked air through his nostrils to calm himself.

Drumming a knuckle on the table, Osman spoke again in their native tongue. Lazarus nodded in vigorous agreement. "He says the moment of reality approaches. He says you must be ready to assist an uprising if one occurs. He says that if you can keep the jihadists away from Puntland, only that, nothing more, will cause an uprising among the masses."

In his peripheral vision, Hari caught a glimpse of Khanfari watching him carefully. "NATO has already launched Operation Ocean Shield to protect…."

Osman cut him short. "Operation Ocean Shield and all the other anti-piracy operations before it, including the European Union's Operation Atalanta, was aimed at protecting the commercial interests of the fishing industries of all those involved. In the meantime, the interests of Somalia are inconsequential. You take our valuable marine resources and send us your aid agencies who hand out a few surplus tents and blankets to the lucky few. Your aid agencies help greatly in keeping us in a state of perpetual niggerdom."

"I would say that's a little unfair, Osman," replied Hari. "I don't doubt your determination to rid yourself of Al Shabaab and its allies from Somalia," he told Lazarus. "But you must, in my opinion, put realities before idealism. The realities are stark and speak for themselves. Since 2006, Al Shabaab has been acting as quartermaster to some of the world's most dangerous organisations. We have abundant evidence that Al Shabaab is using former members of your Coastguards of Puntland to store weapons and explosives ready for distribution to terror groups all over Somalia and elsewhere," said Hari following the pitch he practised with Acharya before he left Delhi. He heard the spymasters voice in his ear. "Always remember to keep it simple, Hari. Focus on Puntland and don't mention India to him."

Lazarus and Osman exchanged dark looks; Hari's information apparently came as a total surprise to them. Khanfari quickly translated to make sure there was no ambiguity as to what Hari was saying. "I can tell you that we have information that in the last seventeen years Al Shabaab have assembled a massive cache of weapons and have stored it in a disused Coptic monastery somewhere in Puntland. I can also tell you that the weapons include biological and chemical agents capable of decimating entire towns." Khanfari slowly translated Hari's words.

Lazarus held up his hand for Hari to stop. "This is Satan's work. What you tell me is diabolical; I know this very well", he said producing a pack of Gunston cigarettes from a pouch in his *malawis*. His hands shook violently as he tried to light the cigarette. "My wife and daughter died because of chemical poisoning. You see, Hari, foreign countries are not just stealing our fish and marine resources," he explained as he inhaled the cigarette smoke, "they are also poisoning our waters and beaches by dumping waste in Somali waters. These evil people know we have no coastal defence, so they dump this waste which is washed onto our beaches and poisons our children. Children like my daughter."

"This began when Salim convinced the Al Shabaab cell in Puntland to work with a criminal syndicate known as the 'Ndrangheta. This syndicate specialises in dumping radioactive waste from developed countries and dumping them in Somali waters," explained Yusuf. "According to Father Umtali, the 'Ndrangheta is a family of Italian mafia groups based in Calabria."

"My brother-in-law Salim didn't just convince Al Shabaab," said Lazarus. "He was the one that negotiated the agreement between the al-Qaeda groups and the Ndrangheta." Under the terms of the agreement waste processing companies in Britain, Europe, America and elsewhere would pay the "Ndrangheta and Al Shabaab a handling fee to transport dangerous waste in ships and dump it in Somali waters."

"The kind of waste we are talking about is the kind that is expensive to process and dispose of. Hazardous waste disposal for a British company can be as high as £2,000 to £6,000 per ton," explained Osman, who worked as a manager at Radio Mogadishu, the federal government-run radio station of Somalia. "Father Umtali's reports identified two companies that are actively colluding with the jihadists and Italians. The China Pakistan Marine Shipping & Freight Forwarding Company which is based in Gwadar Port in Pakistan and a British shipping company called Fauji Shipping & Freight Forwarding Company of Southampton."

Sir Ibrahim Ali

"These two companies are responsible for killing my wife and daughter," Lazarus said quietly. "Two years ago, a ship chartered by the British company offloaded toxic waste to a waste handling company owned and operated by the Ndrangheta which disposed of the material at the port in Puntland. The material was radioactive hospital waste. The Ndrangheta dumped the waste at seventeen sites around the capital city, Garoowe. These people are responsible for killing over a hundred people and poisoning nearly thirty thousand others. Over a hundred thousand of our people had to be hospitalised." He tapped out another cigarette on the table, picked it up and angrily thrust it into his mouth before searching for a lighter. "I can still see the long lines of people waiting for treatment from the UN relief agencies. Some died while waiting," he added. He found a lighter and, igniting it with a thick thumbnail, held the flame to the end of the cigarette. Blue smoke bellowed from his nostrils. "I pray every day that God send an avenging angel to bring justice to our land; to wipe out Al Shabaab and all those that feed on the misery of the Somali people. When will God send us such an angel?" he asked rhetorically.

Hari said, almost in a whisper. "I think God has answered your prayers. The angels you are praying for are, even as we speak, on their way to Puntland to bring justice to the land of your forefathers."

The Somali men around the table looked at each other in silence. Lazarus stubbed out his cigarette and leaned forward looking directly at Hari. "What exactly are you saying? Speak plainly."

"I will, this is the reason I am in Puntland," said Hari. "To deliver this message. To let you know that those who murdered your family by poisoning them will be delivered to the doors of hell. I'm here to tell you that the Al Shabaab cell and the Ndrangheta syndicate's days are numbered."

"Please tell me how," said Lazarus staring directly into Hari's green eyes.

"I will." For the next hour and forty minutes, Hari explained the Puntland plan to the Somalis.

There was a restless silence in the room when Hari finished explaining the operation. Osman was slowly wiping his spectacles. Lazarus aimed a flame from his lighter onto the tip of another cigarette. Yusuf drummed his slender fingers on the metal band of the cheap watch on his wrist. Jabir Khanfari appeared to be dozing with his head tilting up towards the ceiling.

"So, you see, it is crucial to my mission that we locate the whereabouts of this Coptic monastery. Unless we can locate it the murderers of your family will continue to roam free," Hari said grimly.

When Khanfari translated Hari's remark, Osman angrily scraped back his chair came round the table and flopped onto the couch next to him. The two, whispering in Osmanya, got into a lively discussion. It was obvious that Khanfari was trying to convince the bespectacled office worker of something but was having little success.

At the table, Lazarus looked past Hari, staring at a poster pinned onto the wall for a long moment. Hari had noticed it when he first entered the room. It was a reproduction of *St. Michael Vanquishing Satan*, a painting by the Renaissance artist Raphael. When Lazarus turned back to his Indian visitor, his eyes appeared to be burning with fever. "You come to us with a dangerous plan," he began, "but it doesn't take into account the desperateness of our situation here in Puntland, the plight of our fishing community, nor the particular quirks of the Somali character that will compel us to fight against overwhelming odds. We have been at war since the Middle Ages. For us Somalis, the fact that a situation is hopeless only makes it more enticing."

Hari decided not to mince his words with Lazarus. "I was sent here to make certain that you calculate the risks correctly. If you decide to encourage an armed uprising against Al Shabaab, you should do so knowing that India will be standing shoulder-to-shoulder with you. And we will be armed to the teeth. My confessor, Jesuit Father Ambrose Tyrell of Blayney Parke always says that followers of Jesus must have no hesitation in carrying out God's will. The rape of Somalia by these foreign mercenaries is evil. Servants of God must always be prepared to wage war against evil."

The Somalis in the room exchanged faint smiles and Hari understood that he had succeeded in his mission. "I and my friends thank God for sending you to us, Hari," Lazarus said looking deep into his eyes. "I will give you a message to give to our friends in India. According to my confessor, Father Abraham Umtali of the Vatican Secretariat of State, there are three things that push men to war – honour, fear, and self-interest. If we go to war with Salim and Al Shabaab it will be a matter of honour and fear. I trust Father Umtali. He's a great friend of our family," he said smoking intently. "After my father was killed in the Somali Civil War my mother was left destitute. Father Umtali helped keep the family together. He arranged schooling for us children and got my mother a cleaning job in Mogadishu Cathedral. He got me out of Somali and into Egypt. He helped me get a job with the Egyptian El Salam Maritime Transport Corporation where I learned my trade. Without the help of my confessor, I don't think my family could have survived. He kept our family's body and soul together," said Lazarus. "I thank God every day for putting me in his path," said Lazarus looking into a far corner of the room. "We are a community of fishermen who simply want to earn a living and provide for our families. We pray that the Indian leaders, motivated by self-interest, will then calculate the advantages of helping us. So, tomorrow, I shall show you the monastery that Salim uses, Hari. The Coptic monastery is located in a port town in the Nugal region of Somalia. This town is called Eyl. I shall also give you all the files relating to the illegal fishing and the Ndrangheta Father Umtali gave to me. The files contain all the background information you need to write our story."

Then, with Khanfari, Osman, and Yusuf leading the way, Hari took his leave. "I look forward to seeing you tomorrow and thank you for helping us, Brother Lazarus." He followed Khanfari down a narrow corridor to a bedroom in the back of the apartment. Osman and Yusuf pushed aside a large, heavy antique wardrobe, revealing a narrow rug-covered break in the wall of the building that opened into a storage space in a vacant apartment in the adjourning building. Osman and Yusuf remained behind to shoulder the wardrobe back into place and block the secret passage as Hari and Khanfari entered the apartment and let themselves out of its back door, then descended three flights to an old crumbling cellar door that gave onto a different street to the one they arrived on hours earlier.

The two journalists failed to notice the small, dusty van parked in front of a *Qahwa* vendor's shack. As they approached the shack, the van's back doors flew open and three wiry black men armed with pistols spilled onto the path behind them. Other dark figures wearing American baseball caps appeared from behind a rubbish tip and blocked their path. Hari managed a startled, "What the fuck is happ..." as a jute sack came over his head. With his hands twisted behind his back, he was quickly bound with a length of wire. He heard a rabbit punch and a hard kick to the stomach followed by Khanfari's agonising gasp. Strong hands bundled the two reporters into the back of the van, shoving them roughly onto bundles of jute sacking on the floor. The doors slammed shut, the motor started, and the vehicle turned sharply away from the rubbish pile, throwing the prisoners hard against one wall. Hari asked Khanfari if he was hurt but stopped in midsentence when he felt a sharp pinprick of a knife against his throat. He heard Khanfari's indignant "Wait till Al Jazeera hears of this..." cut off by a savage blow to the face.

The battered old van swerved right and then right again, then left, then with the motor suddenly revving up speed carried on straight. After what seemed like an hour but could easily have been two or four the van slowed to a stop. From the distance, the deep hollow bleating of what Hari recognised to be the foghorns of ships could be recognised easily through the head covering. He had spent long enough scouting the vessels belonging to Sir Ibrahim Ali in Southampton to recognise the sounds of the port. He heard someone get into the van. He thought he heard the name of Suleyman. The presence of this person silenced everyone. He heard the metallic snap of a lighter and fought back the panic that rose to his throat. The van started to move again. He had visions of his captors burning them alive in the same manner jihadists burned to death the Jordanian pilot Muath al-Kasasbeh in 2015 during the war against the Islamic State. After torturing the pilot, the jihadists videotape him being burned to death. Hari began to recall details of the film which was released by the Islamic State in a snuff film entitled *Healing the Believer's Chest*. It was only when he got a whiff of familiar-smelling tobacco smoke that the terror began to subside. At that precise moment, his reporter's antenna became tuned to details. Why were these Somalis so quiet? They were normally a noisy rabble. The odour of the tobacco that reached his nostrils reminded him of the Wills Navy Cut brand of cigarettes smoked by so many of Delhi's elite. Why was the person who had just entered so silent? Was it because they didn't speak English, or spoke it with an accent? Was this person an Indian? Had someone betrayed Hari from inside the Wing? As he weighed up many possibilities in the hope that one of them might lead to some logical conclusion, Hari's thoughts began to drift – only afterwards did he realise that he had actually nodded off – and he found himself flicking through a mental scrapbook of memories: lighting his father's funeral pyre; Robbie holding his shoulders as they watched the flames take hold of the wood; his first glimpse of Blaney Parke; how he felt during that beautiful moment when he first saw Jago.

    Hari came back to his senses suddenly when the back doors were jerked open and a fresh sea breeze sept through the stifling van. Strong arms pulled him out of the vans and dragged him across the ground before coming to a halt. After what seemed like an eternity, he became aware of a grinding noise. He had heard a similar noise in Blayney Parke. They were hatch bolts turning in the bulkhead of a warehouse. The door swung open on greased hinges and Hari felt himself being pulled onto a wooden platform before being pushed down a long flight of narrow steps. As he descended into the sweltering bowels of the building the stale air that reached Hari's nose smelled of dried fish. Someone pushed Hari into a room and began to drag the shoes off his feet and then strip him to his underwear. He felt someone examine the amulet around his neck and for a moment felt panic that it would be removed. Hari could smell the man's foul breath as he read the inscribed Quran verses. After another agonising moment, the man released the chain. His wrists, aching from the electrical wiring biting into them, were cut free and he was shoved onto a wooden chair and expertly tied to it, his wrists behind the back of the chair, with shipping rope that was passed several times across his chest and behind the chair. Then the jute sack was removed from his head.

    Squinting hard to keep the harsh spotlights from burning the retina of his eyes, Hari looked around at his surroundings. Khanfari, also stripped to his underwear, was angling his head away from the bright light. Three wiry, bearded men in dirty dungarees were removing wallets and paper from the pockets of clothes and throwing them into a plastic bucket. Another was searching Hari's notebook. A thin, sinister-looking Somali man in an ill-fitting pink shirt studied them from the door. His eyes were hidden behind oval sunglasses. The ghost of a smile appeared on his lips. "Hello to you. I am a friend of Salim, the brother-in-law of your friend Lazarus. Salim sends his apologies that he cannot be here, but he looks forward to speaking to you soon. In the meantime, he has asked me to keep you company," he said, speaking in heavily accented English. As he stepped into the room Hari noticed he was wearing white gloves with washed-out stains on it. One of the sailors came in behind him carrying a bucket half filled with water. He set the bucket in a corner, filled a plastic cup with water from the bucket, and spilt some down the throat of the prisoners. The emaciated Somali scraped over a chair, turned it so that the back was to the prisoners and straddled the seat facing them. He extracted a Chunghwa cigarette from a pack, tapped down the tobacco and held the lighter to the tip. Sucking on the cigarette, he seemed lost in thought. "Admit it," he said, "you are hoping this is an initiation test of our former friend Lazarus to test if you are to be trusted but you are not sure." A cackle erupted from the back of his throat. "I must tell you are on the North Korean cargo vessel *Ji Shun* anchored in Bosaso port while we wait for clearance to put to sea with a cargo of dried fish. Our destination is Wonsan port in North Korea. The ship has already been searched by NATO forces who keep us waiting many hours because they receive pleasure from doing so." He dragged a notebook from a pocket, moistened a thumb on his tongue and began to leaf through the pages. "So," he said when he found what he was looking for. "Which one of you is Jabir Khanfari?"

Khanfari cleared his throat. "I am Jabir."

"I see that you have a degree from Qatar University and studied at the Department of Mass Communications." He looked up. "You carry a laminated card identifying you as an employee of Al Jazeera Media Network."

"Yes, I do."

"What exactly is your work at Al Jazeera?"

"I am a journalist. Specialising in African Union affairs."

"Please Mr. Jabir, I know that you and your friend are spies working for India. We know that you are conscripted into India's spy agency, the RAW based in Lodhi Road in New Delhi. The Research & Analysis Wing of the Union Secretariat, is that not what its formal name is? We know you were sent to work with our former friend, Lazarus. You are a spy, Mr. Jabir. You were recruited in your final year at university. Please do not lie. It will not go well for you."

Hari asked, "What do want from us?"

The Somali sized up Hari. "The first thing I want is for you to forget the story that Mr. Jabir is working for Al Jazeera and that you – Mr. Hari - are working for an Indian aid agency. When you have done this more will be revealed by you – the date you were recruited by the RAW, and by whom, the names of all your case officers apart from Miss Anita Kinnar, known as Golda and Acharya Bhairava, the full details of instruction you received at the MacGregor's Club, and the real reason why you are in Puntland. You will want to tell me details of your meeting with Lazarus and the secrets he has revealed to you. Secrets given to him by his priest Father Abraham Umtali of the Vatican intelligence service."

As the Somali interrogator spoke, Hari felt a paralysing fear run through his body. *How did he know all these details?* He then remembered Robbie's words. It's not the pain that breaks you but the fear. Hari focused on calming his mind.

The reed-like man, it transpired, was the first in a series of interrogators who took turns questioning the two journalists. With the hot spotlights burning into their retinas, they quickly lost track of time. Every time Khanfari dozed off during the inquisition, a sailor would jar him awake with a blow to the head. Working from typed notes, the interrogators walked the captives through the cover stories that had been worked up in Lodhi Road and McGregor's Club.

"You want me to believe that you, Mr. Hari, are working for the Indian Technical and Economic Cooperation Programme."

"How many times do I need to repeat myself, man? Working for the ITEC isn't the same fucking thing as working for an Indian government spy agency. You've been watching too many Bollywood movies."

The cigarette held between the thumb and forefinger of the interrogator was burning perilously close to the skin. "Your godfather is Sir Robert Charles Gage, the former station chief of MI6 in New Delhi, is that not correct Mr. Hari?"

Hari was stunned that the man knew about Robbie. He quickly regained his composure. "You are correct in that Robbie is my godfather. You are incorrect about this MI6 angle," said Hari wearily. "My godfather is a retired Foreign Office official, a former cultural attaché, and celebrated Indologist. He has published many books on Indian history and culture."

"As you are a member of Sir Robert Gage's extended family, it would have been logical for him to recommend you, his godson, to the RAW," said the interrogator adjusting his dark glasses.

"My godfather would never have recommended me for anything without first asking if I wanted to spy for the Indian government," retorted Hari indignantly. His mind was racing so rapidly that he was having trouble keeping up with the fragments of thoughts and memories of his briefing by Golda. It was obvious he had been betrayed, and by someone who knew him personally or had access to the inner circles of Lodhi Road. But who?

The interrogator was about to ask another question when one of the sailors entered the compartment and whispered into his ear. The Somali turned towards Hari and said, "So, the harbour master has at last given us permission to get underway." Beneath the feet of the captives, the floor began to vibrate, faintly at first, then with a distinctly hard throb. "I hope you do not suffer from sea sickness," he said, "we have a very long sea voyage ahead of us." He switched to Osmanya and barked a series of orders to one of the young sailors. Khanfari whispered that he wanted buckets placed next to them in case they threw up. Hari motioned him to be quiet. He sensed something was about to happen. The atmosphere in the room had changed.

And then suddenly there was a commotion in the galley. The door was ajar and men in uniform and caps could be seen lumbering past. The two inquisitors in the room exchanged worried looks. Something was clearly wrong. The thin Somali gestured with his head. They stepped outside and held a hushed conversation in Osmanya with a stocky man wearing the gold braids of a naval officer. Hari noted the man's East Asian features: straight black hair, brown eyes, and pale skin. Khanfari thought he heard "rebel clans and student groups approaching the harbour" and "heavy iron chains", and he was positive he heard "Operation Prosperity Guardian" and "throw them overboard if coalition naval vessels attempt to intercept us."

"What the fuck are they saying, Jabir?" Hari growled.

"They are talking about throwing us overboard into the sea if they are intercepted by NATO vessels involved in Operation Prosperity Guardian."

"Fuck," Hari said. "I happen to know just how seriously the Americans and their allies are taking on the Houthi-led attacks on shipping lanes in the Red Sea. I believe there are thirteen members of the coalition currently involved in the ongoing operation...."

"*Allah yakhthek!,*" exclaimed Khanfari. "If any one of those vessels decides to intercept this ship we are in trouble." His chin sank forward onto his chest, and he began to tremble slightly.

The emaciated Somali, still in the passageway, could be heard talking about "the two Indian spies sent by the RAW," but what he said was lost in the wail of the harbour siren. The Korean naval officer raised his voice angrily, and switching to English, the international language of shipping, he said, "No, no. not with so many coalition vessels. I am officer in charge.... I am the one who decides.... the *Ji Shun* is under my command....in an hour.... sunrise....by cypher... use iron balls and throw them over...."

With a worried look on his face, his brow furrowed, the Somali interrogator returned to the compartment alone. "I have some bad news for you both," he announced in a flat voice. "This is most unfortunate; you are not to blame. You are merely collateral damage in the spill over in the fight against the genocide of the Palestinian people by the Jews. It appears that the American destroyer *USS Carney* wants to board the ship again for another inspection."

Half a dozen sailors barged into the room. Some were carrying chicken wire; others were holding lengths of chain. Another sailor was carrying lengths of rope. The Somali shook his head sadly. "Please believe me, Mr. Hari, it was never my intention that it should come to this," he said in a hollow voice. "I am sorry." He unhooked his sunglasses from his ears; his bulging dark eyes were dead. "You see Mr. Hari the ones we kidnap, we frighten them, but we always let them go in the end after the ransom is paid."

A sailor that Hari hadn't noticed before moved from out of the shadows and stepped forward, standing behind the Somali inquisitor. Clearly a professional military operative, the sailor's head and eyes were locked in a fixed forward position. His eyes and facial expression were blank.

Hari had started to shiver uncontrollably despite the stifling heat in the room. He actually stopped breathing for a very long moment before he felt the panic rising from the pit of his stomach.

From somewhere in the harbour came the crackle of rifle fire; it sounded like fireworks popping on New Year.

"Suleyman will now finish the task. I must leave you now, Mr. Hari. Again, I am sorry. Goodbye."

The sailor called Suleyman stepped forward and aimed his sidearm, a semi-automatic directly at Hari. Forever the reporter, Hari noticed it was an air rifle. The harsh spotlights caused tears to trickle from the corner of Hari's open eye. He closed his eyes. Hari's last thoughts were of Jago.

29

Muridke Madrassa, Punjab, Pakistan

The commander of Lashkar-e-Taiba, Muhammad Hafiz Saeed and his *bacha bazi* boys, were discovered asphyxiated inside a locked Hinopak truck. The vehicle was parked behind the madrassa on the edge of Muridke. The madrassa was the one where Saeed had been educated during his formative years. He was named Hafiz because he had memorized the Qur'an as a child. Muhammad Saeed was a founder member of the Pakistan-based Islamist militant group and was wanted by India for murdering one-hundred-and-sixty-eight people during the Mumbai bombing of 2008. One end of the industrial hose had been inserted into the exhaust pipe and sealed with industrial tape while the other end ran into the ventilation shaft under the hood. Members of the Pakistan Army Medical Corps who responded to the call from the imam smashed the windows with bricks and hammers, switched off the motor, dragged the bodies outside and administered oxygen, but it was too late. The sadistic paedophile Islamist warlord was dead. He had been deeply depressed by the recent exposure of his habitual pederasty, his passion for young boys. The Pakistani authorities concluded that the Sargodha-born leader of LeT was pushed over the edge when the imam of the Muridke madrassa banned him from entering the premises because of his addiction to *bacha bazi* boys. No suicide note was found, and forensic examination revealed no bruises on the corpses and no evidence to indicate there had been a struggle.

The media in India and Pakistan made much of the fact that Saeed was on the run from Taliban rule in Afghanistan where the practice of *bacha bazi* carries the death penalty. Saeed was wanted by the Taliban government for keeping boys in Kunduz Province, some as young as six-years-old, chained to a bed and raping them. The newspapers reported that Saeed paid a local Afghan police superintendent called Abdullah Rahman to find suitable *bacha bazi* boys for his pleasure. The papers in India produced a letter purportedly written by Saeed to his imam arguing that *bacha bazi* does not violate Islamic law because sharia does not forbid sex with boys, only men. In Pakistan, the deaths of Saeed and his dancing boys were listed as multiple suicides, and the case was closed.

30

The Research & Analysis Wing, Lodhi Road, New Delhi

The atmosphere in the corridors of the third floor of Lodhi Road was unusually subdued. Junior research officers and underlings milled around the *chai* and drinks dispensers, whispering in undertones. Something was happening. A crisis was looming. No one knew the exact details. An operation was in serious jeopardy. One of the Wing's agents was in trouble. The head of the Directorate General of Security, Anita "Golda" Kinnar, knew more than most. Massey, who had been woken at four in the morning by the night duty officer reading a HIGH ALERT from the communication officer onboard *INS Indira Gandhi*, brought key personnel for an early morning strategy meeting. The war council gathered in the ornate Longewala room. Leaning forward, Massey brought everyone up to date on the latest information: Hari Vandra, on a mission to Puntland in Somalia under deep cover, had failed to turn up at his hotel the previous evening. A discreet check of hospitals and the local police had drawn a blank. The National Intelligence and Security Agency which monitors all foreigners was saying nothing: yes, they were aware of an Indian delegation, representatives of the Indian Technical and Economic Cooperation Programme, but they had no record of anyone called Hari Vandra who had joined the ITEC delegation at the Al Ahmer hotel; no, they had no information on his whereabouts. Yes, they will check with immigration and passport control, and the port authorities; it went without saying they would investigate the matter and get back to the Indians if they found anything.

"Those dogs at NISA are lying through the skin of their teeth," Massey declared to his officers gathered around the table. "I think if Hari struck out on his own accord, he would let us know. Of that I'm certain. Before he joined the ITEC delegation he committed to memory the whereabouts of an Indian fishing trawler in Puntland for repairs. The skipper is a long-time cutout working for our West Asia desk. His boat is equipped with the necessary communication equipment. Also, we carefully worked out emergency exfiltration protocols to get him out of Puntland if his ITEC cover was threatened."

Forty-five minutes into the meeting Shivananda Menon, came on the speaker phone from the RAW language and training school in Gurgaon, to remind the meeting that the Somali NISA were owned by the Chinese Ministry of State Security. "We should remember the relationship," he counselled softly. "If the Chinese defecate, it's the NISA that flushes the toilet. Remember that Somalia signed a joint letter in 2019 to the United Nations Human Rights Council defending China's treatment of Uyghurs and other Muslim minority groups. Also, Somalia backed the Hong Kong national security law at the UN."

"This is not surprising," said the head of the East Africa Division. "Since 2007, the Chinese have taken over all oil and mineral exploration in the country. They recently trapped the Somalis with a loan of fifteen million dollars to buy large tracts of land. Classic Chinese salami-slicing moves."

The departmental heads brainstormed ideas for another hour. It was suggested that the Ministry of External Affairs, which is responsible for ITEC, file a formal complaint with the Somali embassy in Delhi, though no one held out any hope that this would result in anything worthwhile. A channel would be opened, via the trawler cutout, to determine if Hari has been taken by any networks known to him. The head of the Psychological Operations & Warfare Division suggested using Hari Vandra's social media platforms to let his followers know what had happened to him. "I think that's an excellent idea," said Golda from the end of the table. "Get a team together and begin a social media campaign immediately. Make it aggressive. Name names. Let's get the Pakis and Chinese on the backfoot. Contact the papers in Brighton and let them know Hari Vandra has been abducted while investigating Sir Ibrahim Ali's links to county lines drug dealing in Brighton schools. I believe Hari worked with the *New Brighton Argus* and the *Hove Herald*. Get in touch with them and give them something to write about. Get a campaign going. I want your best people working on this. Do it now."

Mya Noori, still junior enough in the presence of Massey to raise her hand when she wanted to say something, felt Massey's gaze lock onto her when she came up with the idea of putting Acharya on the case immediately; he could meet with his Mossad contacts and ask for help under the terms of the RAW-Mossad alliance. "If they've seized Hari Vandra," she said, "it's because they've penetrated his ITEC cover story. The problem at hand is how to bring him out alive and in one piece and destroy the monastery. Our Israeli friends have a lot of experience in these sorts of situations."

Sipping lukewarm tea from a cup, Massey nodded slowly. "I like the idea of the Israelis bringing their special skills into this scenario." Massey glanced at his watch. "Golda will have to contact Acharyaji. I have to brief the national security advisor. Good work, Ms Noori. I'll authorise this."

31

McGregor's Club, Safdarjung Road, New Delhi.

"I am hearing that you are the rising star in the Wing," Acharya murmured with a mischievous twinkle in his eye. "The Guru wishes to pass on his thanks, he says you were a delight to work with. Also, anytime you feel like a career change you are to call him first."

My Noori smiled. "Thank Guruji for his kind offer but please tell him I am happy at the Wing."

They were in McGregor's reviewing the targeted killings of the perpetrators. Local newspapers and news channels had reported mysterious deaths. Mya Noori brought Acharya up to speed on the latest: WION had reported two in Amritsar (the dead men, killed when their Toyota jeep malfunctioned and crashed into a wall, were Sikh extremists from northern Punjab hired by D-Company to smuggle explosives into Mumbai). Zee News had reported one in Peshawar (a senior officer, from the Joint Intelligence North, the department within Inter-Services Intelligence responsible for Kashmir & Jammu and the Northern Area, who had recruited the Afghan bomb-makers to make the fifty explosive charges used in the 1993 bombing, died when a kerosene-gas cooker exploded in his face resulting in his decapitation). ABP News had reported another one in Muzzaffarabad (an ISI officer who provided Tiger Memon, a leading member of D-Company, photographs of targets in Mumbai, including the Jewish Chabad, Merriman House) was knifed to death outside a homoeopathic remedy shop in a hectic *bazaar*. The man was stabbed thirty-eight times in the neck and chest. "Guruji clearly has not finished his work," remarked Mya Noori. "What is my next mission, Sir? I went to Golda, and she said I was to speak to you because I have been seconded to work for you until further notice. Is this correct?"

"Ahh yes, you have been seconded," Acharya said, "I want you back in England running your agent. Hassan, is it? The time has come for me to tell you something. There was one name that I deliberately left out from the hit list I gave to the Guru. We will deal with him ourselves."

"Can I ask...."

"Sir Ibrahim Ali," declared Acharya, looking directly at Mya Noori. "I have read all your reports and I agree with your conclusions. Ibrahim Ali represents a clear and present threat to India. Make your preparations to leave for London. I will send you instructions in due course. Now I have to leave you," said the wily spymaster, "I have a meeting with an old friend from Tel Aviv."

32

Mossad safe house, Karol Bagh, New Delhi

The veteran Mossad liaison officer in Delhi was waiting for Acharya in the discreet safe house they used for such purposes. The two men knew each other well. In 1977 Prime Minister Indira Gandhi ordered the RAW to formulate a working relationship with Israeli intelligence. Mrs. Gandhi wanted Mossad's expertise as a countermeasure to the military links between Pakistan, North Korea, and China. The task was assigned to Acharya who travelled to Tel Aviv and convinced the then director of Mossad, Yitzhak Hofi, that Pakistani army officers were training Iranians, Libyans, and the Alliance of Palestinian Forces in handling Chinese and North Korean military equipment.

Known as Gideon in the corridors of Lodhi Road, he sported an unkept beard and sideburns and wore spectacles with jam-jar thick lenses that magnified his already bulging eyes. He dressed in his usual uniform of a sleeveless cream-coloured shirt, flannel trousers, and brothel-creeper sandals. He was never seen without his gunmetal grey fedora. "You have caught me at a very distressing time, my dear friend," Gideon confided once after embracing Acharya.

"I would be surprised if you were not distressed, Gideon," Acharya said softly. "Israel is facing its greatest challenge since the Yom Kippur War fifty years earlier."

"The world is reminding me why I live by the biblical commandment: an eye for an eye. Hamas and its Iranian paymasters must be stopped. There has never been a time where the law of exact retaliation and reciprocal justice applies." Gideon stopped talking as a young woman came in carrying a tray with chilled lychee juice. Without a word, she cleared a space on Gideon's desk, set down the tray and disappeared.

"You know that you can count on our support, Gideon. Israel has supported us in every war and conflict since Independence. Lodhi Road is with you all the way my friend."

"Thank you, Acharyaji," Gideon said. "I'm in contact with the head of the West Asia Division at Lodhi Road. Like you, she's someone I can do business with. We will be meeting in the next few days to go over my shopping list of requirements. She is a very sound lady who remembers Israel's assistance to India during the Kargil War. Now, to business, to what do I owe the pleasure of your visit?"

"I'm running an operation in Somalia. The Wing got wind of the Pakistanis and Chinese storing large quantities of weapons in a Coptic monastery somewhere in the Puntland region. These weapons are destined for distribution to various insurgent groups operating in Kashmir and the Red Corridor. The Pakistanis have hired a gang of Somali and Houthi pirates to protect the place. We've had no assets in Somalia since the civil war, so I recruited a journalist and sent him in to make contact with a former member of the pirate gang to see if he will disclose the whereabouts of the monastery."

"So, what's the problem?"

"The Wing has been tracking him from the moment he landed in Puntland. We know he made contact with the ex-pirate, a fellow called Lazarus. But shortly after the meeting we lost contact with our boy," admitted Acharya.

"It's part of the territory, my friend. You of all people know this," said Gideon with sadness in his voice. "Everyone I know has walked through fire. As you know, my son is missing all his fingernails on both hands; they were ripped out by a Hezbollah commander in Lebanon when he refused to reveal the whereabouts of his unit. What are you asking of me, Acharyaji?"

"I have no contacts or assets in Somalia that I can use. So, I'm asking you if you have anyone that I can use to locate our boy?"

After many minutes of silence Gideon said softly, "I don't think I can help………"

Acharya interrupted his friend. "There's a few more things I need to tell you, Gideon, before you answer. The boy in question is Robbie's godson, Hari Vandra. And the second thing is that we have conclusive evidence that the Chinese and Pakistanis have been storing biological weapons in the monastery." Acharya let those words sink in.

Gideon sat motionless for many minutes in silence. The everyday noises of Delhi life sounded deafening.

"Pakistan is one of the most anti-Semitic countries I know of. The retired generals running everything would be overjoyed to see Israel wiped off the face of the earth." Gideon still remembered how Pakistan included Nariman House, a Jewish outreach centre, in its November 2008 Mumbai attacks. He saw photos of how the Pakistanis had butchered Gavriel Holtzberg and his pregnant wife, Rivka. Thanks to the bravery of the couple's nanny and caretaker, Sandra Samuel, their two-year-old son, Moshe, escaped death.

"Yes, old friend," replied Acharya. "On this, we stand united."

"No doubt you have a file for me to read."

Silently Acharya slid a thin blue folder across the table. "Thank you, Gideon; I will see myself out."

"Leave this with me. I will need to make some calls to Tel Aviv. Stay beside your phone, Acharyaji."

"Thank you, Gideon. If Pakistan is willing to use biological weapons against India, it won't be that long before those dirty bombs are in the hands of Hamas and Hezbollah. I will see myself out."

Gideon sat motionless for many minutes. He picked up the phone, "Ruth, book me a flight on El Al, please. Yes, today."

33

Eyl, Puntland

Slowly Hari recognised the voice of one of the interrogators; the one called Suleyman. "Relax Mr Vandra, I'm not going to hurt you. As you will have noticed you are handcuffed to the tuck, but you are not hurt. I simply knocked you out using a tranquiliser dart to sedate you for a while. I used a mixture of etorphine and ketamine to do the job. The groggy feeling will wear off soon. We are not all savages. I am taking you to see Salim." Honking nonstop at bicycles and donkey carts and men pulling wheelbarrows filled with fresh produce, the driver turned in a western direction. They passed an ancient China Motor Bus, its red faded to a washed-out pink, the original signage still visible above the front window, and several Kowloon trucks whose bodies had been repaired a few too many times. Hari noticed that nearly every vehicle was of Chinese origin. "Africa is where China dumps all its unwanted and surplus goods," Suleyman said as if reading his mind. At a signal from Suleyman, the driver pulled up on the road. Suleyman got out of the truck and pointed towards a telegraph pole in the distance.

"With American help, the third Somali president Siad Barre massacred thousands of herdsmen near here in 1978," he remarked. "I apologise for the handcuffs, but my instructions are clear. That you be kept secure but comfortable. My boss simply said that you were a valuable commodity. This is the reason why you are still alive."

"It was a volatile time in world affairs," Hari noted cautiously, "the return of Ayatollah Khomeini to Iran was being planned in Paris, students were preparing to seize the Grand Mosque of Mecca, the battle plan of the Afghan War was being drawn up by the Soviet Union, and the Egypt-Israel peace treaty was being negotiated. The Cold War was in full swing." He was puzzled by Suleyman's attitude towards him. It had changed since the interrogation. But what? He tried to reason things out all the questions buzzing inside his brain, but his head ached too much. "How long was I out for?"

"I was at a United Nations school at the time," Suleyman said, ignoring Hari's question. "I remember my father coming back from work looking as if he'd seen a ghost. When my mother asked him what had happened, my father said he had heard Barre's soldiers had murdered a group of unarmed herdsmen belonging to the clans." He explained how during the 1970's the *Duub Cas* and a unit of the secret police called Victory Pioneers carried out systematic genocide against the Majeerteen, Hawiye and Isaaq clans. Barre's soldiers systematically poisoned water reserves to deny water to the tribesmen and their herds. More than 2,000 Majeerteen died of thirst and an estimated 5,000 Isaaq were killed by starvation. "More than 300,000 Hawiye fled to Ethiopia. Somalia is a sinkhole where armed infants with long memories set out to right wrongs done to the great-grandfathers of their grandfathers," said Suleyman. "What are your first impressions of my country?"

Hari chose his words carefully. "I think places like Somalia and Gaza, Lebanon, and Iraq have a long way to go, and that the world should stop looking for quick fix political solutions to long-term human problems."

"Somalia is a can of insidious worms," Suleyman said looking towards the brown hills. "It's a place where you can trade a Miss World calendar for a twenty-five-year-old bottle of American bourbon, and get your throat slit by a teenage jihadi if you're caught with your feet pointing towards Mecca. Actually, there are lots of wars going on around here: ethnic wars, clan wars, tribal wars, drug wars, religious wars, Hamas versus Fatah, the Houthi movement, the Shi'ites versus the Sunnis, the Iranians versus the Israelis, the Chinese versus the Americans."

"You left out the last but not least." "The piracy in the Red Sea – and the rest of the world."

"There's that war too, though sometimes it gets lost in the shuffle. Look, the truth of the matter is that the world only vaguely understands what's going on here and, more often than not ends up backing the wrong side. They don't know because no one wants to know about Somalia and this part of the world because its medieval. Our story is a tragic one. The monastery is over there", he said pointing towards a cluster of brown hills. "Around twenty or so kilometres down there- Darius's Persians, Alexander's Macedonians, Tamberlane's Tartars, Babur's Moguls all came through here."

"Now it's my turn," Hari said shielding his eyes from the sunlight. "Aren't I the lucky one."

The monastery was nothing like Hari imagined. All he could see was a mass of make-shift buildings and shack-like stalls stacked to boxes and sandbags. It was more like a guerrilla camp. Skinny black youths wearing baseball caps and dirty English football shirts were busy unloading sacks of provisions. Everything was covered in fine sand. Wherever Hari looked there was evidence of the civil war and human suffering: bony black men with missing limbs hobbled on wooden crutches, an old turbaned man was sitting on a crate with his right arm in a sling, a pregnant teenage girl suffering from burn marks and blisters was lying in a foetal position close by. Next to her on a straw mat, a tall Somali youth was sewing his battle fatigues, cartridge belts and black combat boots. Three mules loaded with boxes were tied to a fence near a trough filled with muddy water.

Suleyman signalled for the driver to pull up near a wooden post. He and Hari crossed over to where a group of men had gathered in a small shack with a sign over the door that read, in English: "Best Tetley Tea." Inside, a small boy squatted before a chimney and worked the bellows, heating the kettles above the wood-and-dung fire.

"Welcome to the monastery Hari," said Suleyman. "Now I want to introduce you to Salim."

34

Gwadar Port City, Balochistan, Pakistan

Kai Ling had finally stormed out of his office to escape the sound of the telephone in his office that never stopped ringing. His most important agent in Europe, Sir Ibrahim Ali, called from Marbella to complain about the delays in shipments of the precursors needed to manufacturer the crystal meth. "The Irish are not happy," he complained bitterly, "they say they are running low on acetic anhydride. The Italians are also pissed off. The Ndrangheta are starting to make nasty threats. I need to reassure them all or else they will turn up in Marbella." Ibrahim Ali also reported that the *New Brighton Argus* newspaper was calling him about a missing investigative reporter called Hari Vandra. What should he do? Was it true, deputy minister Tang Yiku wanted to know, that the Indians had succeeded in locating the Coptic monastery? He was calling from the Ministry of State Security headquarters in the Yidongyuan compound in Beijing and sounded agitated. And frightened. Was there any danger of the monastery being traced back to Beijing? The Eight Elders needed to know, the deputy minister insisted, how this matter was being managed. Was there any truth to the rumours circulating in the social media that a British journalist named Hari Vandra had been abducted in Puntland? Was this true? If so, who authorised this? When was he to expect a full report of the Puntland operation? The man sounded hysterical. He had every reason to be worried. Deputy minister Tang Yiku was a minion of one of the Eight Elders, the uncle of a member of the 20th Politburo Standing Committee of the Chinese Communist Party. The Elder was a man with a reputation for making those who disappoint him disappear suddenly and permanently.

Stamping out his Burmese cigar on the gravel, Kai Ling made his way towards the path leading towards the forest. From beyond the trees came the distinctive calling sound of a Houbara bustard. He luxuriated in the smell of the salty sea and breathed deeply. Gazing out over the trees, he thought of his beloved father and how he hated the soft bureaucrats of Beijing. Like his father he loathed weak, feminine men like Yiku. If everything had gone according to the plan, the weapons, including the biological devices, would be ready to be shipped out of Puntland, into the Bay of Bengal and through to India via the Chittagong Port. The sea route had been meticulously planned: Ely in Puntland, the Gulf of Aden, the Arabian Sea, the Hambantota International Port in Sri Lanka where his people will bunker the ship. The Sri Lankan port was owned by China. It was Kai Ling who arranged the negotiations for its ninety-nine-year lease to China Merchant Ports. After bunkering in Sri Lanka, the vessel would sail into the Bay of Bengal and into Chittagong Port in Bangladesh. His people in Bangladesh had already confirmed the gangs of smugglers were ready to transport the goods into northeast India using the ancient smuggling routes that predate the arrival of the British to the subcontinent. To ensure safe transit of the cargo, Kai Ling had arranged security cover from the Bangladeshi terrorist group, the Jamaat-ul-Mujahideen.

Breathing deeply and walking slowly, Kai Ling gently put aside Deputy Minister Yiku. The man was insignificant. What he was orchestrating, using the Compact, was the destruction of India's Research & Analysis Wing by poisoning it from inside Lodhi Road. He was continuing his beloved father's work in removing India as the only significant obstacle to Beijing's total domination of Asia.

The initial stages of the complex planning were to subjugate the Pakistanis. This was achieved through the Compact Accord and the China-Pakistan Economic Corridor. His father had designated the Inter-Services Intelligence agency in Islamabad to be the instrumental part of the Compact. Working slowly and diligently, Kai Ling now controlled the three most important divisions of the ISI responsible for India: the Joint Intelligence Bureau, the Joint Signals Intelligence Bureau, and, crucially, the Joint Counter-Intelligence Bureau. As well as arming insurgents in Northeast India these divisions are responsible for training Kashmiri separatists, Khalistan narcotraffickers, the Houthi rebels in Yemen and Somalia in using Chinese weaponry. Pakistan was very much in Beijing's pocket.

The supply of weaponry and finance to the separatists, jihadists, and militants operating in India always requires critical timing. It's all about the timing, instructed his father. Absolutely nothing must prevent the bioweapons from reaching the Red Corridor. The Balkanization of India was his father's ultimate goal in South Asia. He will finish what his father started. To achieve this his father created what he called his Partition spies to act as instruments of sabotage. His most prized informer in India was agent QIPIAN and his flock of beautiful carrier pigeons. QIPIAN was his eyes and ears inside Lodhi Road. From Kai Ling's point of view, all other informants are expendable. QIPIAN was not. He was to be protected at all costs. He was close to his divisional chief and had access to other senior people in the RAW, and he continued to deliver gold nuggets. But Kai Ling knew from his meticulous study of his profession, learning from the KGB files on how they ran the Cambridge Five during the Cold War that this cat-and-mouse game frayed the nerves of even the toughest agents. He was convinced the shrewd Acharya Bhairava who had been called out of retirement would pick up the tremors of a mole inside Lodhi Road soon enough. It was simply a waiting game.

Kai Ling was playing a subtle version of the *surrounding game* he learned from his father. The new generation of recruits in Lodhi

Road had been weaned on the legendary exploits of Acharya. The legendary spymaster was studied by recruits at the RAW training and language school in Gurgaon. Because of the mystic monk, Pakistan's professional army had never won a war and in 1971 lost half of its land. Though long retired, Acharya was at the heart of Lodhi Road. He was privy to all major operations. Kai Ling had been meticulously studying Acharya after his father's murder onboard Zia's plane in 1988 along with the American ambassador. Kai Ling had watched him from a distance when Acharya was appointed number two at the Directorate General of Security. He had pored over reports on this former Hindu monk from his agents posted throughout South Asia. He conceded that Acharya was a lethal opponent and understood why his father admired him. However, he had a weak spot – his lifelong friendship with the English paederast, the aristocratic Sir Robert Gage. Using the Englishman's godson, Hari Vandra, as a gofer in Somalia was a serious mistake. Kai Ling instantly recognised this fact when he received the carrier pigeon message sent by agent QUINPIN. He would destroy Sir Robert by taking Hari Vandra in Somalia. The Englishman had spent a lifetime as the British SIS representative in South Asia. The wear and tear on his nerves and his mind was apparent. He put on a brave face in public but after four decades in the field, he was dulled by alcohol and grief for the Indian catamite lover executed by General Zia ul-Haq on his father's orders. His father had ordered the torture and execution be filmed and the recording posted to the Englishman at the British embassy in Delhi. "We destroy them slowly from the inside," his father had always instructed.

By capturing Hari Vandra, Kai Ling would slowly push Sir Robert over the edge into paranoia and alcohol-induced psychosis. The military psychiatrists in Beijing had assured him of this. Paranoia would spread inside his mind, infecting him. He will suspect everyone in Lodhi Road, especially Acharya and that brilliant eunuch bitch, Anita "Golda" Kinnar, who had sent Hari to his death. Acharya Bhairava was the target for Kai Ling. Acharya was the man who murdered his beloved father. By using the old English paederast and his homosexual godson he would break Acharya. At which point there would be nothing standing in the way of TUPAC II, Kai Ling's complex and long-term operation to break India's back and take them back to the Stone Age.

If Kai Ling orchestrated this carefully, the paranoid alcoholic Englishman will start chasing shadows within India's clandestine services, causing suspicion and mistrust between Delhi and her QUAD partners. It will cause distrust between the intelligence services of India and her allies. The CIA, the SIS, the Mossad, and the French DGSE will refuse to share information with Lodhi Road as they did during the tenure of Ashok Chaturvedi, the alcoholic chief of the RAW between 2007 and 2009. Periodically Kai Ling would drop an informer or jihadist 'informer' in Delhi, Langley, Tokyo, or Canberra to feed the paranoid narrative he is scripting for them. The military-intelligence alliance between India, the USA, Japan, and Australia will be jeopardised. The threat to Beijing from the Quadrilateral Security Dialogue will be neutralised.

Now, what to do with Mr. Hari Vandra?

A warm, salty breeze drifted in from the sea. Kai Ling savoured the moment before turning back towards his study and the phones. As he walked, he recalled the words of Sun Tzu, "Don't flail against the world, use it. Flexibility is the operative principle in the art of war." It was going to be a long war. He will continue to honour his father. From his study Kai Ling dialled a number in Marbella. Sir Ibrahim Ali answered on the third ring. "Master Kai Ling…….."

35

The Coptic monastery, Eyl, Puntland

They climbed the narrow wooden steps to the private room on the second floor. Salim, a muscular black man around Hari's age with broad shoulders, rose off a rush mat to greet Suleyman. His eyes were glazed and red from chewing *khat*. "Suleyman, my brother's brother," he said hugging him warmly and drawing him into the room. "*Assalamu alaikum.*"

For a split-second Hari froze on the spot as he recognised Salim from the *hammam* on his first day. He recalled Yusuf saying to him, "They say he's a pirate."

Suleyman saluted in Somali and then switched to English so Hari could follow the conversation. "Salim my brother, this is the British journalist I was telling you about, the one who will write about our coastguards. The Chinese and Iranians want him to be treated well. He is a man of respect," he said. Salim understood. It was clear to all that Suleyman outranked Salim. He nodded once at Hari, pausing to take in the unusual colour of Hari's eyes, but did not offer to shake his hand. Hari couldn't tell if Salim recognised him. As the visitors settled cross-legged onto the rugs, a teenage boy shyly approached and filled two tin cups with strong Qahwa coffee.

They talked business for a quarter of an hour – Salim brought Suleyman up to date on what was happening in the Red Sea shipping lanes. "We have recruited over fifty fighting-age men from the UN camps. The army instructors sent by Pakistan are working well in turning our boys into warriors. Also, tell our Chinese and Iranian brothers that I have two boats out scouting," he said. He described a daring attack he had led against an Indian fishing vessel called *The Malabar Goddess* in which the vessel and crew were taken. "There are six Indian fishermen in the basement below," he reported to Suleyman. "Let our brothers know that we did this under the interfering noses of the foreign navies in our water."

"Are any of the fishermen hurt? Have they been given food and water?" asked Suleyman. "The clan elders do not want Indian nationals harmed. We have discussed this before."

"Peace brother! Peace!" said Salim in mock horror. "The Indians who are busy poaching our fish are being well looked after", he said adding. "We are doing our best with what we have – which is not much."

"What supplies do we need, Salim?" Suleyman said. "Our friends, particularly the Iranians and the clan leaders won't have hostages being ill-treated. That defeats the object." Hari detected tension between the two men. Suleyman clearly had no respect for Salim.

Throwing up a palm in defeat, Salim pulled a scrap of paper from the pockets of his pants. "Medical supplies, especially painkillers and antibiotics. Artificial limbs."

Suleyman stood up and headed towards the door. "I'll speak to our Chinese and Iranian brothers and do what I can," he said. "In the meantime, Salim show our guest around the camp. As I said, the Chinese and Iranians want our British friend to be safe; you will see to it that he is treated well." Turning towards Hari, he said, "I have some errands to run but I will return soon. In the meantime, you will remain here."

Salim rose gracefully to his feet. "I, too, will do what I can, brother dear." He threw an arm around Hari's shoulder and steered him towards the window. "Welcome to Puntland, brother Hari," he said loudly. "I look forward to reading what you write about us. I understand you have a big following on social media. We, too, use social media to tell the world about our cause."

Salim turned to Hari and regarded him with a cheerless half-smile. "My brother Lazarus is a good and kind man," he said mesmerised by the reporter's green eyes. "Somalia has a habit of destroying good kind men." The half-smile brightened into a full-blown smile; small lines fanned out from the corners of his dark eyes. "Did you enjoy yourself watching me at play in the *hammam*?" asked Salim with a lecherous grin. "You should have joined us. There was plenty for both you and your friend."

Hari laughed. "It was fun, another time perhaps. Suleyman tells me you used to be a soldier," he said changing the subject quickly.

"I still am," said Salim proudly. "I served with one of the best regiments in all Africa."

"What made you leave the army?" asked Hari.

Salim paused for a long time before replying. "I left in 1991 after the warlords overthrew my boss, Said Barre, and headed back home to Puntland."

"And now you're also a Somali coastguard," said Hari.

Salim regarded quizzically. "My brother Lazarus is a good man, but he is weak and does not want to take any real risks," he said. "He does not realise that what we have got ourselves involved in will attract retaliation from the shipping companies. Already ship owners are hiring security companies with high-tech American and European military hardware to safeguard the boats and crew," he said chewing thoughtfully. "And now we have the added problem of America and her allies firing cruise missiles at us in the stupid belief that they will stop the Houthi movement. Operation Prosperity Guardian will fail. The people of the West will see it as another American-British attack on Muslims and Arabs. The BBC was reporting the other day that pro-Palestinian protesters in central London were expressing support for the Houthis. It seems everyone was chanting anti-American slogans hours after the USA and Britain launched missile and airstrikes on ground targets in Yemen."

"So, if you're not a coastguard what are you, Salim?" Hari asked.

Salim laughed. "You Europeans! Always wanting to put labels on things," he said. "I suppose I'm a hired gun, a mercenary, a soldier of fortune. Our brothers in this jihad – the Chinese, Iranians, North Koreans, and of course, the Pakistanis - leave the actual planning and execution of the hijackings to me while they do other things."

It was starting to get dark outside. In one corner of the camp, a roaring fire was being built and a group of men had gathered for tea. In the distance, Hari could see a large group of young men approaching purposefully towards the camp. "They are the new batch of Houthi boys sent to guard the monastery. Do not worry my British friend, we are well protected," Salim said as he draped an arm around Hari's shoulders. "These boys have been trained by the best Pakistani, Iranian, and North Korean military instructors. You are safe here."

Salim, walking slowly and deliberately, led Hari down a wooden staircase that opened into an ancient sunken stone basement. "You will be locked in your cell while I attend to my men. I am also expecting an Iranian VAJA delegation sometime today," he said. "After which our journey will start." The monastery turned out to be a complex of buildings comprising domestic quarters and workplaces of long-dead monastics. Inside what used to be the chapel, fires blazed in soot-blackened chimneys. Islamic scrolls and calendars depicting Mecca and the Al-Aqsa Mosque in Jerusalem were glued next to a hastily made *mihrab* – the niche that tells the faithful the direction of Mecca. An entire section of the building had been cordoned off with clear plastic. Hari could see men wearing white CBRN defence clothing and NBC suits. "What's going on in there?"

"In there my British friend," Salim said, pausing to watch the activity inside, "we continue the good work of the great Ali Hassan al-Majid. Your Western journalists called him Chemical Ali. Have you heard of him?"

In fact, Hari did know about Chemical Ali. A first cousin of Iraq's Saddam Hussein, he served as Secretary General of the Ba'ath Party during the eight-year-long Iran-Iraq War starting in 1980. During the Al-Anfal Campaign, Saddam Hussein put him in charge of orchestrating the military and intelligence operations against the Kurdish people. "I know he got his name because of his use of mustard gas, sarin, tabun, and VX against the Kurdish people," Hari said grimly, "if memory serves, I think he was responsible for killing over fifteen thousand people."

Salim, a moody man who could explode in rage if he thought Islam was being mocked, snarled, "They were not people. They are dogs. Kurdish dogs. Unbelievers. Defilers of the faith."

Salim started down a wooden staircase. Under his feet, the raw planks of wood creaked. Rats were scurrying everywhere. They made their way across an ancient stone floor of what looked like a vast storage room filled with large crates. "This is one of the storage depots," said Salim.

"What do you store in here?"

He fixed his dark brooding eyes on Hari. It was a look of pure malevolence. "I will tell you only because I will slaughter you before dear brother Suleyman gets back. I like to slaughter an infidel for the benefit of my boys because it wins me respect. In this part of the world, we place much importance on respect. I am sure you understand this, Mr. Hari. Fear not, my British friend, it will be quite painless. I use the same method of throat slitting as the famous

Mohammed Emwazi. A fellow Brit, although you probably know him as Jihadi John," Salim explained softly. "Jihadi John is the type of British export we like in these parts. An excellent product of modern Britain. The Iranians and Chinese tell me this." He walked to a crate and opened the lid. He nodded to Hari. "This is what we store down here." Packed between layers of straw were rifles complete with folded spiked bayonets and milled receivers. "These are Type 56 rifles, a Chinese variation of the Soviet AK-47. Our friends in Beijing always deliver." He walked across to another crate and opened the lid. "These crates will be of interest to you. They tell me you are a famous crime reporter. They are destined for Southampton in your England." Salim pulled out a large plastic bag containing what looked like small shards of glass. "Crystal methamphetamine. This batch is a gift from the Cantonese Chinese syndicate, Sam Gor. The syndicate also supplies us with fentanyl. Our Chinese brothers are generous when it comes to such matters. We have a ship docked in Puntland harbour ready to take the product to Southampton."

Sir Ibrahim Ali.

"What's in there?" asked Hari pointing to a sealed section of the basement guarded by armed militiamen.

"We cannot go in there," said Salim, spitting out a wad of *khat*. "It is restricted and only lab technicians are allowed entry. Besides, I would not want to go there. It is where they make the Chemical Ali bombs. That's what my men call them; it's their little joke."

"Is that what you people are doing? Making chemical weapons like those used in the Iraq-Iran war?" Hari was desperate to keep Salim talking. By now the Wing should know his location and they would have sent a recon team to scout the area. He knew a team of special forces were onboard one of the Indian naval vessels, though he hadn't been told which one. Focusing on Salim, he tried to calm his mind and memorise as much as possible for his story.

"These weapons are not chemical. They are bombs filled with germs," Salim said in a matter-of-fact manner. "The Jews are particular experts in the use of bioweapons. You should make a note of that, my friend. You should let your readers and all your social media followers know that during the 1948 Palestine War, Jews from the Israeli Hagenah contaminated the water supply in the city of Acre. The Jews used Salmonella typhi bacteria to cause an outbreak of typhoid. I was told this by one of the Pakistani scientists working here."

"How many Pakistani scient...."

"And that is not all," intoned Salim. He seemed to be in a world of his own. "The Hagenah militiamen were captured by the Egyptian army in Gaza carrying these germs to poison water wells."

Hari said, "I'm assuming these germ bombs have been made for Hamas or Hezbollah to be used against the Israelis?"

"That is exactly what I thought. Germ warfare is what Hamas must use against the Jews. Only then will the Holy Land be free." Salim snorted bitterly. "But I was mistaken. They tell me the containers that you see over there are destined for India, a place called the Red Corridor." Salim turned away and walked towards the sealed-off section to hold a hurried conference with the armed guards. "We must go to your cell now where I will lock you in. The Iranians will soon arrive. They have important news for us."

As the door to his cell was slammed shut, Hari was suddenly paralysed with fear. Cold fear. He suddenly remembered something. He had forgotten to remove the amulet around his neck despite Acharya's strict instructions that it should be kept away from steamy places. *What if the RAW wasn't tracking him? What if the bloody transmitter around his neck had malfunctioned and wasn't transmitting? He was fucked.*

36

INS Indira Gandhi, **Gulf of Aden**

The communication officer onboard *INS Indira Gandhi*, India's formidable fifth *Talwar*-class frigate commissioned by the navy in 2019, became aware of the flashing light on the portable console. The vessel was fitted with advanced panoramic sonar sensors and advanced weaponry including BraMos supersonic cruise missiles, one of the world's fastest cruise missiles. I may even get to see one fired thought the young officer. The portable console however was not a part of the ship's system. It was bought onboard by the commandos who joined the ship in Oman. The commandos were soldiers of the Special Frontier Force, also known as *Establishment 22*. "I saw the beret," he had boasted to his bunkmate.

The regimental insignia was designed by a decorated Sikh soldier who had commanded the 22nd Mountain Regiment of the Royal Indian Artillery during World War II, Major General Sujan Singh Uban, the regiment's first Inspector General of the SFF. Uban wanted the distinctive insignia of the Tibetan Snow Lion on top of two crossed swords to remind each commando of their illustrious heritage going back to the *Chushi Gangdruk*, the CIA Tibetan Program of 1951, the Tibetan Rebellion of 1959, and their absolute allegiance to the 14th Dalai Lama and his successors. Composed primarily of Tibetan refugees and Gurkhas, the SFF was raised by Nehru's spymaster after the 1962 war with China. Based at Chakrata Barracks, the force is under the direct supervision of the Directorate General of Security, which was currently headed by Anita "Golda" Kinnar, in Lodhi Road.

Like everyone else, the young naval officer was awed by the presence of the SFF commandos. Everyone knew if the Tibetans and

Gurkhas were onboard, the crew was going to see some serious firepower very soon. The counterterrorism task was given to the Special Frontier Force in 1977 by the RAW founder-director Rameshwar Nath Kao when he deployed six hundred Tibetan and Ghurkha commandos to Sarsawa Air Force Station, the former Soviet Union, and then Israel for specialist military training. Because the Tibetans and Nepalese were foreigners and therefore did not have a direct stake in Indian communal politics, they were seen by Kao and the Wing as an ideal, objective counterterrorist unit. Throughout its history, the regiment has fought in every war including the Indo-Pakistan War of 1971, the Kargil War in 1999, and all China-India border conflicts that began in May 2020.

The communications officer logged the details which were relayed back to Delhi in real time. Captain Sharma's instruction had been specific: he was to be notified when they had locked on to the monastery target. The comms officer, who had trained at the Indian naval bases in Visakhapatnam and Kolkata, had not been told who they were tracking. He had no need to know. Looking at the monitor he could see the target was positioned just outside the town of Ely. He straightened up and patted down his uniform.

The SFF commandos had come onboard the ship three days ago and spent hours training on deck. The captain was holed up for hours with his senior officers. There was an immediate change in the mood of the crew as the ship moved out of Port Salah in Oman. Seventeen hours earlier Captain Sharma briefed his senior officers on their mission and objectives. "We have been ordered to take part in an anti-piracy operation in Puntland. Our task will be to provide logistical support in rescuing Indian hostages held captive by Somali pirates in the port town of Ely," he said to the assembled men and women. He then spent the next two hours explaining the details of Operation FLUENCY.

As the captain to his men talked inside the warship the SFF commandos were taking advantage of calm waters to do outdoor exercises, a punishing regime of cardiovascular workouts and stretches. They regularly trained with the Israeli special forces known as Commando Unit 101 and the Russian *Spetsnaz*. Many SFF officers train at the "Swick" in Fort Liberty in North Carolina. In their early twenties and at the peak of physical and mental fitness aspiring candidates for the SFF selection board at Chakrata barracks are faced with a four-kilometre run which must be completed in fifteen minutes; a five-kilometre ski course in twenty-six minutes, a six-metre hand-over-hand rope climb and a fifteen-obstacle assault course which had to be completed within five minutes. These are the only basic physical requirements. On operations, the Tibetan and Gurkha recruit will be expected to travel long distances under Arctic conditions, walking or skiing more than thirty miles a day and swimming across icy rivers and frozen swamps carrying a 100lb load of personal kit.

"Ready to go hunting?" said the SFF team leader to one of his men, Kotex, a seasoned soldier, and the team's medic. The team leader was respected, even lionised by his men. A highly trained and experienced Tibetan from Dharamshala in the state of Himachal Pradesh. His home was known as *Little Lhasa* on account of the Tibetan government-in-exile being headquartered there. His father was a diplomat who spent much of his time in the Netherlands representing the Tibetan government at the Unrepresented Nations and Peoples Organisation in the Hague. His mother was a senior official working in the Tibet Fund which was based in New York.

"All the men are ready," said Kotex staring intently at the barren Puntland hills. "And the pilots, also."

37

Inside the monastery, Eyl, Puntland

Alone in the cold cell, Hari went over to the tiny ventilation shaft. It was covered with a strong wire mesh. On closer examination he discovered it was the same high tensile steel reinforcement mesh sheets the Five Aces used in Blayney Parke. Standing on his toes he could make out a group of men across the courtyard. Walking in twos and threes, a long line of young Houthi teenagers, some holding rifles or machetes, followed behind. The group disappeared behind a large rectangular building. Hari tried the door, but it was heavy and reinforced with iron and refused to move. He decided to concentrate on the ventilation shaft. Lacing his fingers through the mesh he pulled but it was cemented into the bricks.

    Stay calm. Breathe. That's what Stax and the Five Aces would say. *Breathe*. Hari sat on the floor and minutely inspected his surroundings after allowing his eyes to adjust to the low light. It was clear he was in a former monastic cell. The small room was probably used by a monk or anchorite to live and use as a devotional space. The entire cell was constructed from stone. Hari's eyes registered movement in the corner of the cell. It was an African rat. "Hello, little fellow." Watching his cellmate, Hari spotted a glint of metal. It was a short length of what had been a carpenter's hacksaw. He picked it up to inspect it and found it was rust-free and fine-toothed. He recognised the saw was nickel alloy-brazed with diamond particles; the type that Skeezy and Squeaky used in the Parke's Hip Hop Garage Workshop. Hari wasted no time. Using a stone as a step he worked the blade through the outer edges of the wire mesh. He slipped his footing, and the sharp ends of the grille tore his skin drawing blood, but Hari felt no pain. The adrenaline being pumped into his bloodstream prevented him from feeling anything. When he sawed off three sides of the mesh, he pulled and bent the grille out. Finding a niche in the wall he hiked himself up to the windowsill and wriggled his body through the small aperture. He landed softly on the ground below. As he prepared to get up, he heard someone scream an alarm. Many feet clamoured around the courtyard and outside the rectangular building as the Somalis and Houthis raced out to where Hari was pinned down to the ground.

He heard Salim's unmistakable voice, "Did you think for one minute, I would leave you untethered? Now you will have the pleasure of experiencing how I use pain to extract information using all the special skills I picked up in the Chinese camps and Iranian prisons."

"Fuck you," Hari said, "and fuck your mother too."

38

Outskirts of Eyl, Puntland

The Pave Hawk helicopter streaked across the calm moonlit waters of the Gulf of Aden. Up ahead loomed the edge of Puntland. The Galgala Hills were clearly visible. The communications officer onboard had locked onto the exact coordination from the transmitter carried by the RAW agent in the monastery. Kotex and his team had moved to the side doors of the chopper, two men to each side, their feet dangling over the edge, each man clipped to a safety harness in the event the helicopter had to make a drastic, evasive manoeuvre. The commandos were all wearing night vision goggles, giving their eyes plenty of time to adjust. In addition, Kotex was plugged into an in-flight headset so he could communicate with the pilots. As he peered out the port door he listened to the chatter. The pilots were reporting four contacts on the FLIR moving toward the target area from the east. They were right on time.

To mask their insertion the Wing had asked that choppers from *INS Tabar*, *INS Satpura*, and *INS Brahmaputra* as well as *INS Indira Gandhi* to make overflights of the area while they were being inserted. The big CH-53 Sea Stallions would also fly just south of the area while the Pav Hawk comes in from the north under a small ridge line. No one was worried about radar detection because they would be flying too low. In any case, Somalia had no radars. The calm water vanished from beneath them and was replaced by a light sandy beach and then the dusty terrain of Puntland. Kotex looked straight down, peering over the toes of his boots. They were so low he felt as if he could reach down and scoop up some sand. The helicopter began to climb as they worked their way up a ravine using their terrain-avoidance, terrain-following radar to hug the contours of the landscape. The pilot calmly called out one minute to insertion as he weaved to the left and then back to the right as if it were meandering its way uphill.

Kotex tugged on his leather gloves to make sure they were tight and placed a hand on the heavy coil of rope that lay between him and the next man. The pilot called out thirty seconds to insertion; his voice just a touch tighter, and then asked his door gunners to report in. The men, one on each side of the bird, looked out past their 7.62mm miniguns and scanned the area, reporting all clear after just a moment. One by one Kotex and his men undid their safety harnesses and grabbed onto hand straps on the side of each door. His heart quickened and his chest tightened slightly as the helicopter started to slow. He'd gone through this drill hundreds of times and it never changed. He'd seen men die fast-roping in near-perfect conditions in the valleys of Kashmir, the Chin Hills of Myanmar, and the Chittagong Hills. The task at hand was something that needed to be performed with great care and focus. The second he heard the words *"Jai Hind!"* from the pilot he threw the rope out the door and tore off his in-flight headphones. Without hesitation, he reached for the rope with one hand and then the other. He launched himself out the door, pulled the rope close to his chest, and then loosened his grip. He dropped like a stone for the first thirty feet and then with ten feet to go he put on the clamps and slowed his descent. Landing on the soft dusty terrain Kotex moved away from the rope, bringing his suppressed MP-10 up his NVGs piercing the dark recesses of the area. Over his earpiece, he heard each of his men call out as they hit the ground, announcing they were clear. In the wake of the rotor wash the commandos moved quickly and precisely.

The Pave Hawk rotated 180 degrees as the ropes were pulled back up, and then started its descent back toward the beach.

Normally the ropes would have been dropped and left behind, but Kotex and his team didn't have the time to gather and bury them. The entire insertion took less than ten seconds. He and his troopers moved out immediately, never looking up as the helicopter left the area. Assembling quickly, they began moving in the direction of the monastery approximately five miles away.

39

Inside the Coptic monastery, Eyl, Puntland

Chained to a metal rack embedded in the wall of what used to be the refectory, his limbs numb from restricted blood flow, Hari sank into a sleep so shallow he found his mind drifting with many images flashing before his eyes. He thought of his parents, the many schools he attended, Padre, Stax and the Aces, the tranquillity of Blayney Parke, and Jago. Always Jago.

Hari dreamt how he met Jago on a hot, dry, sunny afternoon in Bevendean. Fragments of memories and images of the last two years flash across his mind as he winced in pain, his mind racing; projecting images: a tall, rangy teenage boy jogging topless in Norwich Drive; Hari missing the number 48 bus; *Grey Goose* vodka, marijuana joints and *Red Stripe* lager beer; investigative crime reporting in Brighton and acting lessons in Lewes; slalom boarding and goat curry with rice; graphic novels and iconic '70's blaxploitation films; trail biking across the South Downs; a mixed-race orphan with Jamaican, Irish, and English ancestry; a formidable loving mother and a McDonald dad (living with Jago meant learning a new language. He learned from Urban Dictionary that the term referred to a father who thinks he is fulfilling all his parental responsibilities by taking his estranged child to McDonald's during the occasional parental visit); a hundred movies, and many cosy nights-in spent smooching with *Shaft in Africa*; dreadlocks, identity, and race politics; unique improvisation techniques and Brighton street theatre; learning intimacy; and each other's bodies. These and a million other small, yet significant, things make up the stuff of my life with Jago, thought Hari as he spat out a bloody wad of phlegm.

The door opened and Hari could make out the footfalls of his torturers as they entered the room. Through his swollen eye, he saw there were two of them. One of the men grabbed his thighs and lifted him while the other cut through the knots which tied his hands to the metal rack. Expecting to be dragged off for more interrogation and torture, he was surprised when the men guided him towards a blanket on the floor. The men treated him with gentleness, and Hari realised that something had changed. Through the window, he could make out the sounds of shouting and gunfire. He heard one of the men say something before exiting the room.

He heard a strong and familiar voice in his ear, "I'm going to give you a shot of adrenaline, Hari. I need to wake up and stay alert."

"Suleyman? Is that you?" Hari felt the sting of a needle in his arm followed by a feeling akin to a cocaine hit. Within a matter of seconds, Hari was awake and very alert. Judging from the faded light he reckoned it early evening. The adrenaline was kicking in fast. His ears could hear all the sounds coming from outside. People shouting and hurrying in all directions.

Slowly standing up, he steadied himself using a table. The instruments Salim and his men had used on Hari were laid out on a dirty rag. The blowtorch was next to a box full of pliers. "When I return you will experience my special skills using this blowtorch," Salim had promised during the last interrogation. Those were the Somali's last words he heard before passing out.

"It's good to see you, Hari," Suleyman said, "got here just in time." He was wearing the distinctive blue PPE jacket of a United Nations relief worker.

Why was Suleyman rescuing him? He assumed that the ITEC delegation had raised the alarm when he failed to return to the hotel; and that Golda and Acharya had been alerted. Would Lodhi

Road have raised the issue with the Chinese, Pakistanis, or Iranians? From his reading of Cold War literature, Hari knew that all intelligence organisations have unwritten, unspoken rules of conduct with each other. There are also back-channel communications. Professional intelligence officers don't normally set out to kill each other. Suddenly Hari was gripped with fear. Was he being rescued by Suleyman to be kept captive? Was he to be used by the Iranians or Pakistanis for the purposes of exchange for one of their jihadists in custody somewhere? The flight-and-fight response triggered by the adrenaline was making Hari hyperalert. He was becoming paranoid. He turned towards the window. What was going on outside in the courtyard? It sounded as though the monastery was under attack from a frenzied mob.

From somewhere nearby came the rapid crack of rifle fire followed by more rifle fire; it sounded like firecrackers at Lewes bonfire night that Hari and Jago never miss every November 5th. He heard a rapid burst of an automatic weapon followed by a hideous scream.

He heard Suleyman say urgently, "We have to need to move quickly, Hari. The monastery is under attack in all directions. We need to be careful, and you need to stay close to me at all times."

A young Somali wearing a UNISO university hoodie appeared at the door and breathlessly reported something in the Somali language. Like Suleyman, he was also wearing a blue UN jacket. He looked familiar. Grinding out a cigarette, he went over to the window and, standing on a crate, looked between the wooden shutters. He was obviously worried about what he saw.

The Somali turned to Hari and said, "We got here as fast as we could. Mother Mary was looking out for you today, my brother." It was Yusuf! A fleeting image of the Somali in the *hammam* flashed through his mind. Hari brushed the image aside.

"Yusuf? What are you doing here? Is Lazarus……"

"No time for questions, Hari," Suleyman ordered sharply, "we have to move. Now. A mob of Houthi's and Salim's men are about to take over the monastery. Quickly, we are going by the back entrance."

Hari followed the Somalis through a passage leading to a mechanics' shed and garage. Yusuf shouted to a Somali youth, a scrawny adolescent with buck teeth, who was hunched behind the wheel of a utility truck, its engine purring. The youth was also wearing a UN jacket. Hari recognised a second man on the truck. He was armed with a Uzi slung under his shoulder. He was one of the guards who drove Hari and Khanfari to see Lazarus. Suleyman waited until Hari and Yusuf were inside the truck before sliding in beside them. "Drive."

Throwing the car into gear, the youth moved the truck up a steep ramp and towards the entrance of the garage. Making sure all was clear; the boy slammed his foot down hard on the pedal and the truck lurched out of the garage and onto a dark pathway. At the third crossing, he spun the wheel hard right, causing the truck to skid violently on two wheels, narrowly missing a frankincense tree. The headlights of the truck fell on an unruly mob of youths armed with machetes. Suleyman barked something and the driver slammed on the brakes before reversing and backing up the truck. In the headlights, a young man was waving the black and white flag of Al-Qaeda could be seen coming towards the truck. An armed youth with a rifle was close behind him. He dropped to one knee took aim and fired towards the truck. The front headlight shattered and the truck, lurching widely from side to side, slammed into a tree. Suleyman kicked open his door and, crouching behind it, fired off a clip at the jihadist youths. Suleyman was clearly an expert marksman and Hari saw over ten figures fall to the ground. The jihadists screamed blood-curdling slogans as they encircled the truck. The skinny driver pulled out a pistol from his waistband but was cut down by two shots through his face, blowing away half his skull. A piece of the boy's brain landed on Hari's lap. Suddenly the doors of the truck were wrenched open, and many hands pulled Hari and his companions onto the ground. The guard and Yusuf had nooses placed around their necks and were dragged across the ground to a mud-and-wattle fence and secured against it. Behind him, Hari could the crack of rifle shots. Turning back, he saw two lifeless bodies slumped forward. Raising his arms in an instinctive and defensive position to protect himself, he turned to Suleyman, "We're fucked. I need a gun." A jihadist brandishing a machete was closing in fast. The expression on his face was of pure animal rage.

40

Near Eyl, Puntland

Each step the troopers of the Special Frontier Force took was done with care. Smaller rocks lying at odd angles were avoided while the soldiers searched for firmer footing. Keeping their separation at all times with Kotex setting the pace each man was responsible for not falling too far behind or bunching up. At the Chakrata barracks and the army's Counterinsurgency and Jungle Warfare School in Mizoram, fresh recruits spent countless hours perfecting this art of moving silently through pitch darkness, on an unblazed trail with a thirty-pound rucksack in rough terrain. Clutching his MP-10 in his gloved hands, Kotex looked down through his NVGs, searching for a firmer footing so he could bolt over a rocky edge. As he placed his right foot on a small boulder, he looked up to check on his scout and froze. The Scout was standing completely still, his right hand held up in a fist. Kotex snapped up his fist signalling the commandos behind him to stop. He then signalled to Sniper One to move forward and take position. "Take out everyone not wearing a UN jacket," Kotex reminded him.

Sniping is a life-and-death game played at the highest intellectual level. Snipers will lay in wait for days, slowly, cautiously scanning every inch of the landscape with practised ease. The sniper, a very fit Gurkha, lay in the prone position, completely motionless. His left eye peered through the coated glass of his Unertl scope. He'd already lasered the range to the target and made the necessary adjustments for windage and elevation. He was in a near trancelike state and his heart had already slowed to thirty-two beats a minute. He inhaled a slow steady breath and then stopped all movement. Gently, evenly, his left index finger increased its pressure on the metal trigger. There was the gentlest of clicks before the 57-inch rifle let loose its Raufoss grade A round. The crack of the .50 calibre round shattered the calm of the air and sent every bird in the valley screeching into the air.

A voice snarled something in Somaliya. In the ebbing light, Hari could make out the mob shuffling to let someone through. Salim appeared out of the crowd. He was dressed in army fatigues, a beret and carrying a Type 56 rifle. He instantly recognised Hari and screamed an order to the youths. A muscular young man armed with a pistol darted forward to pull Hari towards him. Before he could reach him the sound of bang followed by echo could be heard from the nearby hills. The Somali was still gripping Hari as a bullet exited his cranium and a large section of the jihadist's skull broke off. A powerful shockwave reverberated through the corpse's brain, propelling a jet of pulverised grey matter, thick pink mist, and bone fragments over Hari. A man wearing an American baseball cap lunged towards Suleyman but was cut down by another bullet. His body was splayed backwards, a flap of black skin attached to his neck, with a splay of blood pouring from his nose and mouth. His head had vaporised leaving the baseball cap perfectly balanced on the exposed cervical vertebrae.

From the hilltop, Sniper Two, a veteran Tibetan sharpshooter, lay in the prone position next to his sniper rifle of choice, the IWI Dan. He was completely motionless. His left eye peered through the coated glass of his scope. Manufactured by the Israeli's, the rifle was chambered for the powerful .338 Lapua Magnum cartridge. He'd already lasered the range to the target and made the necessary adjustments for windage and elevation. He, too, was in a near trance-like state and his heart had already slowed to a meagre thirty-two beats a minute. The Tibetan pulled back one notch and said, "Say the word, Sir."

The team leader took a quick look through his Steiner-Optik binoculars to make sure none wearing the blue UN jackets were about to enter the line of fire. Satisfied, he said, "Take the shot."

The Tibetan also inhaled a slow steady breath and then stopped all movement. Gently, evenly, his left index finger slowly increased its pressure on the metal trigger. There was the gentlest of clicks before the crack shattered through the air, scattering the horde of jihadists below.

Chaos erupted on the ground below. "We need to move, quickly," Suleyman shouted as another skull exploded, sending a pink mist into the air. Behind them, a line of jihadists formed an impromptu firing circle.

"Agreed, but where? There's no fucking cover," Hari coughed, his mouth dry and filled with dust, "hang on; what's that sound?"

From the edge of the hills came the distinctive sound of helicopter motors. Salim screamed a warning as his men opened fire into the sky. One of the Houthi youth's misfires and shoots Salim on his forearm, throwing him onto the ground.

Hovering at five hundred feet, over the hills, was an AH-64D Apache Lowbow helicopter, the worlds most advanced all-weather attack helicopter. Its fire control radar target acquisition system allowed it to classify and prioritise over one hundred and twenty-five targets in a matter of seconds. It could designate the fifteen most dangerous targets and engage them with the Longbows "fire and forget" Hellfire laser-guided missiles or AIM-9 Sidewinder air-to-air missiles.

Originally designed as a tank destroyer the AH-64D carried eight Hellfire missiles, thirty-eight Hydra 70mm folding-fin aerial rockets and 1,200 rounds of 30mm ammunition for their belly-mounted chain guns. Shivananda Menon insisted on including the

Apache during the planning stages of the Puntland plan. "The AH-64D in an important part of the helicopter inventory of the Aviation Research Centre, the Wing's imagery intelligence unit based at Chakrata Barracks," he explained to the NSA during a meeting, "so, let's use them. This is the perfect opportunity for our pilots to test their skills."

Taking on a bunch of lightly armed Somali and Houthi pirates defending a ruined, sunken Christian monastery was not what the Apache had been designed for, however, the SFF pilot flying the Longbow was not about to argue with his boss in Chakrata Barracks. Especially not when his boss's boss was the legendary Anita "Golda" Kinnar, head of the Directorate General of Security. The co-pilot gunners monitored their various instruments as they waited for orders. The order to move came over the encrypted digital communications link. Simultaneously the twin General Electric gas turbine engines increased power and the helicopter began to climb. The pilot moved over the ridgeline, closing in on the kill zone at a cautious fifty knots. With each passing second the fire control computers effortlessly calculated a new solution to each target. In less than eleven minutes the monastery and everything in it would be ablaze.

Flying low from the opposite direction, the Indian naval Chetak helicopter reached the landing zone. The SFF commandos in the cabin leaned forward, poised to unhook their harnesses and rappel down. Side by side, the Black Hawks descended. An RPG-7 launched by a Al Shabaab jihadist sailed between the helicopters, exploding against the side of the hill. "That was too close," yelled the team leader, "watch yourselves." On the plateau below, the Somalis and Houthis fired AK-47s, the rounds clattering off the Kevlar floor mats protecting the aircraft. The Chetak gunners perched over the .50-calibres, firing back in controlled bursts. The brass jackets from spent machine gun rounds poured off the guns and into the night. The helicopter lurched downward, levelling out fifty feet above the ground. The lead gunner raised his left fist, the signal to drop.

"Now!" he screamed above the turbines. "Now!"

Holding the frame of the juddering Chetak, the team leader tugged on his pack: sixty-three pounds of ammunition, grenades, and other essentials of close-quarter combat. A Kevlar cable was coiled on the floor, its end knotted to the helicopter's frame. He threw it down and shimmied down, hand over hand, feeling the cable's rough fibres under his gloved fingers. AK-47 rounds whistled by close to his head. Five feet from the ground, he jumped, landing lightly.

Around the drop zone, he could see the Hellfire missiles had done their job. Burned men were strewn across the monastery courtyard, the acrid smell of flesh and fat heavy in the air. As planned, the attack had caught the Somalis and Houthi rebels building campfires for supper.

One of the choppers settled onto the ground, kicking up a huge ball of dust, another hovered above the monastery and bombarded the camp with air-to-ground missiles. From the sheds and outbuildings jihadists shrieked in terror as phosphorous shells exploded around them. The rebels who ran out of the clouds of dust were cut down by turret gunfire.

Suleyman came up behind Hari. "You need to get on that chopper," he yelled. "Your work here is done."

"Don't be fucking ridiculous, I'll leave when we all leave; including you." He turned towards the monastery. "We have to go back, Suleyman," Hari shouted, "there's a bunch of Indian fishermen in the basement cells. We have to get them out."

Two more DRDO Rudram air-to-ground missiles exploded nearby, forming shallow craters on either side of them. The swirling dust caused by the rotors momentarily blinded them. As it settled, a huge, bearded jihadist, bleeding heavily from a gaping wound where his knee had been, rolled over in the sand and began screaming. Watching him, Hari became aware that his left inner thigh was sticky and damp. Glancing down, he noticed that shrapnel had grazed him and was embedded into the flesh. Suleyman, moving fast, snatched the pistol from Hari and aimed at his chest. "I'm sorry Hari but I have my orders," he shouted, "you have to get on that chopper and get back to Delhi in one piece. That monastery and everything inside it and around it is about to be incinerated by BrahMos missiles. Things are going to get crazy around here. I've heard that Iranian president Ebrahim Raisi has died in a helicopter crash. The Houthis are going mad. You have to go, Hari. You cannot be here."

Hari backed away. He knew Suleyman was right. "We intend to launch BrahMos and Rudram air-to-surface missiles into that monastery, Hari *beta*," Golda had told him in McGregor's Club, "we will be sending a clear message to the Chinese and Pakis that we have the technical means to defend ourselves and are quite prepared to use it." The dust began swirling around them again. "You fucker," he screamed at Suleyman.

"You will understand when you get to Delhi," Suleyman said as he thrust a tightly sealed envelope towards Hari. "Here, take this; it's from our mutual friend, Lazarus, he wants you to have it. He promised you this. It's all the evidence given to him by his priest, evidence you need to write your story. You have to get out of here so you can write the story of what's happening here."

Hari looked at Suleyman with confusion. "I don't understand......."

"No time for questions, Hari; just get onto the chopper," he shouted. "Don't worry, my friend; our paths will cross again. Of that

I am certain. And don't worry about the prisoners, I will get them out. On that you have my word."

"Just answer me this: who the fuck are you Suleyman?"

Suleyman grinned. "I'm your friend from Israel," he said, "now get into that chopper before I kneecap you. *Shalom* to you, Hari."

Hari turned and started towards the chopper, but he lost his footing in a crater and fell forward. He felt strong hands pick him up and a quiet voice said in precise and flawless English, "Namaste Hari Vandra, can I offer you a ride back to Delhi? Your godfather, Sir Robert, is expecting you for tea."

41

Compact headquarters, Abbottabad, Pakistan

Inside the well-guarded Compact headquarters, a grand Raj-era mansion once owned by a former quarter-master general of the British Indian army, arguments raged on around the conference table. "My contacts in Rawalpindi have irrefutable evidence," asserted Major-General Iqbal Khan, a former head of the Covert Action Division of Inter-Services Intelligence, "that India's RAW working with the Jews have succeeded in infiltrating agents into our storage depot in Puntland. The monastery in the Galgala hills is destroyed. The Indians deployed their BrahMos supersonic cruise missiles."

The vast room was tastefully decorated with imported handcrafted Sankheda furniture adorned with delicate lacquerware known for its elegance and durability. Expensive Kutch Rogan artwork hung on the walls, exquisite cloth paintings with natural oil colours blended using the *sil batta*.

At the end of the table, a former vice admiral in charge of naval intelligence, a sharp-faced, clean-shaven man demanded, "Where is our Chairman? Why is he not here to answer our questions? Can you name some names, just a few."

Dressed in the crisp uniform of a Special Services Group officer, Iqbal Khan was only too happy to comply. He identified Hari Vandra as the godson of Sir Robert Gage, a lifelong friend of the Hindu spymaster Acharya Bhairava. "Any fool can see that we are being manipulated by the RAW – it is part of an Indian-Jewish plot to sabotage TUPAC II, our government, and after that our economy and nuclear technology programme. Then the Hindu dogs will destroy our scientific and military research. The ultimate goal of the RAW is the destruction of the Pakistani state and reducing our influence in the Muslim world. We will become the laughingstock of Muslims everywhere."

The twenty-four men, all members of Pakistan's armed forces and the intelligence community, seated around the long *dhurrie* rug on the floor listened grimly. They had spent the last four hours listening to Iqbal report on the latest updates in Puntland and the assassination of Pakistani agents involved in the Mumbai bombings. At midmorning, other retired generals started arriving at the mansion. The guests had sipped mint tea, sampled aromatic *gir kesar* mangoes, and chatted amiably in a large room decorated with wall paintings from Saudi Arabia as they waited for late comers. One senior army official had complained bitterly about the cost of sending his daughter to Roedean, an English boarding school in Sussex and those listening had nodded in empathy. "Education costs in America is even worse," complained a former head of the SS Directorate.

A young Covert Action Division intelligence officer, sitting directly opposite Iqbal, gave a smile of complicity across the table, then turned to whisper in the ear of his uncle, a former admiral in the Pakistani navy. Admiral Rahman was an austere and devout Sunni who made no secret of his deep aversion to Hindus, Christians, and Jews. He nodded in agreement and addressed Iqbal. "General *saab*, the story of Jewish spies may be the thing that breaks the Compact Accord. We cannot upset the Chinese; they are our only lifeblood. We no longer have the Americans in our pockets. We can no longer count on the Saudis because Mohammed bin Salman is tilting towards India and the bloody Turks are too fickle. The Chinese are all we have left."

"I have heard of these rumours circulating among naval people," Iqbal Khan reported to the company of retired generals, air marshals, and admirals. "As I reported earlier, we also have this problem of a young British journalist asking questions. You have read the reports from our communications people that these social media reports orchestrated by the RAW will harm us greatly."

"I agree with my colleagues. We cannot afford to upset Beijing," a retired general of land forces. "We are financially dependent on the handling fees we receive for storing material for the Chinese. I am not just talking about the weapons; I'm also referring to the narcotics money we are reliant on. We need this line of work for our operations. Need I say anymore? Our struggle against India depends on our cashflow from narcotrafficking operations. This has been the case since 1979."

"Our country is facing famine and flooding," claimed an opposition politician, a former finance minister. "The economy has been reduced to chaos by COVID and the floods. Thanks to that gutless cricketer, Imran Khan, the state sector does not work. Ordnance factories have cut production because of lack of materials. The wheat harvest is disorganised because the peasants are facing starvation. Tractors sit in fields because there are no spare parts. Our merchant ships have no fuel. Indian naval vessels are having to recue our fishermen and protect them from pirates. Sugarcane, cotton, and rice cannot be harvested. Our economy is import-dependent and our foreign exchange reserves are running out. We are facing disaster."

"Our beloved Pakistan is going to the dogs," agreed a director of the Army Fauji Foundation. "Federal and state tax rates are so high no one can pay and remain in business. This is the work of useless federal ministers sitting in Islamabad. Army veterans who have devoted their lives to the noble traditions of our armed forces are now reduced to selling their medals and ribbons because they can no longer afford food on their miserable pensions."

A former minister of foreign affairs slapped the table with the palm of his hand. "It's the fault of the monkey-loving Hindus and their friends the Jews," he insisted. "They bear collective responsibility for the troubles of the Pakistani people. Even members of the Organisation of Islamic Cooperation are beginning to favour India. Have you forgotten how the OIC disrespected Pakistani sensitivities when they invited India as guest of honour to the 2019 meeting in Abu Dhabi? And when our foreign minister criticised the OIC for its stance on the Kashmir issue what happened? Saudia Arabia punished us by demanding immediate repayment of one-billion-dollars from the three-billion-dollar loan we had taken in 2018. The Saudis also ended the oil supply credit. I ask you my brothers, did the Saudis forget the *Ummah*? Did they forget that Pakistan is a founder member of the OIC?"

His nephew, a current minister of aviation said, "I wholeheartedly agree with my uncle – I hold that Hindus, Sikhs, and Christians living in Pakistan must be forbidden to emigrate, and most especially to India, until a military tribunal of the Pakistani army has had a chance to weigh their fate. After all, these Hindus were born and educated here at state expense – it is only fitting that Pakistan be compensated. Have we all forgotten the Asia Bibi blasphemy case, no?"

One of the old guards, General Aleem Amir, a distant relation of General Ayub Khan was a bloated figure of a man with yellowish stains in his snow-white beard, added, "The Jews and Hindus are responsible for disco-dance music, drug addiction, inflation, sodomy, and pornography on television."

As the meeting progressed, the generals exposed their resentments and fears. Emotions ran high; there were many moments when several men started talking at once and Iqbal Khan, like a primary schoolteacher of an unruly class of schoolboys, had to point with his baton to someone so the others would give way.

"That cricketer deceived us into thinking he intended to tinker at the edges with defence and intelligence matters. He definitely knew a thing or two about spin. The bastard! He never told us he intended to destroy our military capabilities. What did we expect of a man who prefers London to Lahore and beds a Jewess? The filthy dog!"

"Malicious mockery of all branches of our military is commonplace among the youth; our people have forgotten the glorious history of Pakistan's army."

A current director of the Army Welfare Trust piped up. "The federal and state coffers are empty – the government is always late in paying our soldiers salaries and military pensions. We are at the mercy of the International Monetary Fund and its austerity measures. This is intolerable. Even that vain bastard Bhutto was a better prime minister than the cricketer."

"Pakistan – our beloved country, *yaa!* – has, in effect, become ungovernable. We can all agree on this, no? I can hear Jinnah turning in his grave!"

"American politics is in the hands of the so-called Blue Team in Washington who believe China and its allies are the significant threat to the United States. The Americans are definitely tilting in India's favour these days. According to my information Washington wants greater strategic cooperation with New Delhi. The Blue Team hates us Pakistanis for harbouring Osama bin Laden in the compound not far from here. Islamabad has failed its lobbying in Washington."

"India's rise has a global power under the BJP government continues. When will it stop? India's crafty foreign minister has sold the concept of a free and open Indo-Pacific to the Americans and

NATO members. The Blue Team in Washington loves the foreign minister."

"Let us not forget India's national security advisor," reminded a former director of military intelligence. "The man is brilliant, no? India appoints a fearless tiger to advise the prime minister on national security. Imran Khan on the other hand appoints a second-rate schoolteacher to advise him. Our government is a joke."

"Let us not forget that Imran Khan was also praising the BJP at every opportunity," noted a former counterintelligence chief glumly, "a Pakistani prime minister praising an BJP minister. This is intolerable business!"

Major-General Iqbal Khan listened carefully, noting everything and everyone. The meeting had gone better than he expected. He searched the faces round the table and said, very solemnly, "The only hope is for us to inform the Chinaman of our concerns. Our grave concerns. Action must be taken immediately. The Compact requires a change of direction and leadership."

"General Musharad will never consent to this," General Aleem Amir observed. "Never."

"In that case," Iqbal Khan said, "we will have to consent for him. I ask those who agree with this analysis to raise a hand."

Around the table all hands went up.

Major-General Iqbal Khan closed the meeting by reciting a prayer for the jihadis in Somalia. "When the time comes," he remarked, "we must not be squeamish about people falling aside." He arched his thin waxed eyebrows knowingly. Many around the table permitted themselves a grim smile.

42

McGregor's Club, Safdarjung Road, New Delhi

"Nice of you to stop by at such notice, Hari *beta*," Acharya told Hari, as they sat down in the corner table.

"Except for Robbie later on, I have no pressing appointments," Hari said. He was well rested and dressed in a Blakely hoodie and a light Cotosen vintage suede jacket. He'd opted for a pair of dark brown smart trainers.

Acharya had lit a Wills Navy Cut cigarette and vanished momentarily behind a veil of blue smoke. "I reviewed the" – there was a violent hacking cough – "notes the debriefing team made in Lodhi Road...."

"Yes, I thought you would."

"I was hoping you could amplify and clarify your suspicions about a mole inside the Wing."

"There's nothing to amplify or clarify. I'm certain I was betrayed by a mole inside the Wing; it's not speculation. Anyway, I've already covered this with the briefing team in Lodhi Road."

"I was hoping you might want to go over it with me one more time. I would like to hear it from you, rather than read it from a transcript."

"You recruited me for a mission in Somalia. I went in under deep cover as a member of an ITEC delegation. I met with Khanfari, and we were picked up after our first meeting with Lazarus...."

Acharya began thinking out loud. "So, you could have been betrayed by Lazarus, or his people, Khanfari or any of his colleagues at Al Jazeera, or anyone who saw you in the *hammam* that you visited on your first night."

"You could be right, but I wasn't. The interrogators seemed very familiar with my personal history. They knew, for example, that my parents were dead and had worked at Marlborough House. They knew I was recruited by you. They knew I was briefed in McGregor's Club by Golda. How could they have known all that, for fuck sakes?"

Behind the screen of blue smoke, Acharya's eyes were slits of pure concentration.

"Then there was the business of Robbie," Hari said, taking a big gulp from his glass. "How the fuck did they know he was my godfather? I have been going over the interrogation in my head. When I doze off, I dream about it. I dream I'm back in that ship, in front of that spotlight, back watching them torturing Jabir…"

Acharya brought the conversation back to the table. "Hari, can I ask something of you, *beta*?"

"I think I've given you enough, Sir," Hari said incredulously. "So has Yusuf and his brother. So has Lazarus and his family." After a minute's silence he asked, "What do you want?"

"That you meet Golda and myself at my place tomorrow for dinner. There I will share something with you. Something only a few, including Robbieji, know about." Lowering his voice, he said, "Hari *beta*, you are correct; the Chinese do have a mole inside the RAW, most likely in Operations, maybe even in the heart of the clandestine service, the Sino Division. We have been aware of this for some time, since 1972 actually. We caught one of the Chinese moles and took care of him, but we know there are others working in Lodhi Road, also. Let us not talk of this matter any further here; it's not safe. Meet me and Golda tomorrow and we will explain everything. I want you to know. What say you, Hari *beta*?" It was clear that Acharya was uncomfortable discussing the issue in the club.

Hari asked, "When did you catch this person and how did you take care of him? When you recruited me for the Puntland assignment, you said that trust was the single most important bond between us. If you want me to trust you, Sir, I need you to tell me the truth. Who was this traitor in Lodhi Road and how did you take care of him?"

Acharya smiled thinly. To Hari, eying him from across the dinner table, the spymaster looked like his namesake, Bhairava. In Hinduism, Bhairava is the avatar of Shiva and represents annihilation. In Shaivite temples across India, *chaturbhuja* statues of Bhairava are traditionally situated in a standing posture facing a southern position. He is always depicted carrying the sacred drum, a noose, a trident, and a skull. A ferocious looking dog always accompanies Bhairava. "His name was Rabinder Singh, a joint secretary working in the European division of the Wing. He was passing details of our military ties to Vietnam. The stupid fellow fell for a Chinese honey-trap and false-flag operation in the Hague," Acharya explained, speaking slowly and deliberately. "The Chinese sent in an American woman named Davina Vacalar who convinced our man that he should spy for the CIA. Singh agreed. The counterintelligence people in Lodhi Road became suspicious when he was caught photocopying files and photographs of naval installations unrelated to his work."

"How did you take care of him?"

"I asked a friend of mine in Langley to track him down in Maryland and he did so. I then asked another friend called Guru to arrange a traffic accident in 2016. The traffic accident took care of Rabinder Singh nicely and neatly by snapping his spine," Acharya said sipping delicately from his glass, "apparently the Chinese had washed their hands off him. Now can we get back to celebrating your return and talk about this matter later with Golda. Can we do this, *beta*?"

Hari nodded in agreement. "Yes, but I have other questions that I want answers to. Agreed?"

"Agreed," said Acharya. "Now, let us celebrate your safe return properly. Where is Karim?"

They sat in silence for a while, each lost in their private thoughts. Seated at his usual table in the Nkrumah dining room, Acharya polished off the Old Monk rum and, catching Karim's attention, signalled he was ready to switch to his Sula wine. Hari, no amateur when it came to lunchtime lubrication, reluctantly clinked glasses with him when the first chilled bottle was set on the table. They were seated facing a large Raj-era mirror on the back wall so Acharya could watch the other club members in McGregor's. "Suleyman did exactly what I would have done," he told Hari who had been patched up and given the all-clear by the Wing's chief medical officer. "I sought help from my old Israeli friend, Gideon, here in Delhi for help. We go back a long way. Golda called me after we lost contact with you. I have read the report from the Wing's science division. It appears that the metal enclosure where you and Khanfari were interrogated caused a phenomenon known as a Faraday shield. This shield prevented the homing signals in your amulet from being received by us. After you were snatched outside Lazarus's hideout the Wing formed a war council which recommended I speak to my Mossad contacts. I knew I had to speak to my good friend, Gideon. He is the Mossad liaison man in Delhi. It was he who arranged for an *oter* to protect you in Puntland."

"*Oter*? What's that?"

"An *oter* is an Arab recruited by the Mossad to work with other Arabs and Muslims," Acharya explained. "Suleyman is one of Mossad's best in the field." Leaning towards Hari, he enquired, "I think we should order some food; you need to keep your strength up. Doctor's orders." He put on a pair of reading spectacles and began scanning the menu. "I highly recommend the *palak* biryani; the best in all of Delhi."

Hari ignored him. "What about Lazarus? Is he and Osman safe?" Hari asked directly. "Before I left him, Suleyman gave me a package from Lazarus. It contains everything I need to expose the illegal fishing and dumping of radioactive material by British and European waste disposal companies." He raised his fingers for another bottle of Sula. "Much of the material comes from a Father Abraham Umtali whom Lazarus described as his confessor and spoke very highly of," recalled Hari chewing on a piece of *aloo tikki.* "Whoever this priest is, he certainly has access to some serious material. He seems to know a lot about the Ndrangheta, the Italian criminal syndicate who do the dirty work for the waste disposal companies. Umtali even knows the meeting place of the syndicate bosses. Apparently, it's a Basillian Christian convent called Our Lady of the Mountain." Hari cocked his head. "Quite frankly, Sir, I don't know what to make of this priest. He sounds more than just an ordinary priest to me."

They were sampling a Zampa Insignia wine that Karim had laid in, especially for Acharya. After a moment the spymaster looked at Hari and said, "I was right about one thing, *beta*; you are your father's son. Your instincts are correct. Abraham Umtali is more than just a simple priest. He's a Jesuit priest and a senior official in a department within the Holy See called the *Congregatio Extraordinaria Praeposita Negotiis Ecclesiasticis Orbis Catholici*," Acharya murmured, peering over the top of his reading spectacles. "Since 1814, the Extraordinary Congregation for the Ecclesiastical Affairs of the Catholic World is the intelligence service of the Catholic Church. Lazarus was one of Reverend Father Umtali's many agents in Africa and the Middle East tasked with keeping an eye on the Muslim hordes in Somalia and their overlords, the Chinese and Iranians."

Silently, Hari wondered how Acharya knew so much about Father Abraham Umtali and why he wasn't briefed on the priest by Golda before he set off to Somalia. "You still haven't answered my question about Lazarus and Osman. What happened to them, Sir?"

"Golda woke me up late at night. Things turned nasty in Puntland after you were extracted by the Special Frontier Force but rest assured both Lazarus and Osman are safe and well. Father Umtali has them in a Jesuit seminary in Nigeria. I understand arrangements are being made for them to live and work in Vatican City. The body of Yusuf and the others were recovered. I'm sorry about Yusuf, truly I am. All our fisherman were successfully rescued from the cells and brought home safely."

Hari was afraid to ask the next question but knew he had to have an answer. "Do we know what happened to Jabir Khanfari? Please tell me everything you know. And I mean everything."

After a moment of silence, Acharya said, "Golda told me Jabir's body was recovered from the sea by local fishermen. He had been drugged and tortured before he died. They used a blowtorch on him before cutting his throat," he said quietly. He sank into his seat and took a long sip of wine. His gaze finally lifted, and he noticed the look of pain in Hari's eyes. "I'm sorry, Hari *beta* but it goes with the territory"

There was a heavy silence in the room as Hari remembered the Al Jazeera man. "Thank you for your honesty, Sir," Hari said. He allowed himself to breathe again, though his heart was beating wildly, and his mind was racing.

A waiter brought over a silver salver with their bill folded on it and placed it in front of Acharya. "What plans do you have for your day?"

Hari managed a faint smile. "Robbie is expecting me."

Acharya raised his glass, "To our fallen friends," he said quietly. "*Dhanyavad.*"

"Fallen friends," intoned Hari. "*Shukriyaa.*"

43

Sir Robert's bungalow, Chanakyapuri, New Delhi

Sir Robert led Hari into the garden. Waving him toward an easy chair, he fetched a bottle of single malt whiskey. "Amrut twelve-year Chairman's Reserve, Hari; I've been saving this for a special occasion." He poured two small glasses to the brim and handed one to his godson. "You have no idea how relieved I was when Golda called to say you were safely onboard *Indira Gandhi*. Bottoms up," he said, smiling, carefully clinking glasses.

"To the next adventure, Robbie – this time we get them together." Hari took a long gulp, rose to his feet, and set the glass down on the table. His thigh was still painful after his surgery. Walking slowly helped ease the pain. "You could have told me, you know."

Sir Robert cocked his head. "Told you what, Hari? That my father supported the Indian independence movement and worked closely with Vallabhbhai Patel. That my father hated the India Office and British policy in the subcontinent. The turning point for him was the Bengal famine of 1943. He couldn't live with the fact that four million people had died unnecessarily of starvation on his watch. Father was a changed man after 1943. I see, Hari, you are surprised that I know about your conversation with Acharyaji. We have no secrets, Hari. For the record, my father worked for Nehru's spymaster, Bhola Nath Mullick from 1950 until 1969. Oh, and do sit down, Hari. You're giving me a headache."

Sir Robert's Garden was built around a number of trees including a Devil tree, a Palmyra palm, Indian rosewood, and a breadfruit tree. It was his pride and joy and easily the best feature of the bungalow. The interior of the garden was studded with plants and water lilies collected from the length and breadth of the subcontinent. Vibrant and vivid bunches of Lady's Slipper, Foxtail orchids, and marigolds were everywhere. In a far corner of the orchard grew a Golden Shower tree amidst a carpet of rhododendrons and Siroi lilies. Yellow-footed green pigeons and colourful Hoopoes with their distinctive crown of feathers pecked on the ground for fat grubs. An old shed was covered in the vines of the Cannonball tree and its brilliant red and white flower. The entire garden was scented by flowering jasmine.

Hari murmured, "And you, Robbie? When did you start working for India?"

Sir Robert rested a finger along the bridge of his nose. "I suppose I've always worked for Mother India," he said finally, "I was recruited by father, you see. I'd just turned twenty. I signed up over a good dinner at the East India Club where he stayed whenever he was in London. Best decision I ever made."

"Why was that, Robbie?" Hari asked as a couple of fat Blood pheasants waddled past a bush of a Nag Kesar tree in full pink bloom. "Was your decision not treachery? Betraying your service, your country, and your friends. Does that not weigh heavy on your mind?"

"No, not for a second," replied the English knight. "I instinctively knew that India would be a great nation when its time came. Everything I read on Indology told me so. After the Partition I knew I wanted to play a part, my part, in making sure democratic India is defended from deadly Communist China and the military dictatorships of Pakistan. Your parents thought the same. I wanted to help repay the one-hundred-and-forty-five trillion dollars the India Office and its successors looted from India through trade and peonage during the one-hundred-and-ninety-year British Raj. Your parents wanted to preserve your spiritual heritage, Hari. All of us knew that Britain would tilt towards Pakistan because of the niche Islamabad had managed to carve out for itself within the Muslim world. As long as the oil was flowing London knew which brown arse to kiss."

"London is known as Londonistan," said Hari, "there's a brilliant book by Melanie Philips on the subject. I'll get you a copy."

They sat in companionable silence for a while before Hari said, "Robbie, do you know a priest by the name of Father Abraham Umtali? I heard his name from Lazarus and Acharyaji tells me that he works for Vatican Intelligence. I ask because……"

Suddenly Hari's rang. It was Stax. Signalling to his godfather that he wouldn't be long he answered. "Hey Stax, listen big man can I call you back, I'm just with Robbie…." Hari listened intently to what Stax was telling him. "What! Are you sure about this? When?" He sat very still listening carefully to what his friend was telling him. "Stax, can you tell the Aces I'm catching the first flight to England? I'll call you from Heathrow." He cut the connection.

"What is it Hari; you've gone white as a sheet!"

"That was Stax," Hari said dazed. "Swarnjeet Agarwal's been taken from Blayney Parke by the Skinny Skoda Boys…."

"Criminals inside the walls of Blayney?" Sir Robert spluttered incredulously, spilling his drink over his lap. "Bastards! Why didn't you tell Stax to just shoot them?"

Hari stared at his godfather, visibly shaken. "That's not all Robbie. They've taken Jago as well; they've taken him hostage because I'm running the story on Sir Ibrahim Ali's drug empire." He turned and headed towards the door.

"Where are you going, Hari?"

"Blayney Parke. I need to get back to Brighton now," Hari yelled. "I need to get back now! Taking my boy Jago is a declaration of war by Ibrahim fucking Ali."

"Wait! Hari!" Sir Robert cried out. "I'm coming with you, *beta.*"

Epilogue

Gwadar Port, Balochistan, Pakistan

Under a bleak sky, sailors on the three-thousand-ton *PNS Jinnah*, a heavy Chinese-made corvette singled up all lines and cast them off from the pier. The moment the vessel was no longer attached to Gwadar Harbour, an ensign blew a whistle. Kai Ling, standing in the doorway of a large brick gatehouse, watched intently as the vessel disappeared into a faint dot on the horizon. He had been up since early morning waiting for all intelligence coming in from Somalia and Yemen. By mid-morning, he was satisfied that all loose ends in Puntland had been attended to and the sanitation process completed. Shortly, an army-owned limousine had drawn up outside the gatehouse. General Syed Musharad, walking slowly and looking defeated, entered the building. "The clean-up operation is completed. The threat to TUPAC II is eliminated." He passed a leather briefcase to Kai Ling. "The research data of the scientists who worked in the monastery is in there. As instructed, they and their families have been eliminated."

"And the Houthis and Al-Shabaab jihadists? What of them?"

"My men took care of them using mustard gas in a cattle shed," he reported, "they have been dumped in the sea. I am leaving for Yemen now to personally update the Iranian and Houthi leaders on the Puntland operation."

"I suggest you hurry, General *saab*. You have a lot of explaining to do. I cannot imagine the Iranians, the Yemenis, or our North Korean comrades being too pleased to see your face," Kai Ling of Macau said softly, his blazing eyes burning into the Pakistani soldier. "You have achieved nothing except prove to me why Pakistan is the only professional army never to have won a war. You disappoint me. I will send for you if and when I require your services, General *saab*."

As General Musharad walked along the quay towards a fast patrol boat operated by Pakistan's coast guards, Kai Ling watched as a Foton Tunland pickup slowly made its way towards the gatehouse. By the time the pickup reached the guardhouse, the Coast Guard patrol vessel had cleared the breakwater and turned due west in the Arabian Sea. The boat was carrying not just General Musharad but also his parents, his wife and five children and their nanny. Squinting through military field glasses, Kai Ling found them huddled in a group in the middle of the boat. Musharad's father, a former admiral, was standing ramrod straight. Musharad's wife was dressed in an exquisite blue and white *shalwar kameez*. The nanny was trying to control the excited children. Over the radio in the gatehouse, an early morning All India Radio Urdu program was interrupted for a news flash. There were reports, so far unconfirmed by the BJP government, that India had launched a surgical strike at a Coptic monastery in Puntland, a region of Somalia. The AIR anchorwoman reported that anonymous sources from the prime minister's office were saying the monastery in question was an al-Qaeda weapons depot for stockpiling conventional weapons and narcotics destined for India. "We are receiving disturbing news that the monastery was also used to store bioweapons destined for distribution among Maoist insurgents operating in India's Red Corridor," she said sombrely. When the normal program resumed, Kai Ling walked over to the radio and switched it off. Looking out of the window, he raised the field glasses to his eyes again. The patrol boat was moving away fast; only the flashing lights on its mast and antennae were visible. Suddenly there was a muted explosion, the echo was no louder than a motorbike backfiring. Through the glasses, he could make out the large gaping wound on the side of the vessel. He heard another explosion, followed by another and watched thick, billowing black smoke fill the air. There was a final explosion. Kai Ling smiled and sucked on the sea air. A weak link in the Compact had been buried at sea. Always remove the weakest link, his father had instructed him.

Exiting the gatehouse, the Chinese spymaster caught sight of the familiar face sitting inside the pickup. As people rushed towards the quay edge to see the patrol boat sinking, Kai Ling walked towards the vehicle. The door opened and a trim middle-aged soldier wearing the immaculate uniform of the Special Service Group, complete with the distinctive maroon beret, stepped out. He saluted smartly and opened the back door for his Chinese master. He did not look in the direction of the harbour and sinking patrol vessel.

"Congratulations on your appointment as the new head of the Compact, Lieutenant General Iqbal Akhtar Khan," Kai Ling announced, "I hope your tenure will be longer than that of your predecessor."

"I have every intention of remaining in post until Allah wills otherwise," murmured the former head of the Covert Action Division of the Inter-Services Intelligence agency.

"Excellent," Kai Ling declared. "Together we will execute the operational plan ZULFIKAR. Let us see if you prove yourself in England. I will not tolerate failure from the Compact a second time. I trust myself clear on this. Categorically clear, General *saab*."

"I will not fail you, Sir."

"Good," murmured Kai Ling. "Sir Ibrahim Ali is waiting for you to call on him in Marbella. He will brief you on the Camorra and ''Ndrangheta angle of ZULFIKAR. I expect you to manage these crime syndicates in an acceptable manner. I do not need to remind you of Pakistan's cashflow problems. We must maintain course and direction for all our operations for TUPAC II. The ZULFIKAR operation will ensure we remain financially independent of Beijing. You will find all the necessary information in here," he said passing a thick folder to the Pakistani. "I will contact you in London. You will be staying in the Surrey safe house."

www.ingramcontent.com/pod-product-compliance
Lightning Source LLC
Chambersburg PA
CBHW071951070426
42453CB00012BA/2077